INDIAN MUSLIMS AND REVIVALISM IN TWENTIETH CENTURY INDIA

Dr. Poonam Bawa

© Dr Poonam Bawa 2023

All rights reserved

All rights reserved by author. No part of this publication may be reproduced, stored in a retrieval system or transmitted in any form or by any means, electronic, mechanical, photocopying, recording or otherwise, without the prior permission of the author.

Although every precaution has been taken to verify the accuracy of the information contained herein, the author and publisher assume no responsibility for any errors or omissions. No liability is assumed for damages that may result from the use of information contained within.

First Published in January 2023

ISBN: 978-93-5668-446-1

BLUEROSE PUBLISHERS
www.BlueRoseONE.com
info@bluerosepublishers.com
+91 8882 898 898

Cover Design:
Yash

Typographic Design:
Tanya Raj Upadhyay

Distributed by: BlueRose, Amazon, Flipkart

Dedicated in memory of my Mentor
(Lt) Professor L.S. Rathore

Doyen of Political Science and Ex-Vice Chancellor of Jai Narain University, Jodhpur, Rajasthan

Professor L. S. Rathore

FOREWARD

There are various ideas and ideologies in the modern Indian social and political thoughts. Among them, one of the important school of thought is Muslim revivalism, whose thinkers have received a proper attention in this work title: 'Indian Muslims and Revivalism in Twentieth Century (1885-1947)' written by Professor Poonam Bawa, Former Head, Department of Political Science, J.N. Vyas University and Director, K.N. College for Women, Jodhpur. She possesses a brilliant academic record, with two research degree: Ph.D. and D.Litt. in Political Science.

Among the Muslim revivalist thinkers Prof. Poonam Bawa has included five thinkers – Sir Syed Ahmed Khan, Muhammed Ali, Muhammed Iqbal, Dr. Zakir Hussain and Abdul Kalam Azad, and has examined their ideas in a systematic and balanced manner. In her analysis two aspects are clearly visible. The first aspect relates to their love for the nation and plea for a united India. The second relates to the Islamic revivalism and the need for western education, focused on science and technology, for the progress and advancement of the Muslims and, at the same time, maintaining their pride in history, religion, and culture.

In the 19 th century the most powerful advocate of the revivalism of Islam was Sir Syed Ahmed, who was sensitive to the trends and forces of the times. His aim was to popularize the scientific and nationalistic education of the West for the purpose of enlightenment of the mind, and wanted that the Muslim youth should take to English education. He wished to give place of pride both to secular modern education and to Islamic Theology. He advocates that the Hindus and Muslims really belong to one nation (Kaum), and pleaded that the progress of the country would be positive only if we have a union of hearts, mutual sympathy and love. He often said that our land of India is like a newly wedded bride whose two beautiful and luminous eyes are the Hindus and the Musalmans.

The second Muslim revivalist thinker is Muhammad Ali (1878-1931). He pleaded for Hindu-Muslim toleration. He believed that neither the Hindus can exterminate the Muslims today nor can the Muslims get rid of the Hindus. So if they cannot get rid of one another, the only thing to do is to settle down to co-operate with one another. He represented a synthesis of apparently conflicting trends of Muslim and political thought of India. He stressed the need of modernity and science as well as the need to follow the spirit of values of Islam. Despite his tolerant attitude between the Hindus and the Muslims, he was basically a Muslim theologian, and had a deep faith in the doctrines of Islam. He recognized the communal individuality of the Muslims. He did not think that any artificial unity or romantic patriotism could be imposed on India.

The third revivalist thinker is Muhammad Iqbal (1873-1938). He gave the slogan: 'Back to early Islam'. He was an opponent of nationalism on two grounds. Firstly, he felt that the concept of a united India (with Hindus and Muslamans together as citizens) is against the spirit of Islam as Islam does not believe in territorial nationalism. Secondly, he felt that the concept of nationalism would introduce separate patriotic feelings in the different Muslim countries. He advocated the formation of a consolidated North-West Indian Muslim state. He thus laid the foundation of the historical and ideological roots of the Pakistan movement. He is considered the spiritual father of the Pakistan ideology.

The fourth Muslim revivalist Thinker is Abul Kalam Azad (1888-1959). He favored a reformist and rational approach to the Koran. He felt that in spite of diversities in India, unity has to be achieved. He was opposed to the separatism and sectarian nationalism which was prevailed by the Muslim League. He had full faith in Hindu-Muslim unity and the firm conviction that the

Hindus and Muslims had a common destiny. He challenged the political philosophy of Sir Syed Ahmed and the Aligarh school.

The last Muslim revivalist thinker, Dr. Zakir Hussain was a true patriot and a nationalist. He believed that a Muslim would not be a good Muslim unless he was a true Indian. Being a true Indian, he would not cease to be a good Muslim. Islam did not stand in the path of its followers becoming good Indians. Whatever a good Indian has to do is permissible under Islam. A good Muslim must accept all the principles and perform all the functions that were necessary for nation's development. The social ethics of Islam and the guiding principles of nationalism both were identical. There was no conflict between them.

Professor Poonam Bawa has analyzed the ideologies of the above five Muslim revivalist thinkers in an admirable and objective manner, free from biases or prejudices. All the ideas of Muslim revivalist thinkers, perhaps unsystematic and disjointed, have been weaved together in such an attractive and harmonious manner, enhancing the utility of the work and uplifting the level of scholarly attainments. She concludes that: All the five revivalist thinkers were great men who had great love for their nation India. They succeeded in awakening the Muslims to bring them out of the cocoon, to stir them into acting to interpret Islam in new perspective without damaging the soul of the religion, and to motivate the Indian Muslims towards education. They always advocated Hindu- Muslim unity because they considered themselves to be true Indians. They dreamt of free India with composite culture, though Sir Syed Ahmed Khan, Maulana Muhammed Ali and Muhammed Iqbal are considered to be the promoters of 'Two Nation Theory, whereas Dr. Zakir Hussain and Maulana Abul Kalam Azad stood for united India.'

Professor Poonam Bawa's present book is excellent both in contents and scholarship. The arguments regarding Muslim revivalism or the Hindu-Muslim unity both have clearly expressed and easy to understand. Their role towards the awakening of the Muslims and the consideration of the idea of national unity have been explained in a simple and solid manner without diluting the scholarly tone. For producing such an impressive work, I would like to congratulate Professor Poonam Bawa. I am sure that the book would be of great benefit to the researchers and general readers who wish to know more about the Muslim revivalist thinkers in modern Indian Politics.

(Professor L.S.Rathore)

Emeritus Professor of Political Science, & Former Vice Chancellor,

J.N. Vyas University, Jodhpur, Rajasthan.

PREFACE

The modern Indian Political Thought has acquired a great significance in study and research during the last four decade or so. Whether this emerging field should be styled as 'Thought' or 'Ideas', there has been a lot of controversy regarding the choice of the term, it can be safely asserted that modern Indian Political Thought has come to occupy a prominent place in the curriculum of political science in Indian Universities.

In the realm of modern Indian political thought there are significant ideas and ideologies. The ideologies such as nationalism, rights and freedom, humanism and new humanism, satyagraha and nonviolence, party less democracy and total revolution are the cult of the individual and of the collective whole.

The religious concepts and the two-nation theory and others sprawl over the field in such a way, making the field a confused intertwining for any researcher. These ideologies have developed according to the circumstances and the situations that have developed from time to time, either in the 19th century or in the first half of the 20th century. The ideologies that have cropped up in the domain of modern Indian political thought, or are still developing, are mostly the racy of the soil. These ideologies have a great relevance towards reforming the Indian society, and thereby to build up the healthy social and political bases in the country.

My work seeks to trace the course of political thought of the Muslims in India during the period (1885-1947). The historical and cultural background of Muslim political thought during the span has been provided so as to bring out and explain the prominent features of thought represented by each one of the personalities selected for the study. The personalities have been chosen as representing strands of thoughts and movements in the political and social life of the Muslims and not to make the present work a biographical study. The emphasis throughout has been on the interplay of the forces of religion and politics though prominence is accorded to political ideas and revivalist movements; on the almost total failure of the Muslims in India to achieve a progressive secular outlook; and on their unwillingness to adapt themselves to the demand of the age- reason, liberalism, modernization and secularism.

The partition of the country in 1947 was the tragic finale of the separatist thinking of the Muslims and of the extremism of some sections of the Hindu community. I with a note of optimism believe that though the political situations are still charged with suspicion and distrust and communalism has a vicious hold on some sections of the population, grounds of hope are not wanting and a spirit of understanding, fraternity and common citizenship may be found among progressive sections of all communities. It is on these sections that their increasing influences in the course of time that the future of our secular democracy rests.

The book based on my D, Litt thesis, is divided into six chapters-

Chapter I studies the political and social thought of Sir Sayyid Ahmad Khan (1817–1898) who responded to the collapse of the Mughal Empire in India, following the failed rebellion of 1857, by diverse efforts to revitalize and to reform Muslim intellectual and social life. He made a powerful impact on his community by his insistence that the Indian Muslims must become as well educated as the British. As a descendant of minor aristocrats in the Mogul court and as a historian of Indian Islam, he understood that knowledge and power are linked. The controversies about him are in the areas of religious thought and politics. With respect to religion, he tried to encourage rethinking of Islamic theology and jurisprudence. In political matters, he favored supporting the British and was critical of the Congress Party. He was one of the foremost Muslim modern thinkers of the 19th century. His emphasis on education as a tool for revivalism of Muslims has been analyzed in my study.

Chapter II brings forth the contribution of Maulana Mohammad Ali instilling courage and confidence in the hearts of the ignorant masses who were sunk as if in deep slumber after the failure of 1857 mutiny. He was largely instrumental in dispelling the inferiority complex resulting from relentless fear on many fronts. The extreme poverty and sufferings, to which the Indian masses were reduced to under the British Raj, added fuel to his fiery temperament. It was at a time when no other national leader had the vision and courage to speak on behalf of all Indians. When Sir Sayyid Ahmad Khan's policy of Muslim co-operation with the British Government failed miserably in uplifting the masses, the revolutionary policies of Maulana Mohammad Ali took root among the Indian Muslims. Maulana Mohammad Ali's rise to Indian national scene began in the first decade of twentieth century with publication of his articles in the Times of India. The Weekly 'Comrade' became the voice of the struggle against exploitation and oppression of the British government, and it was recognized as the leading paper of independent journalism. Maulana Mohammad Ali's English translation of the Qur'an was the first achievement in the history of Islam that started to dispel the darkness in the Western countries and spread the light of Islam from place to place. Maulana Mohammad Ali's greatest distinction, destined by God for him and which only he was blessed with, was that in the history of Islam he was the first Muslim who conveyed the message of Islam to Western countries in a Western language.

Chapter III discusses Dr. Muhammad Iqbal as one of the great thinkers of the twentieth century. Most of Allama Iqbal's writings are devoted to revival of Islam. His foremost book Reconstruction of Religious Thought in Islam was intended to secure a vision of the spirit of Islam as emancipated from its Magian overlaying. In this inspirational work, he attempted to show a path back to the scientific and intellectual striving that Muslims once excelled in. He opposed the current methods of teaching and called for a reconstruction of thought. He encouraged Muslims to embrace ideals of brotherhood, justice, and service and to free their mind from the prevailing colonial mentality and narrow self-interests, His masterpiece is 'The Song of Eternity' (1932) and classical work is *"Toloo-e-Islam"* (Rise of Islam).

Chapter IV is focused on Dr. Zakir Hussain. A happy blend of east and west can be seen in his unique personality The Sufi tradition, Islamic knowledge and thought formed the bed-rock of Dr. Hussain's educational ethos. He was an educator and laid emphasis on character building of the students by the educators. Zakir Hussain aimed at instilling the virtues of Nationalism, patriotism and other human values in the Muslims so as to enable them to join the freedom struggle and contribute in the progress of country. He made Jamia an institution where a nationalist took pride in being an Muslim and a Muslim be proud of being a Nationalist. After Independence when the atmosphere of Aligarh was gloomy and when Muslims faced the situation similar as they did after the uprising of 1857, Dr. Zakir Hussain came to its rescue, became the Vice Chancellor of the university for two consecutive terms and restored its glory and prestige. He taught the students and teachers the ideals of nationalism, secularism and humanism.

Chapter V is dedicated to one of the leading tolerant Muslims Maulana Azad, who left a deep impact on the idea of pluralism in Islam. His contribution to Indian nationalism and Hindu-Muslim unity in India, and to the idea of universal humanism is tremendous. Maulana Azad will always be remembered in the history of India but for the role he played in the national liberation movement of the country and also as a

Muslim leader who stood for a dialogue among Muslims and Hindus. As an activist and a revivalist Muslim he was an upholder of pure Islam. In his early career from 1906 to 1920, he was influenced by religious teachings, had an enthusiasm for Muslim nationalism and a passion for the Pan-Islamic theory of Jamaledin Al-Afghani. For Azad every Indian Muslim was first of all a member of the world Muslim brotherhood. After 1920 a radical change appeared in the views of Maulana Azad and he ceased to be a revivalist Muslim and embraced Indian secular nationalism as a political philosophy.

The last chapter is a comparative and critical analysis of role played by these revivalists' thinkers in the revivalism of Muslims and their contribution to restore the lost glory of Islam.

The analysis has two aspects which are clearly visible-

The first aspect relates to their love for the nation and plea for a united India.

The second relates to the Islamic revivalism and the need for Western education, focused on science and technology, for the progress and advancement of the Muslims and, at the same time, maintaining their pride in history, religion, and culture.

What are the roots of Muslim Revivalism? To what extent Muslim Revivalist thinkers have been able to promote nationalism? What have been their contributions towards the awakening of the masses during the freedom struggle? Are these ideologies suitable for a diverse and complex society? Can they promote a composite nationalism and a cosmopolitan outlook? These are related issues that has been discussed and analyzed in this book.

Dr. Poonam Bawa

ACKNOWLEDGEMENT

Any significant achievement has the benevolence of Almighty God to whom I bow with all humility for the courage, patience and wisdom bestowed on me to undertake such stupendous task. My respected parents Shrimati Shakuntla Grover and Shri Dev Raj Grover has always been a great motivational force for my academic pursuits.

I consider an honor to express my heartfelt thanks to Prof. L.S. Rathore, Former Vice-Chancellor, Jai Narain Vyas University, Jodhpur and the doyen of Political Science, my esteemed teacher, my mentor for motivation, encouragement and guidance to undertake this task.

It is my privilege to express my deep sense of gratitude to Prof. P. S. Bhati, Professor Emeritus, Department of Political Science, Jai Narain Vyas University, Jodhpur, for his unstinted support, valuable suggestions and helpful guidance which helped me in completion of this mammoth task.

I am also indebted to the authorities, Prof. Sunita Inayat Zaidi and Prof. Inayat Zaidi (Department of History) Jamia Millia Islamia University who helped me immensely in the collection of material. Indebtedness is expressed to the libraries of Jamia Millia Islamia University and Delhi University who extended an unstinted support to me and made my access smooth to rare books and manuscripts which enabled me to put in proper perspective of my research findings.

Sincere thanks to my esteemed colleagues of the department who helped me in the pursuit of my work.

Finally, I wish to avail the opportunity to place on record the support of my family consisting of daughter Ridhi and son-in-law Gaurav, son Apoorv and my husband Dr. R. K. Bawa who always contributed in numerous ways which helped me in completion of my work.

Dr. Poonam Bawa

TABLE OF CONTENTS

FOREWARD v

PREFACE ix

ACKNOWLEDGEMENT xv

EMERGENCE OF MUSLIM REVIVALISM: 1
   SIR SAYYID AHMAD KHAN 1
   Sepoy Mutiny 1857: The spark for Revivalism 7
   Aligarh Movement: Revivalism through Education 20
   Urdu Verses Hindi Controversy: Conflict of Linguistic Domination 27
   Concept of Indian Nationhood 36
   Attitudinal Change: Crisis of Muslim Identity 39

THE LEANING TOWARDS PAN ISLAMISM: 54
   Views On Islam 58
   Revivalism Through Journalism 60
   Role of Comrade 61
   Hamdard Urdu Daily for Muslim Masses 66
   Muhammad Ali's vision of Progress: National Muslim Education 67
   Beginning of Jamia: The National Muslim University 72
   Jamia Moves from Aligarh to Delhi 74
   Pan- Islamism 75
   Islamic Nationalism 86

THE PROCESS OF CONSTRUCTIVE REVIVALISM: ... 103
   Philosophical Basis to Revivalism 108
   Constructive Revivalism of Iqbal 114
   Political Ideas of Iqbal 120

Education 127
Concept of Nationalism 129
Muslim Nationhood 134
INTELLECTUAL FERVOUR TO REVIVALISM: 152
DR. ZAKIR HUSSAIN 152
Revivalism through Education 158
Nurturing Jamia Millia Islamia 161
A Reformist: Igniting Minds 170
Composite Culture 172
Nationalism: Zakir's dream of United India 179
THE PROPONENT OF NATIONALISM: MAULANA ABUL KALAM AZAD 195
Influences and Rationalism 196
Mental Crisis and Understanding Islam 198
Revivalism through Journalism 203
Understanding Islamic History and Theology 206
Political Strategy al- Hilal (Rise of the Crescent) 209
Nationalism 223
Muslim Politics 226
Religion and Politics 229
United India: Hindu-Muslim unity 235
Khilafat: Maulana's Clarion Call for Revival of Islamic Brotherhood 238
CONCLUSION 248
GLOSSARY 287

EMERGENCE OF MUSLIM REVIVALISM:
SIR SAYYID AHMAD KHAN

Domination of infidelity is ruining Islam.

Had our forefathers not waged *jihad,*

India would not have flourished with Islam.

The power of sword ensured the dominations of Muslims,

Had our forefathers been idle, what would have happened to Islam?"[1]

This poem truly reflected the state of mind among Muslim religious leaders and social reformers in India at the beginning of the nineteenth century. Their perception was that Indian Muslims who constituted a minority of 21 per cent of the population felt persecuted both in their true faith and in their social status as compared to other sections of society. After the Islamic Mughal administration gradually gave way to British colonial power in the eighteenth century, Muslim religious thinkers and the tiny former Muslim ruling elite of princes, landlords, administrators and military commanders had to adjust themselves to their crushing fall from power and to the consequences of the minority status of their religious community. As the Muslim ruling elite was mostly connected with feudal and non-commercial activities, it felt severely hurt by the mounting pressures of emerging colonial capitalism. Muslim landed gentry was challenged by up and coming "commercial men" as communications and trade expanded and cash-cropping increased. Servicemen of the Mughal army found no employment. Muslims were progressively squeezed out of the local administration where they had occupied a pivotal position so far".[2]

It was no easy task for Muslim thinkers in India to favorably respond to new impulses demanding to restore the dignity and grandeur once enjoyed by the Muslim community. Complications were rooted in the structure of the Muslim community in India and in the challenges it faced. By no means did Indian Muslims constitute a coherent social or ethnic community. Unlike in the Islamic heartland of Arabia, Indian Muslims lived more or less dispersed. Besides a few Muslims of foreign descent, who were employed at the court and in the administration of the Mughals, they mainly constituted local population groups hailing from different ethnic communities, castes and tribes all over India. However, such a wide variance in living conditions did not prevent Indian Muslim communities from striving for a common course in religious matters as well as partially in social and political affairs. The urge for unity was there, though it seldom tallied with reality. Emerging colonial capitalism did not much reduce differences among Indian Muslims. Divergent segments like government servants of the United Provinces (UP), the landed aristocracy of Punjab, the *ulema* of the seats of Islamic learning at Delhi, Deoband,

Aligarh or Hyderabad, the traditional weavers of Gujarat or the cultivators of Bengal and of the Malabar coast-all had different interests. It was the Muslim educated urban classes of UP (where Muslims made up for only 15 per cent of the local population) who played a key role both in the reform of Indian Islam as well as in the formation of a bourgeois Muslim political movement in India. Mounting pressure from the colonial administration and tough competition from Hindu bourgeois classes, who more quickly adapted themselves to changing circumstances, made UP Muslims very clearly feel the need to bring about changes in Muslim religious and political thought. Muslims from other Indian regions, where they even constituted a majority (Bengal and Punjab) but were largely engaged in politically less sensitive employment like land cultivation, were less vocal in this respect. In this sense it is no coincidence that Sayyid Ahmad Khan from UP advanced to the peculiar position of spokesman articulating through the experience of his own plight, the fate and faith of a whole social stratum which set out on the path from tradition to modernity.[3]

Sir Sayyid Ahmad Khan, a great thinker of Muslim India was born on 17th October 1817 in Delhi in a respectable family of Sayyid Mohammad Muttaqi & Azizun Nisa Begum. Many generations of his family had been highly connected with the Mughal administration. His maternal grandfather Khwaja Fariduddin served as *wazir* in the court of Akbar Shah II. His paternal grandfather Sayyid Hadi held a mansab, a high-ranking administrative position and honorary name of Jawwad Ali Khan in the court of Alamgir II. Sir Sayyid's father Mir Muhammad Muttaqi was personally close to Akbar Shah II and served as his personal adviser. However, Sir Sayyid was born at a time when rebellious governors, regional insurrections and the British colonialism had diminished the extent and power of the Mughal state, reducing its monarch to a figurehead status. With his elder brother Sayyid Muhammad Khan, Sir Sayyid was raised in a large house in a wealthy area of the city. They were raised in strict accordance with Mughal noble traditions and exposed to politics. Their mother Azis-un-Nisa played a formative role in Sir Sayyid's life, raising him with rigid discipline with a strong emphasis on education.

Sir Sayyid was taught to read and understand the *Qur'an* by a female tutor, which was unusual at the time. He received an education traditional to Muslim nobility in Delhi. Under the charge of Hamiduddin, Sir Sayyid was trained in Persian, Arabic, Urdu and religious subjects. He read the works of Muslim scholars and writers such as Sahbai, Rumi and Ghalib. Other tutors instructed him in mathematics, astronomy and Islamic jurisprudence.

Sir Sayyid was also adept at swimming, wrestling and other sports. He took an active part in the Mughal court's cultural activities. His elder brother founded the city's first printing press in the Urdu language along with the journal *Sayyad-ul-Akbar*. Sir Sayyid pursued the study of medicine for several years, but did not complete the prescribed course of study. Until the death of his father in 1838, Sir Sayyid lived a life customary for an affluent young Muslim noble. Upon his father's death, he inherited the titles of his grandfather and father and was awarded the title of Arif Jung by the emperor Bahadur Shah Zafar. Financial difficulties put an end to Sir Sayyid's formal education, although he continued to study in private, using books on a variety of subjects. Sir Sayyid assumed editorship of his brother's journal and rejected offers of employment from the Mughal court. Having recognized the steady decline in Mughal political power, Sir Sayyid entered the British East India Company's civil service. He was appointed *Sehestadar* at the courts of law in Agra, responsible for record-keeping and managing court affairs. In 1840, he was promoted to the title of *Munshi*.

While working as a jurist, Sir Sayyid focused on writing. From the age of 23 (in 1840), he wrote on various subjects (from mechanics to educational issues), mainly in Urdu, at least, 6000 pages. He published a series of treatises in Urdu on religious subjects in 1842. He published the book *A'thar-as-sanadid* (Great Monuments) documenting antiquities of Delhi dating from the medieval era. This work earned him the reputation of a cultured scholar. In 1842, he completed the *Jila-ul-Qulub bi Zikr-il Mahbub* and the *Tuhfa-i-Hasan,* along with the *Tahsil fi jar-i-Saqil* in 1844. These works focused on religious and cultural subjects. In 1852, he published the two works *Namiqa dar bayan masala tasawwur-i-Shaikh* and *Silsilat ul-Mulk*. He released the second edition of *A'thar-as-sanadid* in 1854. He also penned a commentary on the Bible — the first by a Muslim — in which he argued that Islam was the closest religion to Christianity, with a common lineage from Abrahamic religions. Acquainted with high-ranking British officials, Sir Sayyid obtained close knowledge about British colonial politics during his service at the courts.

Sir Sayyid Ahmad Khan, although a product of the medieval system of education and thinking, was a modern and liberal man with a rational outlook. He was in favor of following a healthy life style and giving up conventional, unhygienic, unscientific traditions and customs. He emphasized clean clothing, nutritious food and a hygienic mannerism. Common men of his times had a general apathy towards western culture and life style. Sir Sayyid always condemned this unjustified attitude of his peer group. He said, "If we hate the culture and life style of different societies, however pristine they may be, because of sheer prejudice or because of age-old traditions, and then what vision and hope do we have for our own development and progress?" [4]

He himself wore western dresses, adapted western mannerism and table etiquettes like the use of a fork and knife.

In this regard he had said, "In all honesty we should accept that eating with a fork and knife is more hygienic and descent than having food by hand." [5] On the religious front, Sir Sayyid Ahmad Khan was a critic of blind traditionalism. He supported the change of religious beliefs with changing times. In his essay entitled, "Time and Religion", he writes, "Just as times change thought, lifestyle, and civilization; beliefs and religions too are influenced by changing times." He added, "There was a time of faith and people believed in anything however irrational it may seem. This was the period of faith *(yaqeen)*. But the present time is the time of suspect *(shak)*. Truth needs proof". [6]

He had an open mind towards religious beliefs. In this regard he has written, "just like ancient and modern philosophies have changed, religious thoughts and faiths have also changed with time. Ancient religious rules teach us that man is meant for religion; modern rule being that religion is meant for man. Old rule tells us to find God blindly within the darkness of a night. Modern rule teaches us to search for God with open eyes, in light of one's vibrant environment".[7]

Sir Sayyid Ahmad Khan was in a strong denial of superstitions particularly miracles, magic and mystic. He had said, "There is nothing more damaging than a belief on superstitions likes miracles and magic for the human mind and for the very existence of humanity." [8]

He denied and was against Pan-Islamism. The concept of *Khalipha* and *Khilafat* was outdated for him. In his article entitled, *"Imam aur Immamat"*, he clarified, "a present-day analysis clearly shows that no one is worth the title of Imam and also no one, not even a head of state, is worth being entitled to be called a *Khalifa* of the prophet. Although Muslim governing area can aptly call their monarch as sultan (king) of that country, and in fact they are actually sultans, what so ever they may call themselves." [9]

He denied any contradiction between religion and science. He said, "Religion is the word of God and our surroundings are the work of God. An explanation of the existence of work of God is science. No contradiction is possible between science and religion as word of God cannot be in opposition of work of God. If a contradiction between religion and science exists in a mind, then it indicates cloudy thinking and therefore one should try to clear his thinking". [10]

A strong supporter of religious understanding he always emphasized the importance of religious tolerance. He has said, "In reality denouncing religious heads of other sects is actually denouncing the religious heads of one's own religion". [11] A great thinker, philosopher and a revolutionary he dedicated his complete life for his nation and especially for his community. Nineteenth century was a hard time for India and especially for Muslims. In the aftermath of 1857 revolt against British colonialism, Sir Sayyid tried to motivate Indian Muslim. In the history of India's transition from medievalism to modernism, Sir Sayyid stands out prominently as a dynamic force pitted against conservatism, superstitions, inertia and ignorance. He contributed many of the essential elements to the development of modern India and paved the growth of a healthy scientific attitude of mind which is sine qua non for advancement, both material and intellectual.

Sepoy Mutiny 1857: The spark for Revivalism

Critical moments in history are like earthquakes. They manifest themselves as convulsions releasing the pent-up stresses of generations. When the tremors are over, they leave behind a legacy, which becomes a prelude to the next major event. The Sepoy Mutiny of 1857-1858 was one such event which marked the end of medieval India died and, in its wake, grew social and political movements that paved the way for the emergence of the modern nations of India and Pakistan.

India was the first country where Muslims were faced with a challenge to define their interface with two global civilizations from political positions. Europeans' arms and diplomacy had smashed their power. The initial response of the Muslims to this debacle was to stay aloof from British, to shun their language, institutions, culture and methods. Withdrawal increased their isolation and set them behind in the race for political and social re-awakening. At the same time Hindus whom the Muslims have dominated for 500 years poised to dominate them. The changing relationships were most acutely felt in the Gangetic plains, in the populous regions extending from Delhi to Calcutta. It was this region that set the tone for the interaction between the Muslims, the Europeans and the Hindus in the years to come.

At the outbreak of the Indian rebellion, on May 10, 1857, Sir Sayyid was serving as the Sub-Judge at Bijnore, but owing to his general versatility and competence, he wielded much bigger influence than is normally the share of a subordinate judicial officer.

When the news of the Revolt (and massacre of Europeans) at Delhi reached Bijnore, the local European officers and their families were perturbed. Sayyid Ahmad Khan, however reassured them and promised to look after them even at the risk of his life. Soon this promise- and all the capacity he possessed for handling men – was to be put to a test. A long big mob, headed by Nawab Mahmud Khan, began to assemble and threaten the Europeans, who had taken refuge in the Collectors bungalow, and it appeared that the refugees would suffer the same fate which Europeans had met in many other places in Northern India. Seeing the position deteriorate, Sayyid Ahmad decided to beard the lion in his den. Unarmed and without any escort, he faced the angry mob and approached their leader. Using all his influence he could command, he tried to convince Nawab Mahmud Khan that it was in his interest to allow the Europeans to evacuate unmolested. He was successful in his plucky mission and the Nawab accompanied him to the Collector's bungalow, and a document was drawn up according to which the Europeans left the place in safety and the territory was taken up by the Nawab. Later the local Hindu local zamindars rose against the Nawab and when the situation confused the Commissioner of Meerut Division asked Syed Ahmad to take over as administrator of the district. He played the role for some time but ultimately the situation became too disturbed for peaceful administration and he had to leave the place and take the shelter at Meerut.

The Mutiny Northern India became the scene of the most intense fighting. The conflict left large numbers of civilians dead. Erstwhile centers of Muslim power such as Delhi, Agra, Lucknow and Kanpur were severely affected. Sir Sayyid and many other Muslims took this as a defeat of Muslim society.

Apparently, Sayyid Ahmad himself had not been affected adversely by the course of events but on studying his speeches and writings of this period reflects that his near and dear ones had suffered terribly during the reprisals which the British encouraged after the fall of Delhi. Deeply affected by the sorrow and anguish, his hair turned grey prima timely, and completely changed the course of his life. His mother was at the Mughal capital during the disturbances, and when he went to visit her after the British occupation of the city, heart breaking sight wet his eyes:

"On reaching his house, he heard that his mother had taken refuge in one of her *syce's* (house-attendant) houses and he followed her there. On his calling out to her she opened the door, crying out, 'why have you come here? All are being killed. You will be killed also." He told her not be afraid, as he had a special pass. He then found out that for five days she had been living on the horse's grain and was very weak. For three days she had no water,"[12].

He took his mother back with him to Meerut, but what she had undergone was too much for her and in spite of the best medical assistance she died within a month. "Sayyid Ahmad's uncle and cousin, whose house adjoined his at Delhi, were slained unarmed by the infuriated Sikh three days after the assault." Graham who has recorded all this adds: "They were as loyal as Sayyid Ahmad himself, but at that dreadful time many innocent men, I grieve to say suffered from the sins of the guilty."

Sayyid Ahmad's personal loss was heavy and when he saw what the Muslim community had suffered, his grief was inconsolable. In the indiscriminate massacre, arson and loot, which followed the British occupation of the city, Delhi, which Sayyid Ahmad had known so well and loved so tenderly, simply ceased to exist.

His speeches and writings of this period reflect his sorrow and anguish. Recalling those fearful days, he stated in a public speech:

"At that time, I did not believe that my people would regain even something of their prosperity and I could not bear to see the condition in which they were at that time......Believe me, this grief aged me and my hair turned grey."

Sayyid Ahmad felt that India was no place for a self-respecting Muslim and wanted to retire from service and migrate to Egypt but luckily, he did not yield to the counsel of despair. Realizing that "it would be an act of cowardice and selfishness to seek a heaven of peace when one's people were in a desperate condition," he gave up the idea of migration from India and chose the stony path of a hard struggle and patient, assiduous labour.

The revolt provided Sir Sayyid with an opportunity to write a book *Asbâb-e Baghâwat-e Hind* (*The Causes of Indian Mutiny*) which at once brought him into the first rank of the leaders of Indian opinion. Sayyid Ahmad's book offers home brewed vintage. He was ignorant of English or any other western language and his book was noteworthy as embodying the political wisdom of a well-informed Muslim who has acquainted with the modern political thought but who was a true heir to the traditions of Mughal statesmanship.

In this book, Sayyid Ahmad Khan stated the basic cause, which ultimately led to the Great Revolt. It was according to him, the absence of any Indian representing the Indian point of view in the upper councils governing the country. Secondly, the official interference in religion.

"There is not the smallest doubt that all men, whether ignorant or well-informed whether high or low, have firm conviction that the English government was bent on interfering with their religions, and with their old-established customs."[13]

Recounting the many causes which led to this belief he stated:

"(It was thought) that government, and the officers of government throughout the country, were in the habit of giving large sums of money to the missionaries, with the intension of covering their expenses, enabling them to distribute books and in every way aiding them. Many covenanted officers and many military men have been in the habit of talking to their subordinates about religion; some of them would bid their servants to come to their houses and listen to the preaching of the missionaries."[14]

He complained about the lack of social intercourse between the British and the Indian sections of public. "There was no real communication between the governors and the governed, no living together or near one another, as has always been the custom of the Mohammedans in countries in which they subjected to further rule."[15] He made it clear that "it was......for government to try and win the friendship of its subjects, not for the subjects to try and win that of the government." [16] He added " Now the English government has been in existence upwards of a century, and up to the present hour has not secured the affections of the people," [17]

He even criticized the handling of the mutineers at Meerut. He believed that they were brave people who had served the East India Company loyally, had won medals and decorations and did not refuse to bite the cartridges even (the biting of which would have "destroyed their castes) because they thought that it "was no crime at all". They were however punished in a manner which thinking men know to have been most wrong and most inopportune".[18] He further adds:

"The prisoners, on seeing their hands and feet manacled, looked at heir medals and wept. They remembered their services and thought how they have been recompensed".[19]

The book was written not to incite the people against government, but to acquaint the authorities with the hardship which people were suffering He sent 500 copies of the book to the India Office of the British government in London and a personal copy to Lord Canning in Calcutta. In India Office, the book was translated into English by Colonel Graham and Sir Auckland Colvin and published in Benares. The book was noted upon, discussed and became the starting point for many reforms, e.g., the appointment of Indians to the Legislative Council which began almost within a year of the publication of the book. A.O. Hume the founder of the Indian National Congress was influenced by Sayyid's book, 'The Causes of the Indian Revolt' and made him to think of establishing on organization like the Indian National Congress.[20]

"It was after reading Sayyid Ahmad's book on the *'Causes of the Indian Revolt'* that first felt the need for having a forum of public opinion in India, and eventually the Indian National

Congress came into existence. But the amazing thing is that when it was started, Sayyid was the first to oppose it."[21]

Sayyid Ahmad noticed that the unsuccessful war of Independence was being represented as a Muslim Revolt, and the Muslim were being suppressed with a heavy hand. He tried to correct the wrong impression of the British officials and started a magazine. In 1860-1861, he published another tract, *Risâlah Khair Khawahân Musalmanân: An Account of the Loyal Mahommdans of India*, in which the faithful services of Muslim noblemen were recorded and wherein he claimed that the Indian Muslims were the most loyal subjects of the British Raj because of their kindred disposition and because of the principles of their religion. He also wrote a commentary on the Old and the New Testament, *Tabiyyan al-kalam fi'l- tafsir al-tawra wa'l-injil cala millat al-islam* (*The Mahomedan Commentary on the Bible*). He attached a *fatwa* (religious decree) by Jamal ibn al-Abd Allah Umar al-Hanfi, the *Mufti* of Makkah, at the end of the book. This *fatwa* stated, "as long as some of the peculiar observances of Islam prevailed in India, it is *Dar al-Islam* (Land of Islam)." This was to counter the religious decrees that had been issued by many Indian *ulema'* stating that the Indian subcontinent had become a *Dar al-Harb,* the land of war. This political overture was favorably received in the ruling circles.

"Now that *Ghadar* is over [22] and whatever had to pass for the Muslims has passed, I am worried about improvement of our nation. I pondered hard and after a long reflection came to the conclusion that it is not possible to improve their lot unless they attain modern knowledge and technologies that are a matter of honor for other nations in the language of those who, through the Will of Allah, rule over us." [23]

The carnage of the Uprising and the subsequent decimation of the Muslim intelligentsia left a major void in the Islamic community of northern India. The initial response of the community to the aftermath of the mutiny was to conserve and withdraw into its social cocoon.

The Architect of Modern India

He strived towards the upliftment of the Indian masses, especially Muslims with modern scientific education and tried very hard to break the shackles of religious orthodoxy and traditional dogma of Indian Muslims. He saw the severe decline and decay of the Indian Muslims after the 1857 revolt. The Indian generally and Muslim specially, having been totally defeated by the foreign power, were sulking. The Muslim community was not inclined to take an active part in mainstream of national life and had almost totally withdrawn from the scene. Muslim youth concerning itself only with traditional and religious learning through the medium of the Arabic and Persian language abhorred European thought, which was in its heyday. They were not only disinterested but were not even aware of the era change. Their own system of life had lost its earlier dynamism and robustness. The doors of *Ijtehad* or re-interpretation of Muslim law had been closed for fear that interpretation in a society dominated by aliens will lead to a total pollution of thinking and action and the norms of Islamic *Shariah* will be diluted and discarded. Meanwhile, some other categories of Indian society had begun to adopt western learning through the English language. This was beginning to give them employment but, more importantly, was making them feel at ease with western thought-patterns and concepts such as democracy, liberty, rule of law, laissez-faire, industrialization and scientific temper.

While the British viewed the Muslims with deep suspicion, the Muslims shunned the British as infidels and foreigners who had usurped what had been rightfully theirs. Hostility and resentment fed upon each other and it looked like the Muslims would miss the opportunity to be a part of the new order imposed by newcomers from the British Isles.

Sayyid Ahmad Khan saw the dangers in this isolationist posture. The Muslim elite had fallen decades behind. He knew that as long as mutual suspicion and hostility persisted between the Muslims and the British, the former would be excluded from participation in the political and social life of the country, and put all his boundless energy behind the idea of pulling them out of their intellectual isolation from world currents and their touch-me-not aloofness in matters of bread and butter.

He had pondered over the tragedy which had overtaken his country and came to the conclusion that it was caused by ignorance. He, therefore, set himself to the task of educating both the ruler and the ruled, and removing the causes of possible friction and misunderstanding. It was during the decade of 1860s, that Ahmad Khan developed his ideas of a "Modern Islam" and a Muslim polity living under the British rule.

As a pioneer, Sayyid Ahmad Khan recognized the critical role of education for the empowerment of the poor and backward Muslim community. As a social reformer and a great national builder of modern India he began to prepare the road map for the formation of a Muslim University by starting various schools. Sayyid Ahmad's principal measure for the spread of knowledge (before he founded Aligarh college) was, however, the establishment of the Scientific society- originally known as the Translation Society- which was started at Ghazipur in January 1864. He instituted Scientific Society and created a scientific temperament among the Muslims and made the western knowledge available to Indians in their own language. While starting schools and prescribing their curriculum, he also realized that the Indian languages lacked useful literature contained in the language of the West. In a speech delivered in 1863 at Calcutta, he said:

"The reason, gentlemen, why we are so backward nowadays, is that whilst we are learned in and benefited by the philosophy, sciences, and arts of antiquity, we are almost ignorant of those of modern times." [24] He supplied this deficiency by organizing Scientific Society for getting useful books in English translated into Urdu.

On January 9, 1864, Sir Sayyid Ahmad Khan convened the first meeting of the Scientific Society at Ghazipur which was attended by Ahmad Khan's future biographer, Colonel Graham also. He was convinced that India could benefit from England's technological wealth. And so, the Society was established with the following goals and objectives:[25]

i. to translate into such languages as may be in common use among the people those works on arts and sciences which, being in English or other European languages, are not intelligible to the natives;

ii. to search for and publish rare and valuable oriental works (no religious work will come under the notice of the Society);

iii. to publish, when the Society thinks it desirable, any (periodical) which may be calculated to improve the native mind;

iv. to have delivered in their meetings lectures on scientific or other useful subjects, illustrated, when possible, by scientific instrument.

Thus, Sir Sayyid became the first Indian to establish and promote the Scientific Society which is active even today at Aligarh. Through this society he propagated methods of reasoning dialogue, experimentation and testing or hypothesis. In essence, Sir Sayyid taught as western empiricism does, that in worldly matters beliefs and views should be held tentatively and not dogmatically, they should be held for the time being in the belief that further experiment, further evidence further thinking will force a change in the old beliefs and positions in favour of new beliefs and postures.

The Aligarh Institute Gazette, an organ of the Scientific Society was also started in March 1866. It was devoted to the spread of knowledge and education and eventually succeeded in transforming the minds in the traditional Muslim Society. The Society translated in Urdu a number of books – including Elphinstone's *History of India,* Mill's *Political Economy*, Malcome's *History of Persia* and many works on agriculture, chemistry and zoology etc. In so far as he prompted a scientific attitude, Sir Sayyid was perhaps the most forward looking of Indian Muslim in the 19th century.

Ahmad Khan and the Society moved to Aligarh in 1867 where he procured a piece of land from the government for experimental farming. The Duke of Argyll, who was also the Secretary of State for India, became the Patron of the Society and Lt. Governor of the N.W. Province its Vice-Patron. Ahmad Khan was the secretary of the Society as well as member of the Directing Council and the Executive Council. In a memorandum of the Society to its President, Ahmad Khan wrote, in May 24, 1877, that for several years "the Society has cultivated wheat and barley according to the methods prescribed in Scot Burn's book on modern farming and showed the results to *Talukdars* (estate holders) of Aligarh; new instruments were used to cultivate corn by Burn's methods; several vegetables were grown from newly developed European seeds and their seeds were distributed to farmers; the Society cultivated American cotton seeds, and demonstrated their superior product."[26]

Sir Sayyid Ahmad Khan devoted all his energies to the Society and contributed a portion of his personal income also. He received small sums from various Muslim and non-Muslim philanthropists and realized that the political realities of India dictated that Muslims should establish their own organizations. So, on May 10, 1866, he established The Aligarh British Indian Association. The inaugural session was held at the Aligarh office of the Scientific Society in the presence of a sizeable number of local landowners and a few European officers but the Association failed to achieve any degree of impact on the decisions of the government and, one after the other, its plans were aborted. Ahmad Khan wanted to establish a "vernacular university" for the N.W. Provinces but was discouraged by the champions of Hindi who wanted such a university to teach in Hindi, rather than Urdu. In 1868, the Association announced assistance for persons traveling to Europe for educational and scientific purposes but at that time, most Muslims of northern India considered social contacts with Englishmen undesirable for their moral and religious integrity.

Thus, we see that Ahmad Khan's efforts to send his Muslim brothers to England for scientific enlightenment failed but he himself had been elected an honorary Fellow of the Royal Asiatic Society of London in 1864 and so he decided to go to England to see the ways of the British in their homeland. And so, at the age of fifty-two, he left his country on his long, expensive and (at that time) most unpopular journey.

He stayed in England for seventeen months and had a very busy time. He had a number of friends amongst the retired British officers and they showed him great courtesy and kindness. Lord Lawrence, for example, used to call him every month and arranged for his visits to important institutions. He was elected an honorary member of the Atheneum. He was received at the India Office by the Duke of Argyle, the Secretary of State, who was also Patron of the Scientific Society (of which Sayyid Ahmad was founder-Secretary) and the insignia of C.S.I was conferred on him.

During his stay in England, he took up two main things through which he rendered a great service to Islam. The first was the preparation of the reply on The Life of Mohamed by Sir William Muir. Sayyid Ahmad had seen the book and in India and one of the objects of his English journey was to collect material for the refutation of this unfair and wrapped biography of the Prophet. During his study of the subject in England, Sayyid Ahmad tried to help and encourage all efforts that were being made to do some justice to this much – maligned personality. He met Carlyle who had been comparatively fair to the Holy Prophet in his *'Heroes and Hero-Worship'*, and favorably impressed the Sage of Chelsa. Sayyid Ahmad helped John Davenport in publishing his book *An Apology for Mohamed and Koran* at his own expense and got it translated into Urdu.

He however realized that a more elaborate and scholarly study of the life of Prophet Muhammad was necessary than was possible for Carlyle or Davenport to write, and set about the task himself. He spent long hours in the Libraries of the British Museum and India Office and after months of patient research, Essays on the Life of the Mohammed was ready for the press. The book was a bulky one and no publisher would publish and bring into the market except at author's experience. Ahmad spent not less than Rs 4000 to see the result of his labour in print, and wrote to his friends in India to sell his library- even his kitchen utensils- to raise the money. The book has, in course of time, been excelled by the other literature on the subject (particularly by Syed Amir Ali's Spirit of Islam) but it ranks high as a pioneering effort and is a worth monument to Sayyid Ahmad's industry, scholarship, robust common sense and devotion to the Holy Prophet.

During his stay in England, he spent a lot of time in removing misconceptions about Islam and its Prophet but he could see that the difficulties of Islam and Muslims would not be solved merely by the publication of polemic or apologetic literature. There were many other things to be set right amongst Muslims, and as a true well-wisher of the community looked to them- even at the risk of his popularity. Sayyid Ahmad was very much impressed by the habits and manners of the English people- by their industry, their cleanliness, their punctuality and their orderly mode of living. Even a maid was servant was polite, well trained and educated. Sayyid believed that the Muslims had to reform themselves in many of these things and felt that right education is the key to all problems.

Towards the end of 1870 Sayyid Ahmad returned to India, and started *Tahzib-ul-Aklaq (Mohammedan Social Reformer)*. The first issue of *Tahzib-ul-Aklaq* appeared on December 24 1870 and, with it Sayyid began a vigorous campaign for improving the morals and manners of his co-religionists. In *Tahzib-ul-Aklaq* he vehemently criticized all the customs and habits which he thought, were holding up the progress of his people. He compared them with those of the nations of the western world and used the strongest language to bring home to his co-religionists their backwardness and intellectual decay.

The effect of *Tahzib-ul-Aklaq* was almost electric, and not exactly what Sayyid Ahmad desired. He had already offended the orthodox in 1868 by advocating a pamphlet that inter dining of Muslims with Christians or Jews was not unlawful. When he criticized the age-old customs and painted in lurid colors the conditions of Muslim society, there was a hue and cry against him and his writings. He did not confine the contents of his magazine to questions of social reforms only but wrote unorthodox articles on religious subjects also. As a result, a number of magazines came into being to oppose Sayyid Ahmad. He was called *'Kafir'* an *'Aheist'*, a *'Kristan'*(Christian). Sayyid Ahmad retaliated spiritedly and was ably assisted by a group of loyal friends. The controversy raged and caused a deep stir in the still waters of Muslim community and this was what Sayyid Ahmad desired of.

Aligarh Movement: Revivalism through Education

Sir Sayyid Ahmad Khan was worried for the scenario in which Muslims remained aloof from British administration, while the Hindus, Parsis and other communities forged ahead in education and social development. The replacement of Persian by English as the language of the higher courts (1835) was resented by the Muslims but was welcomed by the other communities. They embraced English education much more eagerly than did the Muslims. In 1878 there were 3155 college educated Hindus as against 57 college educated Muslims. In a country, growing poorer by the year due to Company practices, government service was a major career path for poor people and the Muslims missed these opportunities. The situation was particularly acute in Bengal and Uttar Pradesh. Since the fall of Bengal in 1757, all of the higher positions in civilian, military and judiciary service were reserved for the British. The more educated Hindus filled the lower positions that were open to Indians. The Muslims were practically shut out. He wanted his fellowmen to understand the importance of education and to use it as a powerful tool to improve their condition.

Sir Sayyid's mind had been molded by western education, and was under the powerful impact of the liberal forces of the modern age in Indian history. He knew that the British had established a stable and powerful government and was fully aware of the changes taking place in Indian society. The 'New', as he envisaged it, was not a change in the government but the symbol of a different pattern of economy and of culture. Therefore, he wanted to make all Muslims realize the significance of the age and take up the challenge of the times. This constituted the basis of his efforts at Muslim awakening known as the Aligarh Movement. Such a movement was necessary because the Muslims suffered from the depressing feeling that they had lost political power for ever and were in danger of losing their culture and civilization. They were frustrated and lacked a sense of direction and aspiration. The *Wahabi* Movement had failed. Shah Ismail and Syed Ahmad Barelvi were dead. There was no hope of the revival of the cherished "Islamic Rule".

He could foresee the imperative need for the Muslims to acquire proficiency in the English language and modern sciences if the community were to maintain its social and political identity, particularly in Northern India. Therefore, he devoted all his efforts to the general education of his countrymen. Graham, his biographer, writes: "Sayyid Ahmad's motto was 'Educate, educate, educate.' 'All the socio-political diseases of India may' he once said to me, 'be cured by this treatment. Cure the root, and the tree will floursih.[27]

Sir Sayyid established schools, wherever he was posted. The first was started in 1858 at Moradabad, and the second at Ghazipur in 1863. So far Sayyid Ahmad's efforts were directed towards the advancement of his countrymen- both Hindus Muslims. The British India Association, as well as the school at Ghazipur, was started with the help of both the communities and the Scientific Society was being managed by Sayyid Ahmad with the help of his lifelong Hindu friend –Raja Jai Kishen Dass. The Society undertook the translation of English works on the physical sciences into Urdu. Its organ, the bi-lingual *Scientific Society Gazatte* (published from 1866 onwards, and later to become the *Aligarh Institute Gazette*), remained impartial towards all communities, and neutral in the religious strife between Hindus and Muslims, urging both sides towards peace and reconciliation.[28]

Both these schools which were established with the support of the Hindu Muslim gentry, roused much more popular enthusiasm than the schools opened by the Christian missionaries, who had a virtual monopoly of modern education in those days. Sir Sayyid's dedication towards the cause of education ultimately made a dent in the Indian social structure and Hindus and Muslims of the country helped him in large numbers to further his cause. It is very important to note that amongst the first 120 people who gave valuable donations for the construction of school building were several Hindus like

Choudhary Sher Singh, Kunwar Lekhraj Singh, Raja Shiv Narain Singh, Raja Ghanshyam Singh, Raja Uday Pratap Singh, Lala Phul Chand, Lala Vasudeo Sahai and others. Their names still decorate the old buildings of Aligarh Muslim University. Thus, the arrival of Sayyid Ahmad Khan on the Indian educational scene is perhaps the most outstanding event in the 19th century in the history of Muslim education.

In 1875, Sir Sayyid founded the *Madarsatul Uloom* in Aligarh and patterned the MAO College after Oxford and Cambridge universities that he visited on a trip to London in 1869. His objective was to build a college in tune with the British education system but without compromising its Islamic values. He wanted this College to act as a bridge between the old and the new, the East and the West. While he fully appreciated the need and urgency of imparting instruction based on western learning but he was not oblivious to the value of Oriental learning and wanted to preserve and transmit to posterity the rich legacy of the past. Dr. Sir Mohammad Iqbal observed that

"The real greatness of Sir Sayyid consists in the fact that he was the first Indian Muslim who felt the need of a fresh orientation of Islam and worked for it--- his sensitive nature was the first to react to modern age".

Mohammedan Anglo Oriental College (MAOC) founded at Aligarh in 1875, the most respected and important educational centre for Indian Muslims was subsequently raised to the status of Aligarh Muslim University (AMU) in 1920. Aligarh Muslim University (AMU), known more as a movement than an academic institution is one of the most important chapters of Indian history as far as the sociology of Hindu-Muslim relation is concerned. Sir Sayyid said:

"This is the first time in the history of Mohammedans of India, that a college owes it neither to the charity or love of learning of an individual, nor to the spending patronage of a monarch, but to the combined wishes and the united efforts of a whole community. It has its own origin in course which the history of this county has never witnessed before. It is based on principles of toleration and progress such as find no parallel in the annals of the east."

Sir Sayyid's famous speech which he made while foundation of MAO College was laid down by Lord Lytton on 18th January, 1877 is the soul of Aligarh Movement. He said:

"From the seed which we sow today, there may spring up a mighty tree, whose branches, like those of the banyan of the soil, shall in their turn strike firm roots into the earth, and themselves send forth new and vigorous saplings".

Since the name of the Mohammedan Anglo Oriental College college was self-descriptive and its orientation was decidedly western and so it faced immediate hostility from the Muslim religious establishment. *Mullahs* denounced him as a "turncoat" and a "*kafir*". Undaunted, Sir Sayyid persisted. He invited a noted Englishman, Theodore Beck to serve as the first principal of the College. As hostility towards his efforts intensified in the areas around Delhi, he traveled throughout the Punjab in search of support and funds. Punjabi Muslims, who felt the British had recently liberated them from the Sikhs, welcomed Sir Sayyid with open arms and generously provided him moral and material support.

A visionary, his ideas were in advance of his times, and he made the times advance rapidly to catch on with his ideas. While his M.A.O. College was primarily meant for the educational uplift of the Muslims, but it was also a college where both communities were being educated together. His broad mindedness led him to mingle the Hindu and the Muslims, the class and the mass. He insisted on equality of rights between all communities in his college and elsewhere and emphasized that the basis of a common nationality was not religion but homeland. In his lectures and writings, he had stated clearly that he regarded the Hindus and Muslims like two eyes of the same person and that discrimination between them was not possible.

Thus in 'Education' he saw as a positive sign for developing mutual brotherhood, so he emphasized that although the college at Aligarh had been set up to improve the condition of Muslim, Hindus also studied in it as equals. He believed that since for an outsider Hindu and Muslims were all like "Indians", the degradation of one community implied that of the other too. He therefore emphasized that they could not earn honor and dignity unless these two 'brothers' were not brought up and educated together, similar avenues of progress being made available to both. He described the college as a source of national progress and an ideal for the 'nation' which for him comprised both Hindus and Muslims and which he fervently desired to 'make a nation'[29]

In one of his lectures Sir Sayyid stated:

"The main reason behind the establishment of this institution as I am sure all of you know was the wretched dependence of the Muslims, which had been debasing their position day after day. Their religious fanaticism did not let them avail the educational facilities provided by the government schools and colleges. It was, therefore, deemed necessary to make some special arrangements for their 'education'. Suppose, for example, there are two brothers, one of them is quite hale and hearty and the other is diseased. His health is on decline. Thus, it is the duty of all brothers to take care of their ailing brother and bear the hands in his trouble. This was the very idea which goaded me to establishment the Mohammadan Anglo-Oriental College. But I am pleased to say that both the brothers get the same education in this college. All rights of the college pertaining to those who call themselves Muslims are equally related to those who call themselves Hindus without any reservation. There is no distinction whatsoever between Hindus and Muslims. Only one who strives hard can lay claim to get the stipends and both of them are treated at par as boards. I regard both Hindus and Muslims as my two eyes."

Similarly, in 'An Account of the Loyal Muhamadans of India' (written in 1860), Sir Sayyid hastens to absolve himself of any charge of partisanship or bias although he was native of Hindustan." In an incomplete and undated letter to an Englishmen, he described himself as a Muslim, a native of Hindustan, and of Arab descent. He apparently accepted such a multiple identity as a matter of fact.

While Sir Sayyid had put forward the need of the hour to get equipped with the modern education to improve the social and economic conditions of Muslims of India but he never discouraged or denied the importance of religious and oriental studies. By his individual means and with the help of Muslim Educational Conference, he always tried to modernize the *Madarasas*, update their syllabus as per the need of the hour.

In the interest of an effective educational programme Sir Sayyid pleaded the students for keeping out of agitation policies. This has sometimes been interpreted as aloofness from the struggle for freedom. Pandit Jawaharlal Nehru correctly saw the spirit of Sir Sayyid's mission which he stated in his Autobiography:

"So, to this education be turned all his energy trying to win over his community to his way of thinking. He wanted no diversions or distractions from other directions it was a difficult enough piece of work to overcome the inertia and hesitation of the Muslims. The Hindus, half of century ahead in western education, could indulge in this post time. Sir Sayyid's decision to concentrate on western education for Muslim was undoubtedly a right one. Without that they could not have played any effective part in the building up of Indian nationalism...... of the new type, and they could have been doomed to play second fiddle to the Hindus with their better education and for stronger economic position. The Muslims were not historically or ideologically ready for the bourgeoisie nationalist movement as they had developed no bourgeoisie, as the Hindus had done Sir Sayyid's activities, therefore, although seemingly very moderate, were in the right revolutionary direction."

Aligarh College soon became a center for Muslim educational and political activities in northern India, although its doors were open to all communities and many distinguished British as well as Hindu Professors served on its faculty. The college served as a magnet for young men and women from families of *zamindars* and peasants alike from all over India. It provided a boost to the Muslims in their competition with the other communities for government jobs. But it was in the political arena that its impact was most profoundly felt. Graduates of Aligarh University were in the forefront of the political struggle in India and their efforts were decisive in the struggle for Pakistan.

AMU's unique achievement is that for over a century it provided quality higher education at low cost in a whole lot of modern fields e.g., sciences, medicine, engineering, literature to a vast multitude of youth from socially and economically deprived Muslim families across the breadth of India. Thus, AMU has truly uplifted the Muslim community of South Asia and has put them on a level playing field with others.

Urdu Verses Hindi Controversy: Conflict of Linguistic Domination

Protracted battle for revival of the medieval pride of Urdu since the early days of British establishment in India is one of the prominent Muslim issues, which widened the Hindu-Muslim divide in the country. A Study of the cause-and-effect mechanism of Urdu controversy, which started in 1837 shows that since the establishment of Muslim rule in the country, this language of urban Muslim elite and of those Hindus, whose economic interest was linked with it, was never acceptable to native dwellers. Gradually its communal, parochial and political influences made this controversy more and more complicated.

Urdu was born out of the socio-administrative requirement of Muslim conquerors, who after repeated plunder, pillage and loot preferred to settle down in regions around Delhi. Initially at the instance of Muslim soldiers Urdu emerged as a synthesis of Khari Boli (Hindi), Braj Bhasha, Rajasthani and Punjabi with some Persian and Arabic vocabulary. Thus, Urdu became *lingua franca* (mixture of different languages used for convenience) for interaction between the alien soldiers and the native dwellers. But gradually its Persianisation and Arbisation were motivated by the foreign rulers to establish their cultural and linguistic hegemony in the region.

Over fifty percent vocabulary have been drawn from Turkish, Persian and Arabic in Urdu language, and this shows that the Arab rulers instead of winning over the hearts and mind of the native dwellers imposed their linguistic hegemony over the native languages without caring for the sentiments of the Indian society. Using Persian as the principal standard written language for administrative purpose, the Muslim rulers with intention to establish their permanent political, economic, cultural and linguistic hegemony in India pushed Urdu as a substitute of the native languages, which had Sanskrit origin and Nagari script. Urdu was gradually saturated with Perso-Arabic script, metaphors, similes, the forms of verse, prosody, about sixty percent of vocabulary, content of mannerism and poetic thought of Islamic and Persian tradition. The birth of Urdu therefore, created the first social division in Indian society.

Till 1837 Persian remained the language of administration and Urdu was used only for literary discourse among the urban elite. But extra honorable status of Urdu in the literary courts of

Muslim rulers made this new language a status symbol of the elite section of Muslims.

At the initial period of British establishment in India when East India Company started exercising executive power on behalf of titular Mogul sovereign, they decreed (1837) to abolish Persian from official use and replaced it with English and native vernaculars. They however, accepted Urdu as *lingua franca* in northern India, where it had already established its dominating position over local vernaculars. The British allowed Urdu to be the language of courts in northern India. This boosted the morale of the Urdu speaking Muslims and some Hindu elite, whose economic interest was linked with this language, when it got recognition in courts of the region.

The Hindu masses however became restive, and demand for official status of Hindi, which was the vernacular in northern India, came to surface. The Muslim elite, who wanted the hegemony of Urdu to continue even though this *lingua franca* was confined to the urban elite, did not like this demand for Hindi. This was the starting point for Hindi-Urdu controversy, which gradually developed communal overtones.

For Hindu masses, linguistic supremacy of Urdu imposed over regional languages always remained a source of irritant for as it disturbed the homogeneity of Indian society. The Hindu masses never accepted Urdu as their language, since it symbolized as an instrument of Muslim barbarism even though a section of their urbanized group accepted this alien language for their economic interest.

Argument that Urdu was developed as *lingua franca* during Muslim rule may be partially correct but its Persianisation and Arabisation at the cost of the native dialect shows that Muslim conquerors never cared for the sentiments of the subjugated natives in their attempt to impose their cultural hegemony over them. Without realizing the emotional attachment of native dwellers with their vernaculars any argument in support of Urdu therefore never convinced the protagonists of Hindi. The supporters of Hindi argue that Urdu was not only developed as *lingua franca* but it was a part of the design of Muslim conquerors to establish their political and cultural hegemony in this region. By creating separatist influence of Persian, Arabic and Turkish tradition on Urdu the alien rulers permanently damaged the possibility of emotional integration of Muslims in the mainstream of Indian society. Hindus developed aversion against this language because of its main vehicle Persian and Arabic, which were alien to their cultural tradition. (An Overview).[30]

The Urdu Hindi controversy broke out in 1867, with the opponents of Urdu refusing to accept it as the vernacular of India, and striving to replace it as the official language, by Hindi written in the *Devnagri* script.[31]

During the last days of the Muslim rule, Urdu emerged as the most common language of the northwestern provinces of India. It was declared the official language, and all official records were written in this language. In 1867, some prominent Hindus started a movement in Banaras in which they demanded the replacement of Urdu with Hindi, and the Persian script with the *Dev Nagri* script, as the court language in the northwestern provinces. The reason for opposing Urdu was that the language was written in Persian script, which was similar to the Arabic script and Arabic was the language of the Quran, the Holy Book of the Muslims. Babu Shiva Prasad of Banares was one of the early proponents of the Nagari script. In a *Memorandum on court characters* written in 1868, he accused the early Muslim rulers of India for forcing them to learn Persian.

On this language controversy Sir Sayyid felt that the Hindus wished to wipe out Urdu which was in fact only an advanced form of *Bhasha* mainly because its foundations were laid during Muslim rule.[32] This onset of the Hindi-Urdu controversy of 1867, saw the emergence of Sir Sayyid as a political leader of the Muslim community.

For him Urdu was undeniably 'our language' and the 'vernacular of Hindustan.' Irrespective of whether or not it was the 'original language of the country', what mattered was that it was the only language which was universally used in India.[33] He was convinced that the Hindus were motivated purely by racial prejudice, therefore unruffled by the displeasure of his Hindu friends, Sir Sayyid never kept silent in the face of attacks on Urdu. He had a lengthy correspondence with the secretary of the committee formed for the restoration of Hindi, which was even made public.[34] There was a great deal of verbal quibbling in these letters of 1868, as to which was the 'current mixed language' and the 'original language' of India: Hindi or Urdu. Sir Sayyid denied that the latter contained numerous Persian words, which he felt were employed only by those who were well versed in Persian.[35]

At that time the demand of the Hindus was turned down, apparently due to the greater currency of Urdu.[36]

The movement was encouraged in 1881 when Hindi in *Devanagari* script replaced Urdu in Persian script as the official language in neighboring Bihar. They submitted 118 memorials signed by 67,000 people to the Education Commission in several cities[37]. The proponents of Hindi argued that the majority of people spoke Hindi and therefore introduction of Nagari script would provide better education and improve prospects for holding Government positions. They also argued that Urdu script made court documents illegible, encouraged forgery and promoted the use of the use of complex Arabic and Persian words.

The movement grew quickly and within a few months spread throughout the Hindu population of the northwestern provinces of India. The headquarters of this movement were in

Allahabad. This situation provoked the Muslims to come out in order to protect the importance of the Urdu language. The opposition by the Hindus towards the Urdu language made it clear to the Muslims of the region that Hindus were not ready to tolerate the culture and traditions of the Muslims.

Hindi-Urdu controversy cracked the unity between Hindus and Muslims last seen during Sepoy Mutiny of 1857. Hindus and Sikhs of Bihar, United Province and Punjab got united to fight against imposition of Urdu on the majority population of the region. Organizations like Arya Samaj, Punjab Brahma Sabha, Sat Sabha and Sikh National Association joined the Hindi movement and placed their opposition to Urdu before the respective units of Education Commission set up by the British to frame the education policy for India. Organizations such as *Anjuman Taraqqui-e-Urdu* were formed for the advocacy of Urdu.[38] Advocates of *Urdu* argued that Hindi scripts could not be written faster, and lacked standardization and vocabulary. They also argued that the Urdu language originated in India, asserted that Urdu could also be spoken fluently by most of the people and disputed the assertion that official status of language and script is essential for the spread of education. It was widely believed that Sir Sayyid prevailed upon the Commission not to take a decision on a matter which according to him was a grave national and political, rather than an educational issue.[39] During a speech in Patna on January 1883 Sir Sayyid described Urdu as the language of neither Hindus nor Muslims, but a new creation- the product of both through interaction.[40]

Urdu was thus for him a symbol of their composite culture, and any attack on it was a blow to their solidarity.

The aggressiveness of Hindi movement "affirmed that for Hindus Urdu was a pure and simple survival of Muslim tyranny".[41]

Introduction of Hindi in Bihar "quickened the pace of Hindi movement in North West Provinces and later in United Province"[42]

Communal violence broke out as the issue was taken up by firebrands. Sir Sayyaid Ahmad Khan had once stated, "I look to both Hindus and Muslims with the same eyes & consider them as two eyes of a bride. By the word nation I only mean Hindus and Muslims and nothing else. We Hindus and Muslims live together under the same soil under the same government. Our interest and problems are common and therefore I consider the two factions as one nation." Speaking to Mr. Shakespeare, the governor of Banaras, after the language controversy heated up, he said "I am now convinced that the Hindus and Muslims could never become one nation as their religion and way of life was quite distinct from one and other."

Taking advantage of his closeness with the British, Sir Sayyid requested the latter to establish an Urdu University as he held the view that this language to be "a common legacy of Hindus and Muslims".[43]

This was really an intellectually dishonest view. Sir Sayyid's observation before the Education Commission (appointed by the British) that Urdu was 'the language of gentry and Hindi that of the vulgar', was repudiated by his contemporary Hindi protagonist Babu Harish Chandar. He retorted that "Urdu was the language of dancing girls and prostitutes"[44]

Sir Sayyid was the first Muslim leader, who turned Urdu-Hindi controversy into a political issue at the cost of Hindu-Muslim unity.

In 1897, Madan Mohan Malviya published a collection of documents and statements titled *Court character and primary education in North Western Provinces and Oudh*, in which, he made a compelling case for Hindi. [45]

The Urdu-Hindi controversy had a great effect on the life of Sir Sayyid Ahmad Khan. Before this event he had been a great advocate of Hindu-Muslim unity and was of the opinion that the "two nations are like two eyes of the beautiful bride, India". But this movement completely altered his point of view. He put forward the Two-Nation Theory, predicting that the differences between the two groups would increase with the passage of time and the two communities would not join together in anything wholeheartedly.

In the fury of Freedom Movement Urdu became one of the issues, which kept the Hindus and Muslims, divided. Sir Sayyid died in 1898 but the followers of his Aligarh Movement under the leadership of Shibli, Hali, Mulk and others carried forward the legacy of battle for supremacy of Urdu even after his death to counter the movement for Hindi. On April 18, 1900 MacDonnell, Chief Commissioner of Oudh abolished Persian script from the language of courts and replaced it with *Devanagari* by adopting *Nagari* resolution. This resolution worked as a catalyst to provoke the educated Muslims of northern India. They took this change as a challenge to the pre-British status of their dominance over Hindu subjects.

Muslim thinkers often project Sir Sayyid Ahmad Khan (1817-1898) as a modernist Muslim leader and a staunch supporter of Hindu -Muslim unity. It is said that Sayyid, the founder of Aligarh Movement was initially in favour of modern education to all Indians and not only to Muslims. But his obsession with Urdu was an indication that he wanted to maintain the supremacy of this language as a symbol of Muslim domination over the cultural and linguistic identity of this country. He got many books translated only in Urdu under the banner of Scientific Society established at his instance in 1863, even though this language was being spoken by only four to five percent of urban elite particularly Muslims. When he found that demand for Hindi language coming to surface, he looked the other way and confined his Aligarh Movement exclusively for Muslims. He was aggrieved to find that Hindus launched a first movement to revive their linguistic tradition for its recognition as the second official language of the North Western Provinces. Urdu-Hindi controversy therefore, originated from the Muslim renaissance movement launched by him after the failure of *Sepoy* Mutiny in 1857.

S. Abid Husain [46] blames Sir Sayyad for taking an "emotional" rather than a "realistic" view of this new trend of Hindu "renaissance"; the assertion by the Hindus of their "separate culture entity"; and efforts to "safeguard their special interests." However, the issue appeared significant to Sir Sayyid perhaps not so much because he saw in it the beginnings of Hindu revivalism and communal consciousness as suggested by Moin Shakir [47] but since he perceived the anti-Muslim, hostile and aggressive character of the movement. Hali treats the eruption of the Urdu-Hindi controversy as a watershed in the life of Sir Sayyad, when for the first time he felt that Hindus and Muslims could not work together as a single nation *(qawm)* for the good of all. Hali observed that Sir Sayyad thereafter began a think in terms of the advancement of Muslims alone, whereas earlier he had always been concerned with the welfare of Indians as a whole. He is even reported to have predicated greater discord and hostility in the future, whereas earlier he has always believed in and acted upon the principle of complete unity. The protests of Bengali newspapers against concessions made by the government of Muslims and their writings against that community further compounded matters. However, Hali acknowledges that in spite of these deterrents Sir Sayyad's desire for unity between the two communities remained unchanged, as is evident from his later public speeches. [48]

From the above account it is evident how strongly Sir Sayyid felt about the attempts to wipe out Urdu and what a keen interest he took in foiling such bids. He was apparently quick to perceive the deep and far-reaching implications of the conflict and that explains why he exerted himself so much in the matter. We however hold that although the outbreak of the controversy caused him great distress and heartburn, he did not allow himself to be embittered by it. This is evident from the fact that even after 1867 many of his plans for the education and upliftment of Muslims were specially molded so as to include Hindus in their purview. Thus, in spite of the challenge posed by the controversy to Hindu-Muslim unity, he never abandoned his conviction that such a unity was possible and continued to work towards it with characteristic determination.

Concept of Indian Nationhood

A very important aspect of Sir Sayyid's political thought is his concept of nation and 'nationalism'. He used the term 'nation' to denote the people. All Indians constitute one single nation. The British rulers in India, according to him, constituted a separate nation. He used the word 'Hindu', also in a broader sense. He who lives in India is a 'Hindu'. In this sense, he was the prophet of the ideal of one 'Nation'. According to him different religions do not militate against the essential unity of the people. 'Hindu' and 'Muslim' are religious denominations, and India could build up a composite culture. In one of his speeches, he said that India is the native land of both Hindus and Muslims, both drink the holy water of the Ganges; both are of the same color. Muslims have borrowed hundreds of customs from the Hindus; Hindus also acquired many habits from the Muslim. This process of assimilation gave birth to a new language, Urdu. Therefore, the preservation and strength of Hindu-Muslim unity is the primary condition for the welfare and progress of both. The Hindus and Muslims of India, he said, are the two beautiful and charming eyes of a bride.

Sir Sayyid repeatedly and explicitly defined Hindus and Muslims as jointly forming a single nation or *qawm* i.e., India, in the speeches of 1884, as on 3 February:

"By the word *qawm* I mean Hindus and Muslims both. This is the sense in which I interpret the word 'nation' *(qawm)*."[49]

In his speeches Sir Sayyid did not hesitate to describe both India and Europe as single nations despite their religious and racial diversity, reaffirming the territorial (as opposed to religious) basis of nationality. A great champion of Hindu-Muslim unity Sir Sayyid addressed a big gathering at Gurdaspur on Jan. 27, 1884. He said:

"Hindus and Muslims! Do you belong to a country other than India? Don't you live on this soil and are you not buried under it or cremated on its Ghats? If you live and die on this land, then bear in mind, that Hindus and Muslims is but a religious word; all the Hindus, Muslims and Christians who live in this country are one nation."

His deliberate use of the English word "nation" suggests that he had in mind its current Western usage and the implied political connotations.

Although there are numerous references by Sir Sayyid in these speeches to Muslims as "my nation" *(qawm)*, at some points he clarified that by "nation" he did not mean only Muslims, but both communities.[50] He even said that if they overlooked their difference of faith, then by virtue of being compatriots in India, they were in reality one "nation".[51]

Sir Sayyid very deliberately and earnestly tried to undermine the argument that Indian Muslims were "aliens". He did so in his characteristically vigorous style, by proving that far from being strangers to India, they had become its native and were therefore, no less "Hindu" than the Hindus themselves. For this he redefined the term "Hindu" not as the adherent of a particular faith, but as a native of Hindustan. As such, it would equally apply to both the communities *(qawm)* living in India. He regretted that Hindus regarded only themselves as Indians and Muslims as foreigners.[52]

In an article written many years later in 1897, he repeated that since Muslims had also been living in India for centuries, like the Aryan invaders before them, they too deserved to be called "Hindu" i.e., natives of Hindustan.[53]

In January 1884, Sir Sayyid undermined the territorial basis of nationhood by saying that Islam had abolished it to create a new national bond that was spiritual; and since Islam was the basis of their identity, Muslim must remain true to it. He also added that that their compatriots of all faiths were their brothers-in social and cultural matters and Islam preached good neighborliness towards all. He defined his nation as the *Ummat* of the Prophet *(Pubh)*, which he loved and desired to serve; he explained that his efforts for its educational upliftment were meant to contribute towards the progress of India as a whole. Yet despite these pronouncements he did not hesitate to express his conviction that neither community separately, nor both together, could rule India.

In 1885, when the Indian National Congress was established Sir Sayyid chose to oppose it. It was not that Sir Sayyid was against the policies of the Indian National Congress but he was of the opinion that "the aim and objects of the Indian National Congress are based upon an ignorance of history and present day realities; they do not take into consideration that India is inhabited by different nationalities; they presuppose that the Muslims, the Marathas, the Brahmins, the Kshatriyas, the Banias, the Sudras, the Sikhs, the Bengalis, the Madrasis and the Peshawaries all should be treated exactly alike and all of them belong to the same culture. The Congress conducted itself on the complacent assumption that all Indian profess the same religion, speak the same language, have the same way of life, that their attitude to history is similar and is based upon the same historical traditions. For the successful running of democratic government, it is essential that the majority should have the ability to govern not only themselves but also unwilling minorities."

In 1887 Sir Sayyid reverted to the view that the different Indian people had not so far intermingled to form a single nation, and nor they were equally matched, He reiterated his earlier opposition to the implementation of pure representation, and felt that due to the backwardness and fewer numbers, Muslims particularly were unfit to compete with others. He therefore advised them to concentrate only on trade and education, and abstain from the political agitation of the Congress fearing that the strong vindictive arm of the government would fall most heavily on them. His reaction was obviously conditioned by his experiences of 1857: he continued to believe that since Indians could not harm the government in the least but would only injure themselves by a confrontation; it was wiser to secure benefits by winning trust through loyalty. He felt that the activities of the Congress would spark off a power struggle between the various Indian communities; and that through it the Hindus hoped to politically subjugate, and even annihilate the Muslim community.

But since 1867 when the Hindi-Urdu controversy started, Sir Sayyid took a very serious view of it. It was to him a symbol of the beginning of communal consciousness and revivalism among the Hindus.

Attitudinal Change: Crisis of Muslim Identity

We perceive a slight change in Sir Sayyid's attitude when in a dateless article he repeatedly uses the phrase *(qawm banana)* exclusively for the Muslim community. He now evinced the belief that in order to make Muslims a nation *(qawm)*, and honored among the "nations" of the world, besides providing good breeding and instruction it was necessary that as far as possible their children and youth should live, study, eat, sleep and play together, with arrangements for their excellent upbringing."⁵⁴

Sir Sayyid had earlier supported both religious education and the teaching of Arabic and Persian but only to popularize modern education too among Muslims. Now he advocated these for altogether different reasons. He believed that at least elementary (if no advanced) religious education (comprising a knowledge of the basic and commandments) should be imparted to Muslim students in order to acquaint them with Islam, which had united different nations *(qawm)* into a single Muslim nation,⁵⁵ and was therefore the very basis of their group identity.

Sir Sayyid even recommended the teaching of Arabic and Persian, not only because these were "superior, modern and scholarly languages, satisfying the needs of Muslims but also because Arabic was "the language of Muslims" and Persian was "closely related to them", besides being "a treasury of Muslim sciences and history." ⁵⁶

Thus, we find a new, deliberate and self-conscious urge in Sir Sayyid Ahmad Khan to preserve the religious cultural and linguistic identity of the community through education, which became a move marked with the passage of time. He repeated nearly identical sentiments regarding the need for residential and religious education, and the teaching of Arabic and Persian, in another speech in December 1893.⁵⁷

"To breathe into them spirit of nationality is even more essential than their education." Without it, the Muslim nation *(Qawm)* would remain dull and lifeless, and would not succeed in any field. He felt that this spirit of nationality could not be instilled into young Muslims unless they were educated collectively at one place. He said that their hearts would then be inspired by the thought of their "national college", and the enthusiasm of being educated in it. ⁵⁸ These sentiments were supported only a day later when he denounced the Indian Nation Congress in his fiery and historic speech.

By 1888, Sir Sayyid had completely abandoned the view expressed in 1884 at Amritsar that India could not progress unless Muslims and Hindus were educated together. Speaking at Meerut on 14 March 1888, he expressed the very opposite view: that a Muslim studying among non-Muslims, who were moreover his superiors in knowledge", would face numerous problems. On the other hand, he would enjoy his studies immensely were he to be educated among "students of his own nation, who are his equals in these attainments." He therefore believed that arrangements should be made for Muslim students to "study in communities."[59]

Sir Sayyid now believed that for their good education and training it was essential that Muslims study, live and eat together and learn "to love one another" as only this could produce the desirable "national feeling and sympathy." He claimed that nowhere in India did Muslim students have so much "national spirit" and brotherly feeling for each other as in the M.A.O. College Although these qualities had not yet attained the desired ripeness, but when they did, national *(qawmi)* honor would be achieved.

Sir Sayyid believed that the effects of being physically gathered together are tremendous. Such an assembly greatly influences the heart and mind, generating unity and a feeling of glory of the "nation" which however vanish on dispersion. Moreover, he felt that "these thoughts will not arise in the minds of men unless they are forced upon their attention. This he believed was the reason why the Prophet *(Pbuh)* had ordered Muslims to meet in daily weekly and bi-annual congregational prayers."[60]

Sir Sayyid summed up these points in two speeches in December 1894, in which his stance is more aggressive them even before. In his almost apologetic tone in 1884, he justified the setting up of a college especially for Muslims. Having come a long way since then, he now assertively defended the need for a separate educational institution for Muslims. He reasoned that not only did the education of Muslims suffer by studying amidst other nations (*quawm*) due to their different needs and modes of life, but they could never thus "become a nation." Their mutual sympathy and "national feeling" which were born by living together would be stifled, and would gradually become extinct by being educated in government colleges where they were very few as compared to other "nations".[61]

In order to keep alive Muslim nationally (*qawmiyyat*) a feeling of "national unity and sympathy" must be generated, which was possible only if students shared all aspects of life together. To illustrate this point, he cited the example of the students of the M.A.O. College, who he believed experienced religious enthusiasm and a feeling of nation (*quawmi*) pride, pleasure and sympathy at the thought of studying in their "national college", which he felt was lacking in progress", and it was only by such education that Muslims would become a "Nation".[62]

By now Sir Sayyid was convinced of the need for religious education hand-in-hand with modern knowledge, but for altogether different reasons- so that:

"A feeling of nationality i.e., "*qawmiyyat*" and national unity and national sympathy which is the first step to national progress should be inculcated among Muslims." For this it was necessary to ensure that they remained Muslims, and the reality of Islam remained firm in their hearts-they should therefore be taught religious tenets and as far as possible made to observe religious obligations. As before, he emphasized that this was necessary alongside elementary religious education since Muslim brotherhood, national unity and in fact nationality itself was based solely on Islam.[63]

Therefore, Sir Sayyid believed that Muslim students should be taught Islamic history, and about the spread of Islam, and Islamic brotherhood, which was stronger than familial bonds. In order to keep alive their nationality (*qawmiyyat*) which he felt was threatened by English education, they must also be taught Arabic (The language of their religion and of their forefather) or at least Persian.[64]

Modern education, for which Sir Sayyid had been campaigning for nearly three decades, had now become quite prevalent, and its ill effects, had also begun to surface. He had told Muslim students on 30th December 1888 that he wanted them to master western knowledge, but while holding on fast to the *'Kalimah'*. Warning them against the undesirable consequence of modern education, and of studying in England, which after manifested itself in indulgence in illegitimate freedom, thoughtless limitation of the darker side of western culture and the flouting of Muslim mores, he urged them to remain faithful to Islam or else they would be excluded from the Muslim nation *(qawn)*.[65]

In 1894 he talked about the threat to Muslim nationality, posed by modern education.

We thus notice a very marked change in Sir Sayyid's ideas regarding nationhood. This was a response to the perceived threat to Muslim identity posed by western education, and the overwhelming majority and dominance of the Hindu population.

He became extremely wary of the latter after the formation of the Indian National Congress in 1885 and publicly gave vent to his feelings for the first time in December 1887 to which time also dates the change in his views regarding Muslim education and identity consciousness. He believed that due to their educational backwardness, the Muslims lacked sufficient political consciousness. Moreover, it was of no use their supporting the Congress because the Muslim society was lacking in a sound middle class. And in Sir Sayyid's mind, the Congress was not a mass organization but a representative of the interests of the middle class. However, support to the Congress and nationalism was not convertible terms. He believed that Congress was harmful even to the Hindus.

Correspondingly Sir Sayyid's delineation of the Muslim "nation" becoming more and more well defined, closely unit, exclusive, and even aggressive. However, these new trends in his thought were neither completely abrupt nor severed from his former views; rather at times we can see their seeds in past experiences.

Shah Abdul Aziz issued the famous and highly significant *fatwa* in 1830, declaring that India had ceased to be a *dar-al Islam,* which amounted to a call to Muslims to mobilize themselves and rise in defiance of the foreign power.[66] Sir Sayyid however did not agree, his views being wholly conditioned by his staunch loyalism.

In the early years (i.e., 1858, 1860 and 1871), he took great pains to show that since Islam enjoins obedience to the ruling authority which provides security and religious freedom (irrespective of its religious beliefs) Muslims should remain, loyal and obedient to the British government.

In the same strain Sir Sayyid ruled out there being any grounds for Muslims to wage a jihad against the British government. In fact, such an uprising by Muslim subjects was unlawful and unwarranted by Muslim law, which according to him recommended either forbearance of migration in the face of oppression by a non-Muslim government. Jihad could however be waged by Muslim subjects of a Muslim ruler, against an infidel country which oppressed its Muslim subjects-provided no worldly or political considerations were involved.

Sir Sayyad clarified that since tumult and disorder are repellant to Islam, it is opposed to aggression and bloodshed for conquest and territorial aggrandizement, as well as for spreading Islam. In order to allay British suspicions regarding Muslim religious zeal and intentions, he clarified that the *Quranic* injunctions to fight polytheists until there is no mischief and religion is for God alone, did not mean that Muslims should continue to fight all unbelievers till such a time as Islam I established as the only religion on earth; since this was both impractical and impossible. He reasoned that rather than being of universal import, these verses refer to the idolaters of *Makkah* at the time of the Prophet *(Pbuh)*. He believed that overlooking the context and purpose of such verses would only excite hostility and criticism against Muslims and embitter their relations with their rulers.[67]

Sultan *Abd-al Hamid* had acceded to the caliphate in 1876, by which time Indian Muslims were trying o influence the British government in the direction of a pro-Turkish policy. The Russo-Turkish war was sparked off the next year and the agitation of the Muslims during it was reflected in the Urdu Press. Huge sums of money were contributed by them to be sent to Turkey.

Sir Sayyid however did not approve of the popular sentiment in favor of the Sultan. He wrote in an undated article that the Islamic "caliphate" or *(khilafat)* as such had ended thirty years after the demise of the Prophet *(Pbuh)*, with the termination of the caliphate of Imam Hasan. The rulers that followed were merely Sultans, although they may have adopted the title of "caliph" for grandeur, which was in reality applicable only to a ruler who had cultivated a complete likeness to the moral and spiritual attributes of the Prophet *(Pbuh)*. He believed that in the present there was none worthy of this title and even if there was, as a caliph his power was limited only to the territory under his sway.[68] Sir Sayyid therefore held that even if the Sultan of Turkey was a caliph, it was only within his own country. Since Indian Muslims were not his subjects, he had on power over them, and was not their caliph in the legal or religious sense. He did not agree with those who advocated a single caliph for the whole Muslim world (and regarded the Sultan of Turkey as such); since he felt that there has never been, and is never been, and is never likely to be, any individual whose political power extends over the whole world.[69]

Sir Sayyid explained the sympathy that Muslim felt for the Turkish sultan on the basis of their feeling of Islamic brotherhood. However, he reminded them that they owed no obligation to the Sultan, their only religious and legal duty being to remain loyal and obedient well-wishers of their government. In the context of the Greco-Turkish war of 1897-9 (in which Britain supported the former), he wrote in the same year that this duty could not be shirked even if the government's political policy was against Turkey. At the most they could pray for friendship between the British and all Muslim states. In fact, he generalized that in the event of a war between a Muslim and non-Muslim government, the Muslim subjects of the latter were strictly forbidden by their religion to support or assist the former in any way.[70]

As we have already seen, Sir Sayyid did not hesitate to preach to Indian Muslims in the name of religion, to abstain from rebellion and remain loyal to the British government. However, it is interesting that in order to counter their pro-Turkey sentiments during the war, he reasoned that religion and politics must be kept apart. He tried to convince them that it was wholly unjustified to give present day wars a religious colouring since they were undertaken not with religious, but purely political motives.[71]

Sayyid Tufail Ahmad in a book towards Sayyid Ahmad says:

"The Indian Muslims realized their decay and downfall only about 1870, and this was the time when Sayyid Ahmad started his movement of reform. At that time the Indian Muslims realized for the first time that the responsibility for their progress and welfare, which was being formerly shouldered by the Muslim government, had now to be discharged by them and their well being in future would depend on their efforts. In short Sayyid Ahmad's movement made them self conscious and they began to use their limited resources to regain their lost glory."[72]

Pannkiar Writes

"Indeed, it could well be claimed for Sayyid Ahmad that not only had he arrested the disintegration of Islam but in the course of a generation he restored it to a position of great importance and undoubted influence."[73] The MAO College that Sir Sayyid established in Aligarh was an intellectual and cultural center in tune with the progressive spirit of the times. It was Sir Sayyid's Aligarh movement that prepared a generation of Muslims who played a prominent role in the struggle for freedom. Maulana Mohammad Ali, Maulana Shaukat Ali, Hasrat Mohani, Liaqat Ali Khan, Khaliquzzaman, Zafar Ali Khan, Dr Zakir Husain, Khan Ghaffar Khan, Shaikh Abdullah, Rafi Ahmad Kidwai and many others were the products of Aligarh Muslim University.

Choudhary Khaliquzzaman repeatedly refers to Sayyid Ahmad Khan as "Father of Muslim Indian" "and "Father of Modern Muslim India"[74] certainly he was.

Sayyid Ahmad not only filled a big void created in the life of the Muslim community by the disappearance of Muslim rule, but he did more. His long life, spanning almost a century, bridged the gulf between the medieval and the modern Islam in India. Himself a relic of the palmy days of the Great Mughals, he ushered in a new era. He gave the Indian Muslim a new cohesion, a new political policy, a new educational programme, a new prose, a new approach to their individual and national problems and built up an organization which would carry on his work. Before him there was all disintegration and decay. He rallied together the Indian Muslims, and became the first prophet of their new nationhood. He could very well say about seventy million Muslims of India:

"They were like a multitude that had cost its bearings in the wilderness; I gave my clarion call, and to, they became a compact caravan."

Sir Sayyid was not concerned with theorizing about Muslim identity in India, his sole aim being the socio-economic, educational, and cultural rehabilitation of his community; and all his efforts were geared towards this end. Accordingly, he supported British rule in India, Hindu-Muslim unity, and the united Indian nationhood which stemmed from the latter, because he felt it was conducive to the attainment of these ends. Yet even in the early period he was astute enough to perceive the inherent antagonism between the different Indian communities. Even before the formation of Congress he felt that Muslims could not compete with to the threat the Hindus in politics, and later opposed it due to the threat that it posed to the permanence of British rule. It was perhaps for him also a symbol of the resurgent Hindu issue, and perceived as a threat to Muslim progress and security.

Therefore, all attempts at categorizing Sir Sayyid's views are bound to fail. However, since both strains are present in his thought, later votaries of both the "nationalist" and "separatist" schools picked on the aspect which suited their purpose, carried to its logical conclusion, and claimed him as their own.

REFERENCES

1. Malik, Hafeez, *Sir Sayyid Ahmad Khan and Muslim Modernisation in India and Pakistan,* New York, Columbia University Press, 1980, p. 260.

2. Reetz, Dietrich, *Enlightenment and Islam: Sayyid Ahmad Khan's Plea to Indian Muslims for Reason;* reprinted from The Indian Historical Review Vol. XIV No. 1-2, pp. 206-218

3. Panipati, Mohammad Ismail, ed., *Rasmo revaj ki pabundi k nukhsanat, Maqalaat-e-Sir Sayyid,* Part 5, Lahore: *Majlees-e-taraqee-e-Adab,* 1962, p. 31

4. Khan Sayyid Ahmad, *Tareeq-e-Zindagi, Tehzeebul Akhlaq.* 13 *jamadi-ul-sahni,* 1288 Hijri, Maulana Azad Library, Aligarh MuslimUniversity, Aligarh. p. 39.

5. Khan Sir Sayyid Ahmad, *Zamane ka Asar Mazhab par,* by Tehzeebul Akhlaq, Yakum Shewal 1311 Hijri. Maulana Azad Library, AMU, Aligarh. p. 14.

6. Panipati Mohammad Ismail, *Mazhabi khayal, (zamane khadeem aur zamane jadeed ka), Maqalat-e-Sir Sayyid.* Part 3, edited by *Majlees-e-taraqee-e-Adab,* Lahore, 1961. p. 23.

7. Khan,Sayyid Ahmad, *Karamat aur Mojeeza, Tehzeebul Akhlaq,* 1296 Hijri. pp. 30-33.

8. Panipati, Mohammad Ismail, ed., *Imam aur Imamat. Maqalat-e-Sir Sayyid.* Part 1, Lahore: *Majlees-e-taraqee-e-Adab,* 1962, p.170

9. *Quran Majeed ki tafseer. Maqalat-e-Sir Sayyid.* Part 2, Reply to the letter of Mohsinul Mulk by Sir Sayyid Ahmad Khan. p. 56.

10. Panipati, Mohammad Ismail, ed., *Ghair Mazhab Ke Peshwaon ka hum ko adab karna chahiye* by Sir Sayyid Ahmad Khan. *Maqalat-e-Sir Sayyid.* Lahore: *Majlees-e-taraqe-e- Adab,* 1962. p. 184.

11. Graham G. F. I., *The life and works of Sir Sayyid Ahmad Khan,* Edinburgh: William Blackwood and sons, 1885, (2 edition), p.21

12. *ibid*, p. 28

13. Quoted in Graham, The Life and Work of Sir Syed Ahmad Khan (IInd edition), p.29.

14. *ibid* p. 16

15. *ibid* p. 35

16. *ibid* p. 36

17. *ibid* pp. 38-39

18. *ibid* p. 39

19. *Khutabat-i-Alia*, Translated from Urdu, Muhammad Ismail Panipati ed., 2 volumes, Lahore. 137

20. Vide the Aligarh Institute Gazette, quoted in Syed Tufail Ahmad Muslmanon ka Roshan Mustaqbil, p.g. 286. Translated from Urdu.

21. The 1857 effort to gain independence from the British rule was called "mutiny" by the British; its Urdu equivalent, *Gadar*, was used by some pro-British writers for this heroic effort which failed due to many reasons, including treason by Muslims and Hindus loyal to the British.

22. Panipati, Mohammad Ismail, *ed., Maqalat-e Sir Sayyid,* 16 Vols. Lahore: *Majlis-e Taraqqi-e Adad,* (henceforth *Maqalat*), Vol. 2, 1963, pp. 199-200

23. Life and Works of Sir Syed Ahmad Khan, IInd edition p.50

24. "*Proceedings of the First Meeting of the Scientific Society*", Ghazipur, January 9, 1864, published in *Fikr-o-Nazar*, April (1963), Aligarh, pp. 8-11

25. Malik, Hafeez, *Sir Sayyid Ahmad Khan and Muslim Modernisation in India and Pakistan,* New York: Columbia University Press, 1980, pp. 88-89

26. Graham G. F. I., *The life and works of Sir Sayyid Ahmad Khan*, Edinburgh: William Blackwood and sons, 1885, (2 edition), p.48.

27. Hali, Altaf Hussain, *Hayat-i-Jawed (A Biography of Sir Sayyid)*, Nami Press, Kanpur, 1901, p. 70, translated by David J. Matthews, New Delhi: Rupa and Company, 1994.

28. *Sayyid Ahmad Khan ka safarnamah-i-Punjab*, Delhi 1979, p.91,

29. http://www.southasian analysis org./paper 675 retrieved on 18.11.2015

30. Hali, Altaf Hussain, *Hayat-i-Jawid. (A Biography of Sir Sayyid)*, Nami Press, Kanpur, 1901, p. 70, translated by David J. Matthews, New Delhi: Rupa and Company, 1994. pp. 89,91 and 94

31. *ibid*, p.93

32. *Muqalat* XII, p. 35 (part of Sir Sayyid's Speech which appeared in form of an article published on 20 September 1867)

33. Hali, *op. cit.*, pp. 95-96.

34. *Maktubat* I, pp. 259-261.

35. Hali, *op. cit.*, p.95.

36. Brass Paul R, Language, Religion and Politics in North India, Universe Incorporated, ISBN 978-0-595-34394-2

37. *ibid*

38. Hali, *op. cit.*, p.95.

39. *Maqalat* XII, p.199

40. *ibid*, p. 90

41. *ibid*, p. 190

42. Abbasi, Yusuf, *Muslim Politics and leadership in the South Asian Sub-Continent*, Islamabad: Institute of Islamic History, culture and Civilization, Islamic University, 1981, pp. 65-66

43. *ibid*, p. 90

44. Jones Kenneth W, Religious Controversy in British India by p124, ISBN-7914-0827-2 Google Book

45. Hussain, S. Abid, The Destiny of Indian Muslims, Bombay, 1965, p. 29

46. Shakir Moin, Khilafat to Partition, New Delhi, 1970 p.22.

47. Hali, Altaf Hussain, *Hayat-i-Jawid*, pp 93-94 and 179

48. *Khutbat* I pp537-38

49. *ibid*, pp. 445-46 and 450

50. *Muqualat*,XII p.119

51. *Safarnama*, pp 195-200; *Khutbat* I, pp537-38

52. *Muqualat,*XV p.41

53. *Maqalat* XV, pp. 199-200

54. *ibid.*

55. *ibid.*

56. *Khutbat* II, pp. 249-250

57. *Khutbat* I, pp. 599-600

58. Malik, Hafeez, *Sir Sayyid Ahmad Khan and Muslim Modernisation in India and Pakistan,* New York: Columbia University Press, 1980, p. 383.

59. *ibid*

60. *Khutbat* II, pp. 290 and 320-21

61. *ibid*, pp. 290-91,321 and 335

62. *ibid*, pp. 286 and 334

63. *ibid*, pp.334-35

64. *ibid*, pp75-77

65. Faruqui, Ziya-ul-Hasan, The Deoband school, and the demand for Pakistan, Bombay, 1963, p.2

66. *Maktubat* II,p.350; *Maqalat* XIII,pp274 and 276-77.

67. *Maqaalat* I, pp 157,167-68,171-72 and 174; Vol.Xiii,p. 432.

68. *Maqaalat* I, pp 158,59 and 162-63

69. *Maqalat* I, pp 168-69; vol.XIII,PP.427-28 and 432; Shan Mohammad Shan, Speeches and Writings of Sir Sayyid Ahmad Khan, Bombay, p.254

70. *Muqualat*, XIII, p.433; Muhammad Shan,Writings And Speeches of Sir Sayyid Ahmad Khan, Bombay, p.254

71. Ahmad, Syed Tufail, *Mussalmanoon ka Roshan Mustaqbil*, Lahore, 1937, p. 1.

72. Pannkiar, K.M., *A Survey of Indian History*, India : Asia Publishing House, 5th Edition, 1960, p.284

73. Choudhary, Khaliquzzaman, *Pathway to Pakistan*, Lahore: Longmans Pakistan Branch, 1961, pp.226-295.

THE LEANING TOWARDS PAN ISLAMISM:

MAULANA MOHAMMAD ALI

"Science shall be in our right hand and philosophy in our left and on our head shall be the crown of "There is no God but Allah and Mohammad is his Apostle."

It is difficult to come across in history men of the caliber of Raisul-Ahrar Maulana Mohammad Ali Jauhar. A renowned Indian Muslim leader, Maulana Mohammad Ali was a prince among the patriots. Maulana Jauhar was unique in many respect: A lover of the land, lover of liberty, lover of Islam, and lover of highest absolute values, who would stake his life to gain his cherished objectives. Well-versed in the learning's of both east and west, Maulana rose to be a political leader of high repute, a poet of great eminence, a journalist *par excellence*, an orator of captivating impact, and more than all a humanist, whose sensitive heart would react emotionally to the sorrows and sufferings of man. Maulana Jauhar was the finest flower of the Islamic renaissance. His thought process was pregnant with the basic Islamic values; steadfastness in faith *(Iman)*, equilibrium *(Islam)* and benevolence *(Ihsan)*. Possessed with a dynamic personality, he towered high above his contemporary Indian politicians and instilled courage and confidence in the hearts of the ignorant masses which awakened them from their deep slumber.

Maulana Mohammad Ali's fearless leadership and selfless devotion to his mission were greatly instrumental in dispelling the inferiority complex, which, the alien rulers had enshrined in the hearts of the teeming millions inhabiting this vast sub-continent and enabled them to brave the onslaughts of the foreign rule with courage and conviction. The policy of co-operation with the British Government, followed by Sir Sayyid Ahmad Khan and his associates, gave place to the revolutionary politics of Maulana Mohammad Ali and Maulana Abul Kalam Azad in which the attention of the Indian Muslims was diverted towards the revival of the Pan-Islamic Movement and the restoration of the Khilafat.

Maulana Mohammad Ali represents a remarkable synthesis of apparently conflicting trends and currents of Muslim religious and political thought in India. He stressed the need to follow the spirit and values of Islam. The name of Mohammad Ali, when he lived, had the power to rally round it forty crores of people in the undivided sub-continent. He was the first political leader of India who was tried for sedition and who openly planned to make the Britons quit India. It was he who transformed the complacent group of the Congressites into a thundering organization and made the Indian National Congress a forum for a united Hindustani nation. It was he who shook the Muslims and inspired them with the passion for freedom. It was he who raised Gandhi to the position of a Mahatma and got him accepted as the spirit behind Hindus-Muslim unity. It was he who made Jawaharlal Nehru secretary of the all-India Congress Committee during his President ship. It was he who had proud distinction of presiding over the sessions of the Indian National Congress, the Muslim League and the Khilafat Conference.

Born in an aristocratic family of Rampur State (UP) on 12 December, 1878, Mohammad Ali was destined to play a glorious role in the Indian politics. His father, Abdul Ali Khan, died when he was two years old, leaving behind three sons, Zulfiqar, Shaukat and Mohammad. His mother, Abadi Bano, popularly known as 'BI AMMAN' being an enlightened lady sent her sons to Bareilly and afterwards to Aligarh to receive the best education available in the country. Mohammad Ali's mother, with all her motherly love and care, inspired her son with a spirit of truthfulness, honesty and devotion to God. Mohammad Ali's life from cradle to grave, demonstrates what a profound and lasting impact the religious instructions and training received in the mother's lap can produce in young minds. That is why throughout his life Mohammad Ali continued to fear God. And because he feared God Almightily above, he feared none down below.

At M.A.O. College, Aligarh, under the brotherly supervision and patronage of his elder brother Shaukat Ali, Mohammad Ali took keen interest in extracurricular activities. He was quite popular as a brilliant debater, poet and writer. He was prominent for his English. M.A.O College was the place from where Mohammad Ali got the qualities of independent thinking and working. He generally used to differ with the professors and spoke in the Union on topics which irritated them. His speeches were forceful, the language plain and very impressive for a young man of his age. He gave full expression to his radical views in the college debates much to the embarrassment of the European staff of his *alma mater* as well as the British Government and was known as a revolutionary. He was a well-known figure in the cricket and football teams in the college and in academics also he did well. Mohammad Ali obtained his B.A. degree at the age of 18, topping the list of successful candidates.

Mohammad Ali went to England for higher studies and joined Oxford and took an Honors Degree in Modern History. In England, he remained for four years and had the distinction of being the first president of the *"Indian Majlis"* in the Cambridge University. He, however, was fortunate in not being selected for Indian Civil Service, which in those days was reserved for a privileged few, otherwise India would have been deprived of the most colourful and dynamic personality of her modern history. Mohammad Ali preferred to devote most of his time in going through the pages of history and literature and with the patriotic spirit which he imbibed at Aligarh, endeavored to acquire more and more of such knowledge as would prepare him for his destined life. Mohammad Ali returned to India in 1902.

On return to India, Mohammad Ali, in his quest for work, offered his services as a professor to his college at Aligarh. His application was strongly opposed by the Principal, Sir Theodore Morrison, who though recognizing Mohammad Ali's abilities and qualifications, did not consider it safe to have a man of his independent character and spirit on the staff of the college. Then Mohammad Ali turned to Indian states. The Rampur State authorities appointed him as Chief Educational Officer but he had to leave the service because of palace intrigues within a year. He served the Baroda State for about seven years as opium officer and as Commissioner of Navsari with a devotion and distinction which won him the confidence of the ruler of the State.

As a thinker and writer and with his dreams of service to his people, Mohammad Ali found himself like a fish out of water in a princely state. Despite his preoccupation with his official duties, he managed time to contribute articles on topics of public interest to newspapers and periodicals and finally made a momentous decision to become a journalist. Without having special claim or training to venture on the hazardous profession, Mohammad Ali decided to switch over to journalism because he felt, under the circumstances, this was the only way to serve his country. In his incomplete autobiography "My life: A Fragment", Mohammad Ali writes: "The reasons which so irresistibly impelled me to take journalism was that the affairs of my country at the juncture made it the only avenue through which I could prove of any appreciable use."

In 1911, began his journalistic career at Calcutta the seat of Imperial Government. He started the *"Comrade"*- 'Comrade of all and partisan to none', as he put it in the very first editorial. Maulana Mohammad Ali represents a remarkable synthesis of apparently conflicting trends and currents of Muslim religious and political thought of India. He stressed the need of modernity and science as well as the need to follow the spirit and values of Islam.

Views On Islam

Mohammad Ali was not prepared to accept anything that conflicted with Islam. According to him, "Islam is not a bundle of dogmas and doctrines that theologians plague humanity with. It is a complete scheme of life, a perfect code of right conduct and a comprehensive social polity as wide as the human race and in fact as wide as the human creation."[1]

Mohammad Ali's philosophy of religion is comprehensive enough to include all the important aspects of life. It guides "man in every concern of life" and teaches "him how to live and how to die"[2] He believed that religion is not a ritual and that it is "an interpretation of life." It is "a culture, a polity, an outlook on life."[3] He held that Islam alone provides an example of such a true religion. Islam was a complete culture, polity and outlook on life. It keeps tradition, reason and mystic intuition "within proper limits."[4] The Qur'an is a book of guidance regulating the activities of all those who profess Islam. It is a "perennial fountain of truth."[5] According to him the Qur'an propounds two basic principles – Unity of God and the establishment of the Kingdom of God on earth. He held that God is "the Supreme Ruler and omnipotent Creator, Sustainer and Developer of all Creation."[6] He learnt from the Qur'an that "The entire universe was one. The unity of the creator postulated, the unity of his creation, and all was one vast Theocracy with Allah for its king and Man for his earthly viceregency."[7]

Man is the servant of the Lord and his function is "the service of his Maker and the fulfillment of His divine purpose."[8] He is the right less slave of God."[9] Mohammad Ali said that surrender to God "will make him free forever and equal of kings and emperors in the greatest of all Republics, and even superior to them."[10]

Mohammad Ali, while elaborating the importance of religion in the life of man, had Islam always in his mind. He was not prepared to accept that all religions are as true and sound as Islam. He never supported the principles of the unity of all religions. To him Islam is the eternal truth. He said: "Islam was unchanging and has remained unchanged in more than thirteen centuries that have passed over"[11] and has been guiding the people in spite of the efforts of theology. He failed to understand that the character of Islam was determined by the prevailing economic, sociological, political and social philosophies. "Ancient Islam" was not concerned with "the individual quest for salvation" and mysticism but with "wealth, power and glory"; even the paradise was pictured as a "soldier's sensual paradise"; the feudal orientation of Islam radically changed its character.¹² Mohammad Ali recognized that there existed no conflict between religion and science, i.e., Islam and Science. As there is no "possibility of conflict between the two and there is nothing to reconcile."¹³

If the interpretation of a particular verse of the Qur'an is rejected and supplemented by a more rational one, it is not a sin.¹⁴ He held that Islam is neither opposed to rationalism nor the mysticism, provided that they do not transgress their limits. The philosophers should not "make Muslim theology their battle ground and divert the energies of Muslims from righteous action.¹⁵

At the same time Islam does not conflict with mysticism. But Islam cannot let "Sufism degenerate into a wild fantastic ritual, or worse still, leading him *(sufi)* to consider his kind above and beyond the claims of Islam's Shariat which prescribed the simplest of duties for all alike.¹⁶ Mohammad Ali's view of Islam was similar to that of the advocates of "romanticism" in politics. The romantic approach to religion and its application to politics imply that Islam is the only criterion of truth and could provide an answer to all the problems that confronted mankind. Its exponents do not see any conflict between Islam and modern Science because Islam according to them is a progressive force, a rational and scientific system. But the limitations of this approach are obvious. Mohammad Ali did not recognize any hostility between Islam and positive science and non-conformist philosophy.¹⁷

Revivalism Through Journalism

Mohammad Ali wrote a series of articles, in 1907, on the 'Aligarh of To-day' and on some other questions dealing with the M.A.O. college. This series was the result of Mr. Lovat Eraser's request, the then editor of the Times of India. He wrote for the 'Hindustan Review' also. But the most notable production of his, "India, Past and Present," published in the latter, brought home to the readers his keen insight and sober judgment. He was endowed with a keen incisive wit which showed itself in his journal, the *'Gup'* published from Allahabad. Unfortunately, only two issues of the paper appeared, as for some unavoidable reasons it had to be stopped. Mr. Mohammad Ali's articles were very humorous and attracted the keen attention of the Aligarh students and trustees with whom the Ali Brothers have been little less than idols.

Mohammad Ali did much in rousing the public life from the "sleepy hollow" and in upholding the cause of the masses. He played a vital part in preparing the Muslims in particular and Indians in general for the final struggle of freedom. Thus, to a great extent, he was responsible for shaping their political destiny. Under his dynamic leadership, Muslims grew into a virile and self-assertive nation. His heart which surged with the love of his countrymen awakened their self-respect. Being an ardent anti-imperialist, he virtually dominated the national stage for the first quarter of the twentieth century. Along with Mohsin-ul-Mulk and Waqar-ul-Mulk, he was present in Dacca when the Muslim League was founded in 1906. On their suggestion, he wrote in his immaculate style an account of this historic session in the form of a pamphlet called, "The Green Book".

Role of Comrade

Mohammad Ali was in the Baroda service when he matured his scheme of bringing out a weekly paper. Mohammad Ali launched upon this plan, because he earnestly wanted to devote himself to the service of his community as well as that of his country. The extreme poverty and suffering of the Indian masses under the alien yoke added fuel to his fiery temperament and so he left the job and shifted to Calcutta to start his weekly *Comrade* on January 1st, 1911.

Its first number appeared on the 14th of January, 1911. Once he was asked as to why he had adopted journalism as his profession, and his crisp and brief reply was that the requirements of the community demanded that he should take up the work, and consequently he had done it. Writing in his autobiography "My Life a Fragment" he mentions the reasons which impelled him to take up the career of journalism 'The reasons which so irresistibly impelled me to take up journalism was, that the affairs of my community at the juncture made it the only avenue through which I could prove of any appreciable use---I felt, I should now assist my community in taking a proper share in the political affairs of the country.'

An interesting story throws light on his determination to fight for the cause of the people through the press. He was prevailed upon by H.H. the Nawab of Jaora and Sir Michael O'Dwyer to accept the portfolio of the Chief Minister of the said State. A personal interview was also granted to him. But as Mohammad Ali had made up his mind to start a paper, he did not budge an inch from his position in spite of Sir Michael O'Dwyer's personal recommendations. He did not open the letter of appointment until the first issue of his paper was out. Maulana Mohammad Ali was an ideal journalist, and the high standard of professional integrity set by him will serve as a beacon light for the coming generations.

The *Comrade* played an important role in moulding the political policy of Muslim India. In assessing the influences which radically changed the outlook of Muslims about 1912, it is worth quoting that the *Comrade* started more than eighteen months before Abdul Kalam Azad,s *Al- Hilal* saw the light of the day, and the pioneering work which this newspaper and *Zamindar*, edited by Maulana Zafar Ali Khan, another Aligarhian, did has to be duly acknowledged. In most matters, Maulana Mohammad Ali agreed to Viqar-ul-Mulk, and his *Comrade* reflected the new era which had been inaugurated at Aligarh. In internal politics, its policy was dubbed as that of 'Communal Patriot'. It was fearless in denouncing discrimination and hardships to which the editor's countrymen were exposed, but it also systematically criticized 'The Bengalee', 'The Tribune' and other Hindu newspapers, which opposed the newly organized All-India Muslim League, or the efforts of Aligarh leaders to secure suitable safeguards for the Muslims. When the Bengal was partition Maulana Mohammad Ali wrote a series of articles dealing with "The Announcement"

He devoted his paper more to education than to anything else. All the while he acted as the Editor; he worked with exemplary zeal and fervor. He was assisted by the Raja Gulam Hussain, the founder and editor of the brilliant but very short-lived *New Era*. As regards the policy and aims of the *Comrade*, they can best be described in the words of the Editor himself:

"We are partisans of none, comrades of all. We deeply feel the many dangers of increasing controversy between races and races, creeds and creeds, and earnestly desire a better understanding between the contending elements of the body politic of India." As to the relations of the rulers and the ruled, his earnest desire was that the line of demarcation between the two should be obliterated altogether, so that the poet's dream might be realized;

"I became Thou, thou became I, I became life and

Thou became Body,

"That none may henceforth say, I am different and

Thou art different".[18]

"When this obliteration is accomplished," he continues, "the present dangers of criticism will cease to be. The opposition will then be as responsible as the Government and responsibility all the world over goes hand in hand with sobriety of judgment and temperate expression."[19]

Mohammad Ali was alive to the differences that prevailed in the Indian society itself, he was also conscious of the gulf which existed between the East and the West. To Rudyard Kipling it may be true that

"Oh, East is East and West is West,

And never the twain shall meet;"

But to the vision of Mohammad Ali the "twain can meet." And consequently, he wrote: "We may believe in the gulf but refuse to believe it as unbridgeable. Remove pride and suspicion on the one side, and prejudice and suspicion on the other, and it will not be difficult to throw the cantilever bridge across the yawning chasm. Be it as it may, there is no gulf between races which individuals cannot bridge."[20]

The *Comrade* was a great advocate of a Hindu- Muslim *entente*, and always prevailed upon the Hindus and the Mussalmans to work side by side, with the object of uplifting their Mother India. On this topic Mohammad Ali wrote: "But while providing for to-day, we must not forget the morrow. It is our firm belief that if the Mussalmans or the Hindus attempted to achieve success in opposition to, or even without the co-operation of each other, they will not only fail, but fail ignominiously. But every step has to be taken with caution."

The *Comrade* was published from Calcutta, because Mohammad Ali wanted to remain in touch with the Government of India whose then seat was Calcutta but at the same time it is true also that the *Comrade* "combated in a spirited manner the inordinate claims of the Hindu community which was then the pet aversion of the officials, having been till then practically the only political party that demanded a share in the monopoly of the civilians. But he had not set out to fight the battle of the civilians and the controversies of the Comrade with the organs of Hindu opinion had their genesis in the conviction that Muslim assertiveness would teach the Hindus to moderate their claims and make them prove to co-operate with the Mussalmans for the good of India on an equitable basis"[21]

The "Comrade" was transferred to Delhi in 1912, when the Indian Capital was shifted from Calcutta to Delhi in 1911.

Maulana Mohammad Ali Jauhar stood for Muslim brotherhood and Islamic unity across the globe. In his unfinished biography, the Maulana says that when he started *The Comrade*, he did not think that he would have to devote much time and space to affairs outside India. Fate had, however, decreed otherwise. Soon after the publication of The Comrade, Turky was involved in war, at first with Italy and later with Balkan powers. The sympathies of Indian Muslims were deeply stirred. As a distinguished alumnus of Aligarh college, with a deep veneration for Sayyid Ahmad Khan and an emotional nature, Mohammad Ali responded to the religious revivalism and Pan-Islamism creed preached by Abul Kalam Azad. He not only echoed the sentiments expressed in *Al-Hilal,* but soon found concrete means to express them.

The *Comrade* did not start with any bitterness towards the British government, but the annulment of the partition of Bengal and the political tension engendered by the Tripoli and Balkan wars affected its attitude. There were other causes which fed the fires of hatred. The controversy about the Muslim University and the serious trouble at Cawnpore after the demolition, by the Public Works Department, of a portion of a Mosque, Maulana took active part in the agitation for the restoration of the mosque and towards the end of 1913, headed a deputation consisting of himself and Sir Sayyid Wazir Hasan, Secretary, All India Muslim League, to place the Muslim case before the British government. He also supported the inclusion, in the aims and objects of the Muslim League, of efforts for the establishment of "a suitable form of Self-Government of India."

Comrade was the first of the newspapers that covered the foreign issues of war in Muslim state. He waged full-fledged support for the salvation of Khilafat in Turkey because it was a source of spiritual unity of Muslims of the world. He also played a vital role to present a Turkish point of views during the war when the First World War started with Turkey and Germany an alliance. In 1914 when Turkey was at war Maulana Mohammad Ali after a continuous sitting of 36 hours wrote his memorable editorial "The Choice of Turks" a befitting to the insulting article to the "London Times" under the same caption. The Indian government forfeited its security and he was marked as a dangerous man by the authorities. *Comrade* remained closed for 10 years from 3rd November 1914 to 1924.

Comrade played a great part along with *"Al-Hilal"* of Maulana Azad and *"Zamindar"* of Maulana Zafar Ali Khan in the awakening of the Muslim masses and in forming their political outlook. Mohammad Ali also started *"Hamdard",* an Urdu Daily, from Delhi in 1913.

Hamdard Urdu Daily for Muslim Masses

Mohammad Ali knew the power of journalism as a means to educate the masses on all the public affairs. The Comrade being in English could not be advantageously studied by them. He, therefore, started the *Hamdard* in 1913, and that was the only Urdu daily which was printed from moveable type. This was an altogether new departure in the Muslim journalism, and was maintained at an enormous personal sacrifice, as his idea was to get together a good number of Muslim writers and make them write in Urdu, books on all subjects—literary syndicate like the *Anjumans i-Taraqq-i-Urdu*—maintaining them with a subsistence allowance of Rs. 75, and giving them large share of the profit. Unlike the *Zamindar* and other off-shoots, the *Hamdard* was sold at two pice a copy instead of one, and in spite of it, its circulation had reached 9,000. And that was a proof of Mohammad Ali's popularity with the masses. The staff of the paper consisted of some of the ablest hands. Mir Busharat Ali Jalib of the *Hamdam* and Qazi Abdul Gaffar of the *Jamhoor* were working on it, besides many others; and they continued to conduct a paper even after the Editor's internment. But as the Government had saddled it with a whimsical censor who wanted to see nothing but trash in it, the *Hamdard* ceased to exist after some time. Its disappearance from the field was a death blow to Urdu Journalism and an end of all the political education of the masses.

Mohammad Ali wrote practically very little for the *Hamdard*. But he always found time to discuss in his green room almost all the points with his sub-editors who were given sufficient time to study all the possible aspects of a question. The discussion was always friendly and everyone was free to say what he thought right. The relation between him and the sub-editors was not that of the master and the servants, but really speaking, they enjoyed a sort of family life. And this is a feature which was unique in Urdu journalism and which was mainly responsible for the quality of everything that appeared in the *Hamdard*.

If the masses in general have begun to take a greater interest in the affairs of the country; if they have begun to throb with new life and if they have ceased to be dumb and mute "like cattle" as in the good old days of the bureaucratic regime it can safely be ascribed to the training of the *Hamdard*, which will long be remembered by all the lovers of freedom and of free press.[22]

Muhammad Ali's vision of Progress: National Muslim Education

Inspired by the Aligarh Movement he was fully aware of the historic importance of Sir Sayyid's role during the latter half of 19th century. He considered that the Aligarh movement and the western system of education were in the interest of the Muslims in India. However, at the same time he thought that the western system should not be blindly copied, or the oriental and Indian tradition recklessly discarded. He was also fully aware that Sir Sayyid, while supporting the western system, had advocated the need to synthesize philosophy, science and religion. While retaining all personal regards for Sir Sayyid, he was convinced that the Aligarh movement was in need of reform.

Mohammad Ali vehemently criticized the system of western education which was in vogue in India. "The present generation is an immature product of modern education with crude, half-formed ideas, not familiar with orders of thing new as well as old,"[23] wrote Mohammad Ali. He held that the western education, "tended to breed in the student an arrogant omniscience, and to destroy along with age-old beliefs in superstition all respect for tradition and authority."[24] He believed that the system of education which had come into vogue was not suited to the genius of the people or even the needs of the modern age. He complained that the modern education had produced men who were "more communal than religious" and who know "so little of their religion and their orthodoxy was more than supect."[25] Although Sir Sayyid's influence on Mohammad Ali was decisive, circumstances obliged him to modify Sir Sayyid's programme radically.

Thus, when the *Comarade* was first founded it was intimately associated not only with Muslim politics but also with Muslim education, and in fact it set out to discuss everything that was connected with the progress of Indians in general and Muslims in particular. He said that if the universalization of *Charkha* is the immediate need of to-day, it is not to be gainsaid that ultimately the greatest need of the Muslim community is national education, and the *Comarade* must not neglect it any longer.[26] He believed that there is the need to reexamine the present situation of the national education which was the offshoot of Sir Sayyid Ahmad Khan's rebel against official control of education.

The principle underlying State education in India was shaped by expediency and low utilitarianism. 'The main idea of the government has been to train men for the ministerial posts in the public services, and naturally enough the type of public instruction hitherto in vogue in this country, has provided a mere mechanical training of a few intellectual faculties. It has absolutely failed to train personality, because it has been innocent of ideals, has been inspired by no collective will and has consequently failed to touch character and mind with a unifying purpose- public government, cannot become national in the broad sense of the term". "It may produce useful and clever men. After immense labor and expense, it may even produce men with highly trained faculties and initiative to strike out new lines of career, men who may succeed in business enterprise or become captains of industry, but it will rarely give birth to men of large purposes and great ideas who would sum up in their personality the hopes and the intellectual and moral possibilities of the race, and would in turn enlarge the scope of those possibilities, and enrich the common life with new hopes."[27]

Maulana Mohammad Ali believed that only a national education can evolve this virile, ample and gracious type. He further said that a truly national education for India is a remote possibility, and all plans for the training of the younger generations are, at present, to be in the nature of compromise. For, it cannot be too often repeated that the only efficient instrument for the organization of modern education is the State. Decentralization may be good for some administration purposes, but the vast problem of education can be treated satisfactorily only on wholesale principles. This is especially true of 'elementary education'. A person without elementary education of the things necessary for a purposeful existence cannot be a good citizen. The contrivance of civilization for a rapid circulation of ideas and the dispatch of the work of daily life which the knowledge of the three R's represent, is as much necessary for the purposes of efficient citizenship as the organization of the social services and the apparatus of public justice. Every recognized duty of the state means, in a sense, a corresponding surrender of individual right. Public law implies compulsion. The state in its modern sense is an instrument of social re-adjustment according to the varying needs of the community. It has already some of the most intimate personal prerogatives of the present. The collective will and mind, as expressed through state organization, have been declared to be far better fitted to look after the training of: the younger generation than the caprice, the inadequate will and imperfect intelligence of the individual. Elementary education therefore is one of the primary duties of a modern state and the Indian government can never have an easy conscience as long as that duty remains un-discharged.[28]

Mohammad Ali emphasized on the need of communal education to concentrate the attention on the peculiar needs of the Muslim community. "To our mind the greatest need of Muslims is that they should be Muslim in the truest sense of the word, and for the purpose we should not tolerate the lacerating difference between temporal and spiritual things nor encourage any differentiation of species among the Muslims such as the clergy or the laity."[29] He said that the evils from which the Muslim society in India is suffering had to be clearly understood, and the remedies had to be devised therefore incorporated in the scheme of studies. The goal that was always kept in view was to turn out from these instructions not only young men of culture according to modern standards, but true Muslims imbued with the spirit of Islam and possessing enough knowledge of their religion to be able to stand by themselves as sufficiently independent units in the army of Islam's missionaries.

He never denied the usefulness of the western system of education but he thought that the western system should not be blindly copied, or the oriental and Indian tradition recklessly discarded. Criticizing the system of western education which was in vogue in India, Mohammad Ali "The present generation is an immature product of modern education with crude, half-formed ideas, not familiar with orders of thing new as well as old,"[30] wrote Mohammad Ali, and that the western education, breed in the student an arrogant omniscience, and destroy the age-old beliefs as superstition with no respect for traditions."[31] Mohammad Ali advocated the genuine spirit of enquiry, the search for truth as well as respect for tradition. He complained that the modern education had produced men who were "more communal than religious" and who know "so little of their religion and their orthodoxy was more than suspect."[32]

Regarding secondary and higher education, Mohammad Ali believed that the highest results can be obtained only if the organization and control are in the hands of the Indians themselves. The only key to the solution of this aspect of the problem is to encourage private enterprise. He believed that Indian government, by its very character and constitution, can only be a very clumsy instrument in evoking the collective mind of India. The state schools and colleges and universities, however efficient and well-equipped, cannot train character and personality on national lines. It is only a Hindu or a Muslim University that can furnish the necessary ground for the germination of the people's genius. "The restriction of the scope of these universities, from the stand-points of India's collective educational needs, is the most short-sighted blunder committed by the Secretary of State. The impulses for wholesome national life, which a contact with western culture, has called forth amongst the Indian mind want a home for a full, many-sided expression."[33]

"National system of education can be evolved only on national lines and in accordance with the inspiration of national "hopes and genius." The control and direction of high education must be in the hands of the Indians themselves if India is to grow through unity of purpose and training to a vigorous and complete national life."[34]

Beginning of Jamia: The National Muslim University

Mohammad Ali regarded Sir Sayyid as "an arch-rebel" and not a loyalist of the British Empire for he said that "It is my firm conviction that he had always aimed and intended to produce staunch Muslim and patriotic Indians, even if he could not contemplate a near enough future for India."[35]

He said that Sir Sayyid Ahmad Khan in his enthusiasm credited Europe and western education with every good quality in which he found his own people deficient; but never wavered for a moment in his belief in the eternal truth of Islam and in the capacity of Muslims to rise to the highest pinnacle of human greatness. Aligarh did produce a fine amalgam of East and the West in many things, they were progressive enough and they were proud enough of their faith; but they were far too ignorant of it. There is no doubt that a communal consciousness among the students but it was far more secular than religious; and also, they considered Islam to be the final message for the mankind and only entirely true faith and they could strenuously and even intelligently enough, argue about the superiority of its chief tenets but were "shamefully ignorant of "Islam's teachings and of its world-wide, centuries old history."[36]

Sayyid's vision to build a bridge that would connect his ancient faith with new science was the ideal which Mohammad Ali placed before himself while framing his scheme of Muslim University of the future.

Mohammad Ali prepared a scheme of a university which was to provide for the youth of his community religious as well as secular education. It was to create for young Muslims a center with the true Islamic atmosphere so that its alumni would not merely be educated and cultured men, but educated and cultured Muslims. With this aim the organizers of Jamia Millia Islamia, or the National Muslim University of Aligarh set out to reform. For this purpose, an intimate knowledge of Holy *Qur'an* was considered an indispensable foundation.

Mohammad Ali's said, "Science shall be in our right hand and philosophy in our left and on our head shall be the crown of "There is no God but Allah and Mohammad is his Apostle."[37] The Muslim masses read in the efforts of their leader's signs of the future glory of Islam and were happy at the idea that Islamic learning would be revived and that Aligarh would become a second Cordova or Baghdad.

The Mohammad an leaders of the country thought and believed that these things were possible provided their long-cherished desire of establishing a Muslim University at Aligarh was fulfilled. The Muslim masses read in the efforts of their leader's signs of the future glory of Islam and were happy at the idea that Islamic learning would be revived and that Aligarh would become a second Cordova or Baghdad. These ideas were extensively diffused among the Muslim masses by men like His Highness the Aga Khan, Mohammad Ali and the Raja of Mahmudabad. "The Mussalmans," he wrote, after the *fiat (farmaan)* of the education department, "want to evolve a certain type of education suited to their need and genius, and they want an All-India organization for that purpose."[38]

The proposed Muslim University was primarily designed to furnish that organization (Islamic). Mohammad Ali thought that if that University is to be deprived of the power of guiding Muslim education throughout India by a well-planned system of Government affiliation, the main object underlying the University movement, falls to the ground. On the 10th of April, 1916, in Lucknow, under the president ship of the Raja of

Mahmudabad, it was decided that the "decisions" of the Secretary of State for India in regard to the Muslim University, though "final," should never be taken as such, and that the government ought to be approached on the subject again. The meeting was fairly representative, as delegates from all parts of India were present there.

Under the colonial British rule, two dominant trends joined hands and contributed towards in the birth of the National University Jamia. One was the anti-colonial Islamic activism and the other was the pro-independence aspiration of the politically radical section of western educated Indian Muslim intelligentsia. In the political climate of 1920, the two trends gravitated together with Mahatma Gandhi as a catalyst. The anti-colonial activism signified by the Khilafat and the pro-independence aspirations symbolized by the non-cooperation movement of the Indian National Congress helped to harness creative energies and the subsequent making of Jamia Millia Islamia. Rabindranath Tagore called it "one of the most progressive educational institutions of India".

Born out of political crisis, it seemed for a while that Jamia would not survive the heat of the intense political struggle for the independence of India. Jamia saw itself in a great financial crisis because the little financial assistance that the Khilafat had been giving it was stopped. Even prominent people started deserting it and Jamia's total collapse virtually became an imminent possibility.

Jamia Moves from Aligarh to Delhi

The saying, 'when going gets tough the tough gets going' cannot be truer about Jamia. As the crisis loomed large, Hakim Ajmal Khan, Dr. Mukhtar Ahmad Ansari and Abdul Majeed Khwaja—the first trio—supported by Gandhiji shifted Jamia from Aligarh to Karol Bagh, in New Delhi in 1925. Gandhiji boosted the morale of Jamia, saying, "The Jamia has to run. If you are worried about its finances, I will go about with a begging bowl". Jamia followed Gandhiji's constructive programme for self-reliance while it took to 'Charkha; and 'Takli' as favored vocations.

Although Gandhi's contacts helped to secure financial help for Jamia, the risk of helping a Congress-backed institution under the British Raj dissuaded many willing benefactors. Orthodox Muslims viewed Jamia as a threat to Aligarh Muslim University, the 'Muslim Oxford'. During those difficult days, it was Hakim Ajmal Khan who met most of Jamia's expenses from his own pocket. Dr. M.A. Ansari and Abdul Majeed Khwaja toured India and abroad, explaining the importance of Jamia and collecting funds for this noble enterprise. Their collective intervention did avert a collapse that was almost certain.

Pan- Islamism

The Balkan War was declared in 1912. The machinations of the European powers against Turkey brought Maulana Mohammad Ali in the arena of active politics. He appealed for funds in aid of Turkish victims. A medical mission was despatched to Turkey under the leadership of Dr M.A. Ansari, which included Messrs A. R. Siddiqi and Shoaib Qureshi as well. This was the first embassy of practical goodwill sent by Muslim India to a foreign country. The mission performed valuable service, which was acknowledged by the Turks with gratitude at that time.

The brutal firing of Machhli Bazaar, Cawnpore, in 1913, sent a wave of resentment throughout the length and breadth of the sub-continent. It was a painful incident for the sensitive Mohammad Ali that shook his heart and made him an active agitator from an armchair politician. As stated earlier he led a deputation to England accompanied by Sayyid Wazir Hasan, secretary of the Muslim League. He canvassed there day and night, lecturing, writing in papers and interviewing the high British authorities for securing an honourable settlement of the Cawnpore (Kanpore, Kanpur) episode, but all in vain. When he came back to India, he found that a Great War was declared in Europe in 1914. Turkey was an ally of Germany and Mohammad Ali wanted that the British government should take into consideration the feelings of Muslim India.

His bold and inspiring criticism of the imperialist powers could not be tolerated by the British government during the war and he was interned for a period of about five years, ranging from November 23rd, 1915 to 1919. When he was released in 1919, the international scene was totally changed. The Great War had come to an end. The Turks were badly pressed in the "Treaty of Versailles" and their very existence was at stake. Turkey was in danger of total extinction and Lloyd George was contemplating to obliterate her from the map of Europe. Political storms were raging on the Indian horizon too. The Indian political atmosphere was tense and explosive. Martial Law had been proclaimed in the Punjab following the great tragedy of Jallianwala Bagh in 1919. These political developments only served as an incentive for the fiery Mohammad Ali. It was the most tumultuous period of his life.

He made extensive tours of the subcontinent during the period extending from October 1920 up to his arrest for the Karachi trial on September 1st, 1921. This period was spent virtually in the Railway compartment. He roused the Indian masses from their torpor and infused in them a new political consciousness. He never aspired for any position or privilege for himself. The Indian political consciousness was the result of his 8 years' untiring efforts---a remarkably short period for such a gigantic work. India was echoing with this song:

"Boleen Amman Mohammad Ali Kee

Jaan Baita Khilafat Pai Daido"

(So spoke the mother of Mohammad Ali: My son lay down your life for the sake of Khilafat).

A resolution was adopted at the *Khilafat* Conference held at Karachi in 1921 according to which it was considered an irreligious act for the Muslims to enrol in the British army. This resulted in the Karachi trial which commenced in October, 1921 in which Maulana Mohammad Ali, Shaukat Ali, Husain Ahmad Madni, and three others were awarded two years' rigorous imprisonment. His imprisonment evoked a country-wide protest. The resolution for which he was prosecuted was adopted and published throughout India. The statement given by Mohammad Ali before the court brings out his truly Islamic spirit. He acknowledges the supremacy of the Divine Law over the man-made legislations. The boldness and daring exhibited by him before the court were amazing. He was still in prison when Mustafa Kamal abolished the Khilafat, and hence the movement in India for its revival also crumbled down.

Mohammad Ali's belief that Europeans regarded Pan-Islamism as a 'movement' directed against Europe could be proved by the intelligent perusal of the articles which appeared from time to time in English and continental periodicals. 'The Times' notorious article written immediately after the "Kanpore Affair" was one of those articles which found a favored place in the columns of that reactionary paper. Mohammad Ali found it strange that in India too, there were certain leaders of thought and men of influence who unhappily fell in with the views of the charitable critics of Pan-Islamism. He thought Mr. Bipin Chandra Pal to be one of them, and regretted that a man of his education and caliber had sided with the adverse critics of Islam. To him the movement was entirely political and a distinct challenge to every non-Muslim State authority holding sways over any Muslim population. Mohammad Ali wrote "the dictum that the Indian Mussalman is first a Muslim and then an Indian, has a very sinister meaning behind it."…"Mr. Pal also accuses the Government of India of unwittingly strengthening the Pan-Islamic sentiment in this country by pandering to the vanity of the Muslim leaders by giving them preferential treatment in the constitution of the recently Reformed Council, but the meaning which the aforesaid writers have attached to the Pan- Islamic movement now on foot in the Mohammad an world, is not only far-fetched but ridiculous. The designs behind these writings need no comment, especially when it is perfectly known that Pan- Islamism has been a source of constant trouble to a set of Orientalists, "who are more concerned with the creation of bogeys than of books."[39]

Pan-Islamism is a movement based on religious fraternity, and its foundation was laid 1300 years ago by our Holy Prophet at the time when he proclaimed loud and wide that Muslims are brothers in religion. It is not in any sense a new movement at all though it appears so to non-Mussalmans. This term came into prominence during the Balkan war when a great wave of sympathy for Turks was felt throughout the Muslim world. Nothing can be farther from truth than to say that Muslims wage war against Christianity. To enter into a general crusade against Christendom is contrary to the spirit of the Koran. It needs no reasoning to prove that no such thing is contemplated in future. Pan-Islamism means nothing but the general uplifting of the depressed Mussalmans to the platform of equality, justice and liberty.[40]

To Maulana Mohammad Ali Pan- Islamism also means the general strengthening of commercial relations, based as they would be on religious ties, among the Muslims of the world. Thus, the Chinese and the Turks, the Indians and the Persians, the Arabs and the Africans, will unite not only in the common bond of religious brotherhood, but also of commerce. It is, in a way, also political, but stripped altogether of diplomatic bearings and designs, religious, social and commercial, and in no sense whatever will it ever be politically aggressive. Mohammad Ali, in the best sense of the term was a Pan-Islamist as all Muslim leaders were, and was perfectly in accord with the views expressed above. The following appeared in the *Comrade:*

"Pan-Islamism, when we come to consider its etymology, is a meaningless tissue of passion and prejudice. If it means anything, it refers to the existence of a community of sentiment and aspiration among the Mussalmans of the world as brought into existence by their religion. In that case, Islam bears exactly the same connotation, being the name of a set of beliefs and ideals common to the entire Mussalman races.[41] Interpreting the word in this sense, no Mussalman need be ashamed of its application. His sympathies are co-extensive with his religion and a race and a country has never captured him to the extent of the utter immersion in a narrow patriotism of the ideals which the acceptance of Islam had made his. But if we take the phrase to mean as some scare-mongers of the Yellow Press in Europe tell ns it means, some hidden political tendencies of modern Islam, struggling into an organized combination in order to throw back the tide of European aggression, we cannot but regard it as a figment of some heated brain. The progressive forces of modern civilization have no doubt produced a spirit of restlessness in the Mussalman populations of the world. But the unrest is entirely the outcome of their consciousness about their intellectual and moral degradation. They want to rcform their society, to grow in knowledge and self-respect and to enjoy all the amenities of an age of -progress and freedom. Every Mussalman sympathizes with his brother Mussalman in this desire, be they as far apart as Morocco and China. Surely there is nothing dangerous and immoral in this aspiration. The Mussalmans have proved their loyalty as subject races under alien systems of government. In China and Russia their patriotism has never been called into question. They have developed the true civic sense and the necessary political consciousness as citizens of State. Islam does not hamper such development; Territorial patriotism is not at all incompatible with the spiritual catholicity of a religion that has declared in a set of common ideals the brotherhood of man, and the supreme shallowness of the distinctions reared by the prejudice of color and race...... Mussalmans know this that Pan-Islamism is the cry of the aggressive Europeans, and that from race prejudice it has grown into a cult. If Pan-Islamism is anything different from every day Islam, the Mussalmans do not believe it. Its real significance can be explained by some of those gentlemen who founded the Pan-Islamic society of London."[42]

Mohammad Ali is considered to be the initiator of Pan-Islamism in India. This is partly true. In India Pan-Islamism was the concomitant of romanticism of which the best representative was Maulana Azad. Mohammad Ali did not employ the term Pan-Islamism to describe the efforts of the Muslim world to bring about united opposition to the Christian powers of Europe[43] as it was used originally in the eighties of the 19th century. It was advocated because the spirit of Islam called for the unity of Muslims. Patriotism and Pan-Islamism were not irreconcilable; Mohammad Ali said "If patriotism has a rationale, surely it can be nothing else but the similarity of culture and civilization, whether due to similar ethnic origin, geographical unity or identity of historical associations- expressing itself in similar laws and institutions. Now the rationale of the brotherhood of Islam or Pan-Islamism is exactly the same rationale of patriotism, with the difference however, that the Islamic fraternity has not achieved an identity of laws and institutions through an identity of ethnic origin or geographical unity, but has received it as a direct gift from God."[44]

Mohammad Ali believed that Islam as a spiritual force would one day dominate the world, and with its simple rationalism purge it of the dross of superstition as well as of Godless materialism." In the words of Mohammad Ali - "What was the essence of the Islamic civilization? It was not Art, though Art formed the basis of Greek culture. It was not Metaphysics, though Metaphysics supplied a substratum to Hindu civilization. And it was not politics, though politics is the foundation of modern European society. It was social ethics. Islam was a *mazhab*- pathway — and neither contemplation nor conquest can be the true *mazhab* of humanity. If the puritanic character of that faith had discouraged music; if its ideality had checked the growth of sculpture and painting; if its *tagwa* or God- fearingness had choked the channel of Arab poetry of the Days of Ignorance, with its free loves and wars of vengeance; if its horror of subtleties had made it unattractive of the abstruse thinker, it had at least supplied the Muslim with a single guide of conduct. Not that the flow of Art or music could be checked for ever for in calligraphy, in carpet-weaving and in architecture the Muslim found outlets for his genius, and, as in architecture so in music, the Muslim graft on the original Aryan plant improved the first beyond recognition. Not that in Literature, Philosophy or Science, thirteen centuries of Islam have been barren; for the names of Firdausi and S'adi, Hafiz and Khayyam, Abu Nawas and Mutanabbi, Mir and Ghalib, Averroes and Avicenna, Gazzali and Razi, Shah Waliullah and Sayyid Ahmad Khan, are proof enough that the Lamp of Letters was kept alight. But more than all these, the glory of Islam has been that not a soul in the philosopher's closet or the kitchen had been left without the consolation of religion in its adversities and its perplexities, and that no human being could fail to find readily an easily intelligible rule of conduct in the Koran, that most practical of all codes of ethics for all aspects of life, for all the functions of father or son, husband or wife, neighbor or friend, citizen or subject, king or conqueror."[45] Now, this fraternity of Faith, as is shown above, was brought into being by the Prophet himself. Individuals have felt sympathy and a brotherly feeling, but an organized brother- hood is yet not fully developed. To develop it to the full is what is connoted by Pan Islamism.

Mohammad Ali asserted that Pan-Islamism is nothing more or less than Islam itself, the "Super national Sangathan of Muslims in five continents."[46]

Islam as a religion and social polity binds all Muslims together. It recognizes neither the sanctity of color nor the virtue of geography, and by offering a set of common ideals, offers the only rational basis for unity and cooperation among its flowers. The sympathies of a Mussalman are co-extensive with his religion because they have been bred into him by the unifying spirit of his creed.[47] According to the Mohammad Ali the basis of Pan-Islamism is one God, One Prophet, One *Ka'ba* and One Book, the *Qur'an*. But "this spiritual unity would have been of no avail if it did not provide a social unity .... a common social policy."[48] He put great emphasis on "the main principles underlying the social synthesis.... throughout the Islamic world."[49] Pan-Islamism is not an institution. It is not concrete. But Pan-Islamism has been more an abstract and emotional factor than a pragmatic concept. It was not motivation by hatred against the non-Muslims. Mohammad Ali, therefore, held that Pan-Islamism and Islam are synonymous and neither is aggressive and provocative.[50] He declared, God before everything God before loyalty, God before King, God before patriotism, and God before my country, God before my father, mother and child. This is my faith."[51]

He preached Pan-Islamism from the Khilafat Committee as well as the Congress platforms. Mohammad Ali wanted to accomplish this is India. "To die for a cause is not difficult. The harder thing is to live for a cause, and if need be, suffer for it ... and the cause we must live and suffer for must be the realization in India of the Kingdom of God."[52] Mohammad Ali declared.

Mohammad Ali acknowledged B.G. Tilak as his political 'Guru'. Like Tilak, he believed in providing a popular basis to the nationalist movement in the country. The influence of Tilak made Mohammad Ali the leading exponent of extremist Muslim nationalism. Because of Tilak's influence Mohammad Ali had realized the necessity and significance of mass contact or associating the common people with the political movement. Tilak and Mohammad Ali both, of them used religion to provide a mass base to Indian politics.[53]

But Mohammad Ali's anti-British stand was the outcome of the British policy towards the Muslim countries. Moreover, the supranational character of Islam awakened and strengthened the latent feeling of Pan-Islamism amongst the Muslims in India.

Mohammad Ali believed that the basic teaching of Islam is peace and not war and hatred. Therefore, he had no hesitation in joining the Non-cooperation movement launched by Gandhi. Although Gandhi exercised some influence on Mohammad Ali, he was very conscious of "communal individuality". He said "I do not believe either in the spiritualism or the institution of Gandhiji. I also do not consider him the saint of God. His religion is different from my religion. But I regard him as my political leader. He is the greatest and most sincere leader of the country. We can become free from the British subjection only through his leadership."[54] Mohammad Ali with all his association with Islamic politics did not lag behind in lending support to Gandhi in the freedom struggle. Political expediency brought him closer to Gandhiji. He held that "there is no clash between Hindus and Muslims. The real conflict is between Malaviaism and Gandhism. I am supporting the latter to serve India and Islam.[55]

Thus, for good or ill Mohammad Ali got an opportunity owing to the Turkish problems immediately after the First World War to advocate Pan-Islamism in the form of the Khilafat movement. He said that the question of Khilafat lay at the root of Islamic polity. To him the Khilafat is "the most essential institution of the Muslim Community throughout the world."[56] He held that "the foundation of the Khilafat unites both temporal and spiritual work, which Islam believes it is charged with doing. There has been no such thing as merely the spiritual headship of Islam. Islam, as we regard it, is the last word in ethics and the last word in guidance and all over affairs."[57] Therefore, the Khilafat question assumed greater importance than all the other problems in India.[58]

Besides political consideration, religion was the dynamic factor behind the Khilafat question. Mohammad Ali declared that "our sympathy with Turkey was not political or territorial but religious, for the sovereign of Turkey was the successor of the Prophet and the commander of the faithful.[59]

So, the Muslims were asked to do their best for the preservation of the institution of Khilafat. Mohammad Ali expiated the Khilafat question for propagating Pan-Islamism. He found no conflict between the Khilafat and the independence movement in India. To him freedom of India was only a springboard for "the realization of Eastern Federalism."[60] He advised Muslims to fight for the country's freedom. For, a "slave India will be of scant help to the Turks and the Khalifa." This gave birth to what can be termed as Islamic Nationalism. Both Khilafat and Islamic Nationalism were the logical result of the Pan-Islamism of Mohammad Ali.

The Khilafat movement led to the emigration of a large number of Muslims from India. Mohammad Ali lacked balanced outlook and a sense of realism. He characterized India as *Darul Harb* while Sir Sayyid had said that there could be a country like India which is neither *Darul Harb* nor *Darul Islam*. Mohammad Ali felt that if the Muslims could not protect Khilafat, the symbol of Pan-Islamism, and if the British Government would not help them do so, the Muslims should leave India and migrate to some Islamic country. Such propaganda produced its inevitable and unhealthy consequences. The latent Muslim feelings of hatred against unbelievers sprang up; the old Muslim religion of the sword was reasserted; the exclusiveness of Arabia was revived; the extra territorial allegiance to Afghanistan which was shown by Muslim leaders nourished Pan-Islamic tendency; the primary allegiance of Muslims to Muslim countries stressed; the dream of establishing Muslim Raj caught many Indian Muslims; the loyalty of Indian Muslims to India was found to be spurious."[61]

Gandhiji supported Mohammad Ali in order to attract the support of the Muslims for the Nationalist Movement. Gandhiji, by supporting Mohammad Ali, wanted to save the cow. But Thompson says that "he never met a Hindu who thought Khilafat claims anything but nonsense, and rather immoral nonsense at that."[62]

Even the educational institutions were made, the hand mind of the ever-shifting exigencies of politics."[63]

Mohammad Ali, however, never recognized that "the fiasco of the *Hijrat* (Khilafat emigration) revealed the superficiality of religious sentiment" which was unable"[64] to save the Caliphal empire from dissolution and to prevent that dissolution from following largely national lines." Mohammad Ali was not prepared to abandon romanticism and accept realism, or to recognize the increasing role of nationalism, divesting it of the context of religion.

Nevertheless, Mohammad Ali was able to create a stir among the Muslims in India and to invest Pan-Islamism with the fervor of a mass movement. The Muslims "felt the impulse of the same social upheaval as shook their Hindu compatriots from their age-long resignation and apathy...it was the revolt of the exploited masses still unconscious of their purpose."[65]

Interpreters of Indian history like L. Hutchinson and Hiren Mukherjee, explain the significance of the Khilafat movement in Marxist terms: "The wretchedness of the Hindu peasants found expression in the National Congress: that of the Muslim peasants in the otherwise absurd Caliphate movement."[66]

Hiren Mukerjee insists that the content of the Khilafat movement was anti-Imperialistic or anti-British.[67] The credit for the mobilization of the mass energy goes to Mohammad Ali. This was earlier accomplished by the Hindu extremists in the history of the Indian nationalist movement. Religion for the Hindu extremists however was not an end but a means whereas to Mohammad Ali religion was an end in itself.

Islamic Nationalism

Mohammad Ali was not only the author of Pan-Islamism but also the most important spokesman of Islamic Nationalism. If Pan-Islamism was a reality to him, "Indianism" was no less so. This was no doubt illogical but he was not prepared to surrender either of the two. What Mohammad Ali attempted was a compromise between Pan-Islamism and Indian nationalism. In the Khilafat movement he appeared to see the blending of the two. We see in Mohammad Ali's thought the struggle between two irreconcilable lines of thought – Islamic universalism and Indian (Muslim) nationalism. He declared, "Where God commands I am a Muslim first, and Muslim second, and a Muslim last, and nothing but a Muslim....but where Indian is concerned .... I am an Indian First, an Indian second, an Indian last, nothing but an Indian."[68]

He said "I belong to two circles of equal size, but which are not concentric. One is India and the other is the Muslim World."[69] In India the Muslims are "the blood-brothers of the Hindus" but outside India there are millions who share their faith. It "is a priceless heritage, the wonder of the age, the most vital and binding human cement." But the fiasco of the Khilafat Movement obliged him to think in terms of Islamic nationalism. In practical politics it was an emphasis on separateness of the Muslim community as a distinct cultural and political entity.

Mohammad Ali's love of Islam and the Muslim world should not lead to doubt his devotion to Indian nationalism.

Though his Indianism was subordinate to his loyalty to Islam, he was a true Indian. He accepted one reality-God. But God also made it obligatory to serve the people of one's own country. Thus, the country was a fundamental as the faith. Islamic theocracy assigns no place to territorial nationalism as it does not make any distinction between an Arab and non-Arab. Mohammad Ali writes : "The theocracy of Islam naturally condemned the narrow prejudices that created nationality and killed humanity, for to God, the universal King, there would be no distinction between Arab and Ajam, of Aryan and Semitic, of Anglo-Saxon and Teuton, I had seen in this terrible war the natural consequences and culmination of nationalism."[70] He held that Islamic theocracy is "super nationalist" in character and therefore opposed to secular nationalism which is the work of Satan and not of God. Nationalism and religion are poles apart. One divides and the other binds.[71] Nationalism without religion kills our sense of right and wrong.[72]

A true Muslim should true away from the shrine of nationalism that has for its creed "My Country, right or wrong." Whereas nationalism demands worship of one's country, Islam recognizes one sovereignty alone, the sovereignty of God, which is supreme and unconditional, indivisible and inalienable.[73]

Thus, the excess of territorial and secular nationalism disrupts the peace of God and sets nation against nation.[74] But nationalism would become acceptable if it is based on Islam, for it would then cease to be territorial or secular and become "non-spatial and non-racial."[75] This attitude perfectly agreed with Mohammad Ali's approach to Islam or Pan-Islamism. To him the more important question was the liberty of conscience and the preservation of the sanctity of souls.[76] It was an attempt to retain the institution of Khilafat on the one hand, and the unity of the people and independence of the country on the other.

Gandhiji was also convinced of the sincerity of Mohammad Ali and the purity of his faith in Islam. "The brave Brothers

(Mohammad Ali and Shaukat Ali) are staunch lovers of their country, but they are Muslim first and everything else after and it must be so with every religiously minded man. The Brothers have for years past represented all that are best and noblest in Islam. No two Mussalmans have done more than they to raise the status of Islam in India.... They have shown themselves true nationalists"[77] wrote Gandhiji. Gandhiji was so much influenced by Mohammad Ali that "the action of Gandhi in launching non-cooperation on (20th August, 1920) was the direct outcome of the Khilafat movement."[78] It should be noted that Mohammad Ali stressed more on Pan-Islamic ends than the nationalist objects. The Khilafat movements could mobilized Muslims but did not bring about the unity of Hindu and Muslims. To achieve this end, Mohammad Ali himself wrote that "The communal temper must change and interests must grow identical before the Hindus and Muslims can be welded into a united nationality."[79]

Mohammad Ali's had a real passion for the liberty of the individual and the freedom of the country, Mohammad Ali got inspiration from Islam in his efforts for freedom for he believed that Islam was opposed to all kinds of subjection except subjection to God. He, therefore, said that when the Mussalmans of India voiced their demand for complete independence, they were only repeating the command of the Qur'an, which was made 1310 years ago."[80]

Mohammad Ali supported the non-cooperation movement as proper means for achieving the independence of the country. He argued that it was sanctioned by the Qur'an: Co-operation in righteousness and piety, but not in sinfulness and transgression.[81]

But these objects could not be obtained without making sacrifices especially in the cause of religion and freedom.[82] He explained to the Muslims that "Swaraj means Swadharma and if you value religious freedom more than others as you think, yours must be the larger sacrifice.[83] He also advised his countrymen in general and Muslims in particular, not to join the British Army. For God's Command was, "I want you to serve Me and not a creature of Mine."[84] Mohammad Ali applied the Islamic concept of liberty of the Indian situation. He was therefore committed to complete independence. [85] In his speech at the Round Table Conference, he declared, "I want to go back to my country if I can go back with the substance of freedom in my hand. Otherwise, I will not go back to a slave country. I will even prefer to die in a foreign country."[86] This meant to him equal freedom for all communities in India and not for the majority community only. On this issue Mohammad Ali even parted company with Gandhi. "We refuse to join Mr. Gandhi." he said, "because his movement is not a movement for the complete independence of India but for making the 70 million of Indian Muslims dependent on Hindu Sabha."[87]

It is generally said about Mohammad Ali that after the end of the Khilafat movement, he turned out to be a communalist. This is far from true. Nationalism in India is not and has never been a concept with a definite meaning accepted by all the leaders of all the communities. To Mohammad Ali nationalism implied independence of the country as well as freedom for the communities from the fear of domination by one another and continuity and preservation of what is best in Muslim culture. He also thought that nationalism was unacceptable and harmful to the Muslims if it violated the spirit of Islam. He therefore argued that "in India the nation could be the synthesis of various races and creeds on the political and to some extent, on the social plane." [88] Commenting on B.C. Pal's concept of nationalism Mohammad Ali said that Pal's definition of nationalism was more in terms of Hindu religion and culture than in terms of Indian geography or in terms of the variety and complexity of Indian society. Indian nationality cannot be viewed as coextensive with the Hindu religion because it leaves out millions of different creeds[89] who have considerably influenced Indian society. Mohammad Ali had always been apprehensive of Hindu-oriented Indian nationalism which was upheld by communal patriots. It alarmed the Muslims and had driven them into a position of sullen isolation. "The veils of separation can be broken down only if a radical change takes place in the concept of communal duty and patriotism,"[90] he insisted. Mohammad Ali who once regarded the demand for separate electorates as untenable found it necessary later to support it. What he regarded as the extremist character of Hindu leadership made Muslims suspicious even of the demand for Swaraj. He pleaded for communal representation and separate electorates because the Muslims became "suspicious of Swaraj becoming a Hindu Raj in practice."[91] He was of the opinion that the interests of the Muslims were separate and distinctive and required to be safeguarded by separate electorates.[92]

Mohammad Ali's nationalism cannot be regarded either chauvinistic or a glorification of everything Indian. It was not a fanatical and irrational revulsion against everything Western"[93] On the country, it was based on the faith that Europe had much to teach"[94] and that India, the East, required to be quickened and enlightened by the rapid diffusion of scientific knowledge.[95] But while he emphasized the need for material progress, he warned the country against gross materialism.[96]

Mohammad Ali's ideas of nationalism and religion are interwoven. His concept of nationalism was so much tainted by Islam that ultimately it was difficult to separate the two. Nevertheless, this agrees at some points with Gandhian nationalism which insists on spiritual foundations and that of Nehru and Mohammad Ali had been internationalist in their own ways. All of them believed that internationalism is possible only when nationalism becomes a fact. They, at the same time, condemned the exclusiveness and narrowness of nationalism. It has, however, been mentioned that Mohammad Ali contributed more to the promotion of the feeling of Pan-Islamism than of national consciousness among the Muslims in India.

Mohammad Ali's ideas on nationalism had a practical bearing on the growth of Muslims in India. His was an extremist type of nationalism. There are many similarities between Hindu and Muslim extremist nationalisms, for instance, their violent anti-British tone and the employment of unconstitutional means. The only and perhaps not so very important difference[97] was that the former was inspired by Islam and Muslim domination in India and the latter by Hinduism. The Hindu as well Muslim extremists clearly constitute a break from the loyalist policy of the moderate Congressites and liberal Muslim Leaguers. The basic differences between the nature and spirit of Islam and Hinduism constituted the complicated communal problem in India. The Indian Muslims being part of an international community have had a feeling of loyalty and belongingness to the cause of Muslims all over the world. But there could be no real political and economic unity, even among the Muslims in India. Religion was only a factor of identity among them. But to Mohammad Ali it was more that. Islam, to him, was more than a religion. It was a source of inspiration for the struggle against the alien British rulers. When Mohammad Ali protested against imperialism and pleaded for the national liberation of the Indian people, he was motivated by the feeling that the British were the moral enemies of Islam. It was the aggressive spirit of Pan-Islamism which was inspired by the triumph of the young Turks.[98] The analysis of this trend shows that it was the "latent reactionary resistance"[99] which was stronger than the reform movement in Islam. And thus, the orthodox Nationalism of the Hindus as well as of the Muslims becomes" a political outburst of the forces of reaction.[100] Seen from this angle, ideological Mohammad Ali's Islamic nationalism would appear absurd, but politically it played a positive role in creating a mass basis for Indian politics. A careful scrutiny would reveal that Mohammad

Ali's political ideas were dominated by consideration of religion and loyalty to the restricted Muslim community.

Thus, we find that Mohammad Ali's concept of nationalism was dangerous. It could not offer a constructive solution to the problems of composite nationalism. Religion of the basis of nationalism would produce competitive nationalities and communal conflict in the country and would always act as a disruptive and destructive force. Mohammad Ali argued that nationalism based on Islam alone would be healthy as Islam was a world religion. Muslim nationalism could be hardly separated from Pan-Islamism. In practice it would mean a Muslim Raj in India with unspecified loyalties, looking outward towards Muslims rather than towards fellow citizens of different faiths. Mohammad Ali believed in the supremacy of Islam. He was so convinced of the righteousness of Islam that an adulterous and a fallen Mussalman were according to him better than Gandhi. True to his genius for inconsistency, he also advocated to ideal of the "united faiths in India." He perhaps did not see that unity of faiths was incompatible with his aggressive and illiberal view of Islam. Mohammad Ali also considered deeply about the establishment of a democratic federation in the country. But he failed to reconcile the cause of Islamic nationalism with a non-Islamic government. Mohammad Ali raised questions but did not answer any.

Mohammad Ali said that women should be encouraged to participate in public affairs for Islam does not discountenance such participation. That "Ayesha was often consulted particularly in matters of women's affairs and in matter of Law generally"[101] showed that there was no such restriction imposed by Islam. Mohammad Ali held that "the Muslim society in India in the days of decadence had sinned against the light in nothing so much as in condemning womanhood to all but universal ignorance."[102] He advocated that "women should not be "confined within the four walls of the Zenana."[103] Their cooperation is needed in the settlement of communal and national problems. He, therefore, hoped that the conventional *Pardah* would not last.[104] There should be as many opportunities for female education as possible. In spite of the fact that Mohammad Ali cherished the religious ideal of Pan-Islamism he emphasized to the Muslims in India that India was their homeland and that their political loyalties ought to be centered on India and not outside. In 1923 he pointed out to the delegates of the Indian National Congress that "if you carefully examine the history of the last dozen years (you) will come to know how our disasters in foreign affairs have thrown us back on you. We feel grateful for the concentration of the Mussalman on foreign affairs outside the confines because it has made us realize that we must after all come to Indians for the proper solutions of our difficulties in the foreign countries abroad."[105]

He followed this attitude to its logical end. Mohammad Ali was not a gifted philosopher. He had neither the mind nor the time for philosophical exercise. He was a passionate propagandist. His preoccupation with journalism was not conducive to philosophizing about religions and politics. He was essentially a revolutionary. His western education and the influence of Islam molded his ideas. Khaliquzzaman rightly said that Mohammad Ali "was not a man to accept facts as facts. He was a born revolutionary aiming to destroy all that did not conform to his ideal, even though he might not be able to reconstruct what he had destroyed." And as a revolutionary he was an egoist interested in his own self with an effort to identify himself with Islam. Afzal Aqbal says, "He started with the life of the Prophet and ended with his own."[106] He carried in his self "the pathos of a great but fallen race."[107]

Mohammad Ali's loyalty to Islam was unquestioned. His aim was the glorification of Islam. Though educated in western ideas of liberalism, he always regarded Islam as his guide. All his political activities were inspired by his love of Islam. One can say that Islam was the source of inspiration in his political life and thought. In his thought religious and political ideas converged. According to him political power is co-extensive with faith. Both Mohammad Ali and Iqbal aspired for the betterment of all the Muslims of the world. But Mohammad Ali wanted to achieve his ends through political means like agitation and revolution while Iqbal relied more on spiritual purification, intellectual revolution and assertion of the self. The Khilafat movement was based on the unrealistic assessment of the internal conditions of the Muslims countries. [108]

It demanded that the Caliphate of Turkey should be maintained as an effective international religious organization.[109] The failure of the Khilafat movement did not make him a pessimist. Even after the Khilafat Committee alive and continue to fight against the British to concede real independence to the Arab world with a view to liberating the liberated. [110] He had to doubt about the efficiency of democracy. He described himself as a "confirmed republican."[111] His concept of democracy is significant because it is a statement of the elements of Muslim political thought and in the name of Islam, he wanted to establish a democratic federation-that became a reality after the independence of the country.

Mohammad Ali's contribution to Muslim politics is of great value. He carried forward the legacy of Sir Sayyid. He himself was the product of the Aligarh movement. The movement rescued the Muslims from ignorance, lethargy, and hopelessness. Mohammad Ali taught them "to discard foreign influences in life, to learn self-reliance, live for cause and die for them."[112]

Mohammad Ali was the first leader who consciously and successfully attempted to explore the possibilities of bringing together the *Ulema* and the western educated youth. He thought that this would strengthen Islam as well as promote Indian Independence. The *Ulema* as well as the western educated youth would be benefited by such cooperation. The *Ulema* would inspire religious spirit among the Muslim youth. The Khilafat movement symbolizes the unity of the *Ulema* and the western educated youth by purposively subscribing to the single object of the solidarity of the Muslims. After the death of Mohammad Ali, the gulf between the *Ulema* and the educated youth widened. The legacy of association of the common people with political movement which Mohammad Ali left behind was utilized and exploited by both. Both the *Ulema* and the educated youth began to outbid each other in courting the support of the masses the only lesson they seem to have learned from the teaching and activity of Mohammad Ali. It is a sad reality that those who followed the technique and strategy of Mohammad Ali "fought the battle of Pakistan and won it."

References

1. Ali, Mohammad, *Comrade,* 15th June, 1925, p. 347

2. Iqbal, Afzal (ed.), *Ali Mohammad: My life, A Fragment: an autobiographical sketch,* Lahore: Sh. M. Ashraf, 1946, p. 125

3. *Iqbal, Afzal* (comp. & *ed.*), *Select Writings and Speeches* of *Maulana Mohamed Ali, Lahore*: Shaikh Mohammad Ashraf, *1944*, p. 465

4. *ibid.*, p. 165

5. Sen, Sachin, *The Birth of Pakistan*, Calcutta: General Printers & Publishers, 1955, p. 74

6. Choudhry, *Khaliquzzaman, Pathway to Pakistan*, Lahore: Longmans Pakistan Branch, 1961, p. 320

7. *Punjabi,* A. (Pseudo), "*Confederacy of India*", *Lahore, 1932*, p. 72

8. Iqbal, Afzal (ed.), *Ali Mohammad: My life, A Fragment: an autobiographical sketch,* Lahore: Sh. M. Ashraf, 1946, p. 43

9. *ibid.,* p. 95

10. *ibid.,* p. 96

11. *ibid.,* p. 164

12. Weber, Max, The *Sociology of Religion,* Boston: *Beacon Press,* 1963, p. 264

13. Ali, Mohammad, *His Life, Services and Trial,* Enlarged Edition, Madras: Ganesh & Company, 1921, p. 167

14. *ibid.,* p. 168

15. *ibid.,* p. 209

16. *ibid.,* p. 209

17. Shakir, Moin, *Islam in Modern India,* Mainstream, June, 1967

18. Ali, Mohammad, *His Life, Services and Trial,* Enlarged Edition, Madras: Ganesh & Company, 1921, pp. 13-14.

19. *ibid.,* p.15

20. *ibid.,* p.16

21. *ibid.* p.17.

22. *ibid.,* p.31

23. Ali, Mohammad, *Comrade,*1st March,1913, p,180

24. Iqbal, Afzal (ed.), *Ali Mohammad: My life, A Fragment: an autobiographical sketch,* Lahore: Sh. M. Ashraf, 1946, p. 18

25. *ibid.,* p.42

26. Iqbal, *Afzal,* (comp. & ed.), *Select Writings and Speeches* of *Maulana Mohamed Ali,* Lahore: Shaikh Mohammad Ashraf, *1944,* p. 413

27. Ali, Mohammad, *His Life, Services and Trial*, Enlarged Edition, Madras: Ganesh & Company, 1921, p. 50

28. *ibid.*, p. 51

29. Iqbal, Afzal, comp. & ed., *Select Writings and Speeches* of *Maulana Mohamed Ali*, Lahore: Shaikh Mohammad Ashraf, *1944*, p. 414.

30. Ali Mohammad: *Comrade Selections from Mohammad Ali's Comrade*, Mohammad Ali Academy, 1965, 1st March 1913, p.180

31. Iqbal, Afzal, (ed.), *Ali Mohammad: My life, A Fragment: an autobiographical sketch*, Lahore: Sh. M. Ashraf, 1946, p.18

32. *ibid.*, p.42

33. Ali, Mohammad, *His Life, Services and Trial, Enlarged Edition*, Madras: Ganesh & Company, 1921, p.52.

34. *ibid.*, p.54

35. Congress Presidential Addresses, 1923, p. 617

36. Iqbal, Afzal (comp. & ed.), *Select Writings and Speeches* of *Maulana Mohamed Ali*, Lahore: Shaikh Mohammad Ashraf, *1944*, p. 416

37. *ibid.*, p.415.

38. Ali, Mohammad, *His Life, Services and Trial*, Enlarged Edition, Madras: Ganesh & Company, 1921, P.27

39. *ibid.*

40. *ibid.*, pp. 57-58

41. *ibid.*, p.59

42. *ibid*, p.60

43. *Encyclopedia, Britannica*: Vol. 17, 1951, p. 185

44. Iqbal, Afzal (comp. & ed.), *Select Writings and Speeches* of *Maulana Mohamed Ali*, Lahore: Shaikh Mohammad Ashraf, 1944, p. 101

45. Ali, Mohammad, *His Life, Services and Trial*, Enlarged Edition, Madras: Ganesh & Company, 1921, pp.61-62

46. Iqbal, Afzal (comp. & ed.), *Select Writings and Speeches* of *Maulana Mohamed Ali*, Lahore: Shaikh Mohammad Ashraf, 1944, p. 389

47. Ali Mohammad, *Comrade*. 12th April, 1913, p. 290

48. Iqbal, Afzal (comp. & ed.), *Select Writings and Speeches* of *Maulana Mohamed Ali*, Lahore: Shaikh Mohammad Ashraf, 1944, p.102

49. *ibid.*, p. 101

50. *ibid.*, p. 61

51. *ibid.*, p. 23

52. *Congress Presidential Addresses*, 1923, p. 657

53. Shakir, Moin, *Myths in Muslim Politics*, Mainstream, October, 1966

54. *ibid.*

55. Iqbal, Afzal (comp. & ed.), *Select Writings and Speeches* of *Maulana Mohamed Ali*, Lahore: Shaikh Mohammad Ashraf, 1944, p. 170

56. Abbas, M.H., *All About Khilafat*, Calcutta: Ray and Raychaudhuri, 1923, pp. 91-92

57. *Congress Presidential Addresses,* 1923, p. 639

58. Iqbal, Afzal (ed.), *Ali Mohammad: My life, A Fragment: an autobiographical sketch*, Lahore: Sh. M. Ashraf, 1946, p. 138

59. *Congress Presidential Addresses*, 1923, p. 709

60. *ibid.*, p. 709

61. Sen, Sachin, *The Birth of Pakistan*, Calcutta: General Printers & Publishers, 1955, p. 72

62. Thompson, Edward, *The Reconstruction of India*, London: Faber and Faber, 1930, p. 123

63. Husain, Azim, *FazJ-i-Husain—a political biography*, Bombay: Longmans Green, 1946, p. 107

64. Roy, M.N., *The Problem of Freedom*, Renaissance Publishers, *Calcutta, 1945*, p. 238

65. *ibid.*

66. Hutchinson, L., *The Empire of Nobody*, p. 217

67. Mukherjee, Hirendranath, *India's Struggle for Freedom*, Calcutta: National Book agency, 1962, pp. 101-102

68. Iqbal, *Afzal* (comp. & ed.), *Select Writings and Speeches* of *Maulana Mohamed Ali*, *Lahore*: Shaikh Mohammad Ashraf, 1944, p. 465

69. *ibid.*, p. 465

70. Iqbal, Afzal (ed.), *Ali Mohammad: My life, A Fragment: an autobiographical sketch*, Lahore: Sh. M. Ashraf, 1946, p. 125

71. Iqbal, *Afzal* (comp. & ed.), *Select Writings and Speeches* of *Maulana Mohamed Ali*, *Lahore*: Shaikh Mohammad Ashraf, 1944, p. 465

72. *ibid.*, p. 165

73. Sen, Sachin, *The Birth of Pakistan*, Calcutta: General Printers & Publishers, 1955, p. 74

74. Choudhry, *Khaliquzzaman, Pathway to Pakistan*, Lahore: Longmans Pakistan Branch, 1961, p. 320

75. Punjabi, A., *Confederacy of India*, Lahore: Nawab *Mohammad Shah Nawaz Khan* of *Mamdot*, 1939, p.72.

76. Iqbal, Afzal (comp. & ed.), *Select Writings and Speeches* of *Maulana Mohamed Ali*, Lahore: Shaikh Mohammad Ashraf, 1944, p. 158

77. Gandhi, Mahatma, *To the Hindus and Muslims*, Edited by Anand T. Hingorani, Karachi: The Editor, 1942, p. 27 (Gandhi Series Part- III)

78. Majumdar, R.C., *History* of the *Freedom Movement in India*, Vol. III, Calcutta: Firma K.L. Mukhopadhyay, 1988, p. 75

79. *ibid.*, p. 62

80. Gopal, Ram, *Indian Muslims*, *A Political History 1858-1947*, Bombay: Asia Publishing House, 1959, p. 206

81. Iqbal, Afzal (comp. & ed.), *Select Writings and Speeches* of *Maulana Mohamed Ali*, Lahore: Shaikh Mohammad Ashraf, 1944, p. 349

82. *ibid.*, p. 350

83. *ibid.*, p.369

84. *ibid.*, p. 211

85. *ibid.*, p. 461

86. *ibid.*, p. 460

87. Coupland, Sir Reginald, *India, A restatement*, London: Oxford University Press, 1945, p. 136

88. Ali, Mohammad, *Comrade*, 5th April, 1913, p. 264

89. *ibid.*, p. 264

90. Iqbal, Afzal (comp. & ed.), *Select Writings and Speeches* of *Maulana Mohamed Ali*, Lahore: Shaikh Mohammad Ashraf, 1944, p. 69

91. Ali, Mohammad, *Comrade*, 7th August, 1925, pp. 61-62

92. Iqbal, Afzal (ed.), *Ali Mohammad: My life, A Fragment: an autobiographical sketch*, Lahore: Sh. M. Ashraf, 1946, p. 50

93. *ibid.*, p. 50

94. *ibid.*, p. 50

95. *ibid.*, p. 50

96. Desai, A. R., *Social background of Indian Nationalism*, Bombay: Popular Prakashan, 1946, p. 265

97. Roy, M.N., *The Problem of Freedom*, Renaissance Publishers, *Calcutta, 1945,* pp. 227-228

98. Ali, A. Yousuf, *The Making of India*, A. & C. Black, 1925, p. 286

99. Roy, M.N., *The Problem of Freedom*, Renaissance Publishers, *Calcutta, 1945,* p. 189

100. Ali, Mohammad, *Comrade*, 31st may, 1913, p. 436

101. Kemal, Rahimuddin, *The Concept of Constitutional Law in Islam*, Hyderabad: Fasé Brothers, 1955, p. 92

102. Iqbal, Afzal (ed.), *Ali Mohammad: My life, A Fragment: an autobiographical sketch*, Lahore: Sh. M. Ashraf, 1946, p.14

103. *ibid.*, p. 254

104. Ali, Mohammad, *Comrade*, 4th December, 1925, P. 254

105. *Congress Presidential Addresses*,1923, p. 626

106. Iqbal, Afzal (ed.), *Ali Mohammad: My life, A Fragment: an autobiographical sketch*, Lahore: Sh. M. Ashraf, 1946, p. VI

107. Iqbal, Afzal (comp. & *ed.*), *Select Writings and Speeches* of *Maulana Mohamed Ali*, Lahore: Shaikh Mohammad Ashraf, 1944, p. 140

108. Hussain, Abid, *The destiny of Indian Muslims*, Bombay: Asia Publishing House, 1965, pp. 80-81

109. Noman, *Mohammad, Muslim India*, Allahabad : Kitabistan,1942, p. 203

110. Choudhary, Khaliquzzaman, *Pathway to Pakistan*, Lahore: Longmans Pakistan Branch, 1961, p. 69

111. Iqbal, Afzal (comp. & *ed.*), *Select Writings and Speeches* of *Maulana Mohamed Ali*, Lahore: Shaikh Mohammad Ashraf, 1944, p. 481

112. Choudhary, Khaliquzzaman, *Pathway to Pakistan*, Lahore: Longmans Pakistan Branch, 1961, pp. 109-110

THE PROCESS OF CONSTRUCTIVE REVIVALISM:
DR. SIR MUHAMMAD IQBAL

Burst into song, oh nightingale!

So that from your melody the spirit of the royal falcan may arise in the delicate body of the dove!

The secret of your life is hidden in your breast- then tell it;

Tell the Muslims the account of the burning and remaking of life.

You are the ever-powerful hand and tongue of the eternal God;

Give birth to a certainty, of negligent one, for you are laid low by doubt

The goal of Muslims lies beyond the blue sky;

You are the caravan, which the stars follow as dust on the road.

Sir Muhammad Iqbal, also known as Allama Iqbal, was a philosopher, poet and politician in British India who is widely regarded to have inspired the Pakistan Movement. He is considered one of the most important figures in Urdu literature, with literary work in both the Urdu and Persian languages. Iqbal is admired as a prominent classical poet by Pakistani, Indian and other international scholars of literature. Although most well known as a poet, he has also been acclaimed as a modern Muslim philosopher. His first poetry book, Asrar-e-Khudi, appeared in the Persian language in 1915, and other books of poetry include Rumuz-i-Bekhudi, Payam-i-Mashriq and Zabur-i-Ajam. Some of his most well-known Urdu works are Bang-i-Dara, Bal-i-Jibril and Zarb-i Kalim. Along with his Urdu and Persian poetry, his various Urdu and English lectures and letters have been very influential in cultural, social, religious and political disputes over the years. In 1922, he was knighted by King George V, giving him the title "Sir".

Iqbal is known as Shair-e-Mushriq meaning Poet of the East. He is also called *Muffakir-e-Pakistan* "The Inceptor of Pakistan", and *Hakeem-ul-Ummat* "The Sage of the Ummah". Pakistan has officially recognized him as its "national poet". In Iran and Afghanistan, he is famous as *Iqbal-e Lahori* (Iqbal of Lahore), and he is most appreciated for his Persian work.

Iqbal (1876-1938) was born in Sialkot, within the Punjab Province of British India (now in Pakistan). Iqbal's ancestors were Kashmiri Pandits, the Brahmins from Kashmir who converted to Islam. In the 19th century, when Sikhs were taking over rule of Kashmir, his grandfather's family migrated to Punjab. Iqbal often mentioned and reminisced about his Kashmiri Pandit Brahmin lineage in his writings. Iqbal's father, Shaikh Noor Mohammad, was a tailor, not formally educated but a religious man. Iqbal's mother Imam Bibi was a polite and humble woman who helped the poor and solved the problems of neighbors.

At the age of four years Iqbal was sent to the mosque to learn the Qur'an. Iqbal began his education in a Maktab (religious school). He was, however, fortunate to have a teacher in the person of Moulvi Sayyid Mir Hassan who was an excellent teacher and a great scholar of Persian and Arabic. It was under Mir Hassan that Iqbal developed interest in Persian and Arabic languages and literature. It was on Mir Hassan's advice that Iqbal was sent to the Scotch Mission School at Sialkot. He passed his matriculation in 1893, and joined the Scotch Mission College (now called Murray College) for his intermediate examination.

It was about this time that Iqbal sent some of his verses, mostly lyrics to the well-known Urdu poet Dagh for correction. After correcting some pocms, with great appreciation Dagh wrote back to Iqbal that his poem did not need any revision.

After passing intermediate with honor, he was awarded a scholarship from the Scotch Mission College. The same year, Iqbal shifted to Lahore and joined the Government College. The subjects Iqbal studied for the Bachelor of Arts degree included Arabic and English literature and philosophy. He graduated cum-laude and was also awarded a scholarship for further study leading towards a master's degree in Philosophy. Two years later in 1899, he won a gold medal for the unique distinction of being the only candidate who passed the final comprehensive examination. Iqbal obtained his master's degree in 1899.

In May 1899 he was appointed Macleod – Punjab reader of Arabic at the University Oriental College of Lahore. However, he resigned from the position of reader and taught as Assistant Professor of English at Islamia College and at the Government College at Lahore.

Iqbal went to England in 1905, for further studies. He studied in both Britain and Germany. At the Trinity College of Cambridge University, he enrolled as an undergraduate student to earn a Bachelor of Arts degree. He remained in London for three years and read voraciously all what he could in the rich library of Cambridge. He also studied philosophy with the noted Hegelian, Prof. McTaggart. This enrollment was unusual since he already had a master's degree in Philosophy from the University of the Punjab, Lahore, and was simultaneously preparing to submit a doctoral dissertation in Philosophy to Munich University.

He continued with his Ph.D. degree, and received admission to the Faculty of Philosophy of the Ludwig Maximilian University in 1907 at Munich. Iqbal worked under the guidance of Friedrich Hommel, and published his doctoral thesis in 1908 entitled: 'The Development of Metaphysics in Persia'. This dissertation, which was published the following year in London, was dedicated to T.W. Arnold.

After three years in England and Germany when he returned to India with a new and vibrant message. Certain aspects of European life made a forceful impact upon his sensitive and brilliant spirit. He was impressed by three things in particular, out of which he constructed a message for Indian Islam. First was the immense vitality and activity of European life, the exuberant initiative of the people whom he saw, the confident restlessness whereby if they did not like a thing, they changed it. Secondly, and related to this, he caught a vision of the tremendous possibilities before human life--the potentialities of which the Orient had not dreamed, but which Europe was already realizing, and intended to keep on realizing more and more. Man could think, do, be a thousand things for which Iqbal's fellows back in India were not even striving and once man had attained those things there would be a thousand more calling for endeavor. Thirdly, Iqbal the critic noticed the severe and damning limitations to which European life, in spite of all its promise, was subject to.

Along with the dynamism of European life Iqbal witnessed the soul-destroying frustration in the lives of the individual of a prospering capitalist society. He saw the bestial competition between fellow-men, and, more obviously destructive tendencies between nation and nation. He appreciated the much of 'value' in parts of European life, but realized that the European life could never be a model for perfection, not good enough to serve as his ideal. Iqbal felt with ardor that the thousands of young middle-class Indians, who were devoting themselves simply to copying Europe, were being grossly misled. The West was good but devoid of the virtues and values of Islam, the religion of his fathers.

At the turn of the century, he was attracted to the surging nationalism of the day, and wrote expressing the ideal of Indian unity and Indian freedom. He appealed strongly for Hindu-Muslim solidarity, and wrote inspiringly of the glorious land of India and of the honor, love, and devotion due to her. His "Song of India" (*Taranah i Hindi*)[1], one of his patriotic poems, is today loved as a national anthem by thousands of all communities in India. He also wrote Islamic poems, and he was sponsored by the chief local Muslim society, but even when addressing that group, he pleaded for inter-communal co-operation.

In 1908 Iqbal returned to Lahore and set up a barrister's practice. Primarily a poet, he elaborated the message of dynamic activism, of a potentially glorious future, and of the supreme value of Islam. He soon became recognized as the outstanding thinker and litterateur of the Indian Muslims and gradually he acquired a prestige among the middle classes which can hardly be exaggerated.

In 1915, Iqbal published his major Persian philosophical poem *"Asrar-i-Khudi"* (The secrets of Self) Its continuation, *Rumuz-i-bekhudi* (Mysteries of the selflessness) appeared in 1918. These poems initiated a series that included *Payam-i-Mashriq* (The message of the East, 1923) a response to Goethe's West Ostriches Divan; *Zubur-i-Ajam* (Iranian Psalms, 1927); and *Javid Nama* (1932) which has been called "an Oriental Divine Comedy".

His generally shorter, more lyrical Urdu poems were also published in several collections, notably *Bang-e-Dara* (The call of the Caraven Bell, Lahore, 1924) and *Bal-e-Jabril* (The wings of Gabriel Lahore, 1935). A collection of his English lectures on Islamic philosophy was published titled: 'The Reconstruction of Religious Thought in Islam' (1930). This work demonstrated knowledge, certainly not superficial, of European thought.

In 1926 he became a member of the Central Legislative Council and in 1930 became the president of the Muslim League. In 1928-9 he delivered 'Six lectures on Islam' at Madras, which attracted wide attention and impressed Lords Irwin and Lothian enough to have him invited to lecture at Oxford. These lectures[2] in English were his only important prose publications, except a few polemic pamphlets, his fame was acquired chiefly by the constant succession of his vigorous and brilliant verses, Urdu and Persian.

Philosophical Basis to Revivalism

Basically, in its origin, Iqbal's philosophy is an extension of the tradition of Islamic thought alone. Iqbal's thought is organically linked to his own Muslim background. Iqbal's concept of the Truth, God, the universe, *Khudi* and *Mard-i-Mumin* themselves have roots in Islamic thinking. He himself traces the roots of each of his concepts to the history of Islamic philosophy, and when he finds the affirmation and support of his concepts in Western science and philosophy, he cites them as additional support. In his creative thinking he first presents his own theories about the truth, life and the universe and then tries to obtain further explanation and proof from western learning and researches of western philosophers.

Motion or dynamism is the principle which molded Iqbal's thought. He writes about dynamic thinking: "In its essential nature, then, thought is not static; it is dynamic and unfolds its internal infinitude in time like the seed which, from the very beginning, carries within itself the organic unity of the tree as a present fact. Thought is, therefore, the whole of its dynamic self-expression, appearing to the temporal vision as a series of definite specifications which cannot be understood except by a reciprocal reference."[3]

In the multi-dimensional sphere of Iqbal's thought the Holy Qur'an occupies the central position, like the nucleus of the atom or that of a biological cell. Like the former the Holy Qur'an emanates the light of the Truth, and like the latter it controls all the details, which together, constitute Iqbal's thought. The raison d'etre of Iqbal's poetry is the elucidation and elaboration of the wisdom of the Holy Qur'an and of being 'a vehicle of its secrets', as well as to be the instrument of the renaissance of the Muslim *Ummah* and its consolidation into a united entity, as required by the Holy Qur'an, is clear from a study of his works as well as from his own admission. He says:

Do not consider my seemingly disjointed song as poetry

As I am aware of the inner secrets of the tavern

I have opened the secrets of *qalandari*

Iqbal refers to (*qalandar* who is a *dervish*, not following all the injunctions of the religious and social law and is often taken for the highest mystical symbol) so that the thinking of the school and the monastery may be freed. Freedom of thinking to Iqbal does not have the conventional meaning. It means freedom of Islamic thought from the fetters of un-Islamic alien philosophies like Greek philosophy.

'There is a vast difference between poetry and me,

Poetry is only an excuse; I am pulling the unbridled she Camel into the line'.

This truth is contained in Iqbal's "Reconstruction of Religious Thought in Islam" like a seed and blossoms out in his poetical works. Iqbal molded poetry so as to make it the vehicle for Divine message, for revealing Divine secrets to mankind, for expressing his internal inspired feelings in a language which would awaken the sleeping *Ummah* from their deep torpor and create in them high thinking and freedom of thought. So equipped, they could visualize the coming age of the *Tawhâd-i-Insaniyat* under pan-Islamism and thus fulfill the Divine trust and accomplish the original mission of the creation of Man which was to be the vicegerent of God on earth (Holy Qur'an 2:30). He was fully conscious of his mission.

Dr. Annemarie Schimmel has unveiled this attitude of Iqbal in her famous book "Gabriel's Wing".

"Iqbal continued to establish connection between Islamic traditions and new Western research by comparative studies. His stand was that Muslims should learn Western knowledge and wisdom for, as the West has been indebted to Islamic civilization for learning and wisdom, Muslim would not lose anything by learning Western science and technology".[4]

Dr. Ishtiaque Hussain Quraishi explains after detailed analysis in his paper "The Psychological Sources of the Philosophy of Iqbal"[5] that the centuries old static life of the Muslim *Ummah,* their declining preparedness, the destruction of the *Khalifah,* the fall of Samarqand, Bukhara and Spain, the

Hindu stratagem of absorbing the Muslims in, and the conditions militating against their organization as a political power, in the Indian Sub-continent were movers for disturbing Iqbal and creating a storm within him. He criticized all those theories which were against the concept of dynamism in life and the universe. Iqbal's concept of life and the universe was that of having 'a soul in motion'. Motion or dynamism is the basic component of his philosophy.

The greatest opponent of Iqbal's dynamic philosophy of life and the universe was the belief of *Wahdat-ul-Wujud*. This belief in *Wahdat-ul-Wujud* whose rationale was based on Plato's theory of the universe, developed later in his system as a static monastic way as part of mysticism, diverted Muslims from the Islamic thinking of conquest and consolidation of the world towards the shame-ridden attitude of divorcing all worldly relations. As a result of this the Islamic world developed the monastic attitudes of inaction, pacifism and other worldliness, and the whole Islamic world was engulfed in a paralytic mystic state. Becoming estranged from the understanding of the universe, and from performing an active role in the reconstruction, shaping, conquest and organization of the world, it became progressively caught into slavery.

The Arab writer Najla Izzuddin[6] analyzed this state of affairs as follows: "The decline of the internal creative power and expeditionary zeal of the Arab civilization was more devastating than the misfortunes and catastrophes that befell if from outside. The ardent desire for intellectual inquiry and the pride of performance which were characteristic of the early times were throttled by the strong pressure of religious dogmas and centralization. Freedom of thought was banished and conservatism reigned supreme. Unbridled search for Truth was branded as atheism and irreligious. The fearless and bold people of the earlier times were relegated to obscurity. The brain trust engaged itself in preparing the explanations and abstracts of well-known subjects instead of using their intellect in discovering new avenues of knowledge. "Freedom of thinking" to Iqbal does not have the conventional meaning. It means freedom of Islamic thought from the fetters of un-Islamic alien philosophies like Greek philosophy.

This state of affairs perturbed Iqbal. He revolted and rejected every theory which was against his dynamic concepts The basic concept of Iqbal's thought is the concept of a living and dynamic God, who is not identical with the universe, but who is Unique, Unparallel, Unequal in His own Being and essence. The universe and life are expositions of His Creativeness which are vibrant with life.

Dr. Ishrat Hassan Enver in his book "The Metaphysics of Iqbal" has explained that to Iqbal[7] God's Zat Essence is dynamic and extremely creative. His words are "Consequently, the nature of God as revealed by intuition is, firstly, dynamic and highly active in its essence. "Reality is one infinite life. It is a self-directing, self-conscious energy, continuously active. Every act of it is itself life which in turn is a self-directing energy. Looked at from outside these acts are spatial things and events. Some of the acts in the course of development have become self-conscious. These are 'I' and 'you'[8]

Khudi, which can also be called "Gnosis of self" or "Gnosis of Zat" is found in Socrates' philosophy as "Know Thyself" and which also appears in the famous saying, "He who knows his Self knows his God." Iqbal himself writes in his Fourth Lecture: "What then is matter? A colony of egos of low order out of which emerges the ego of a higher order, when their association and interaction reach a certain degree of co-ordination... The emergent, as the advocates of the Emergent Evolution teach us, is an unforeseeable and novel fact on its own plane of being, and cannot be explained mechanistically... We have seen that the ego is not something rigid. It organizes itself in time, and is formed and disciplined by its own experience."[9]

In his Reconstruction of Religious Thought in Islam, Iqbal tries to remove what is old and anti-Qur'anic in the traditions. However, he sticks to the genuine spirit of the Qur'an which he attempts to revive. His struggle is above all against the conceptions which have made religion "a body of doctrines" rather than a vital fact. He wants and he explicitly admits not to return to the past but "to re-construct" in the modern spirit.

The religious philosophy of Iqbal is based on his particular emphasis on the idea of 'Self'. Prof. Mc Taggart, the great Hegelian and his teacher in Cambridge, wrote to him a letter in 1920 after reading the English translation of his *Asrar-i-Khudi* (Secrets of Self). An interesting passage from the letter is as follows:

"Have you not much changed your position? Certainly, at the time in which we discussed together the problems of philosophy you were more of a pantheist and a mystic and this attitude you don't show at present." In fact, his emphasis on 'Self' is a reaction, adopted from a most noble "practical motive". It is love for his decadent co-religionists oppressed by the foreigner. It is a reaction against the ascetic other-worldly and fatalistic mysticism in which the people of the Orient and particularly the Muslims have fallen.

Particularly the Muslims because — and it is the discovery of Iqbal as a result of his reading of the *Qur'an* — the early spirit of Islam is altogether different from asceticism and other-worldliness. "The *Qur'an*", — is the first sentence of his Lectures on the "Reconstruction of Religious Thought in Islam—"is a book that puts emphasis on deed rather than on idea."

As an eminent and multi-dimensional philosopher, Iqbal's thought was 'creative' as well as 'harmonizing'. It was creative in the sense that he showed a new direction to his period by his philosophy of *"Khudi",* and theory of 'dynamism'. It was harmonizing in the sense that, looking critically into the thoughts of the Eastern and Western philosophers in the light of his creative theory he established harmony between them and gave his own opinions.

Iqbal was not among the philosophers who get engulfed in abstract concepts and theories and engage themselves only in the super fineness of linguistic and logical excellence. He was a revolutionary philosopher, and in accordance with the saying of Marx that the much greater function of philosophy is to alter the normal conditions existing around it rather than subjective analysis of the universe. Iqbal also, with his original thinking, established a system of thought which aimed at revolutionizing the conditions existing in his time. The main aspect of his entire system of thought was practical, dynamic and revolutionary. He discarded every thought, concept and theory which preached inaction, and which a great obstacle to Iqbal in the task was also of changing and activating the existing conditions of Muslims.

Constructive Revivalism of Iqbal

Iqbal demonstrated in his thought an evolutionary process. Iqbal stood as a revivalist and struggled hard throughout his life since 1905 until his death for the revival of Islam and Islamic civilization. He wrote:

Now, along with the renaissance of Muslim community, the renaissance of Islam also is needed. I pray to God Almighty that He, for the sake of his beloved, the Prophet, peace be upon him, produces such an interpreter among Muslims who gets at the 'lost wisdom' once more and offers it to *ummah*. Our demise is not near at hand. The Qur'an still holds on.[10]

The revival of Islam and its civilization to Iqbal was absolutely necessary for peace, security and prosperity for the entire mankind in this modern age. No one, therefore, he contended, should misunderstand in any way that the revival of

Islam is either a backward step or against the interest of humanity; rather, it is for the survival of humanity as humanity.

The Islamic revivalist trend in Iqbal's thought can be easily gleaned through an exploration of his views on spirituality, ethical values of Islam, and his critical insights into the ideologies of democracy and nationalism, his views on the institution of *Khilafah* and the need for *Ijtihad* and the necessity of Islamic political system. An exploration into all these areas and his political thought unfold understandings about Iqbal and reveal the fact that to Iqbal, the modern west and western thought have lost the credibility to claim the leadership of mankind for they failed to guide mankind to achieve peace, security and prosperity. Therefore, Iqbal said that to fill up this gap of leadership, Muslims should come forward. For this purpose, at the very outset, they must realize that they first need to understand clearly the weaknesses of Western thought on one hand and on the other the spiritual and moral force of the teachings of Islam.

Iqbal endeavored for the revival of Islamic civilization and argued that unless mankind submits itself to the teachings of God, and accepts Islam as the way of life, it cannot achieve the noble goals of peace, security and prosperity.

This philosophy of Muhammad Iqbal summoned the sleeping Muslims to awake. The bourgeoisie heard his penetrating voice and responded eagerly. Iqbal devoted himself to inciting activity, to insist eloquently that life is a movement in which action is good and that the universe is composed of processes and not of static things. He bitterly attacked the attitudes of resignation and quiet contentment the religious valuation of mere contemplation, passivity, and withdrawal from strife. The mystic *(sufi)* and idealist world-denying tendencies in Islam were rejected by him only as dimmable Iranian and Hellenistic importations in to an originally vigorous Arabian religion. His Islam repudiated the conception of a fixed universe dominated by a dictator God and to be accepted by servile men. In its place he put a view of an unfinished growing universe, ever being advanced by man and by God through man. Iqbal's prime function was to lash men in to furious activity and to "imbue the idle looker on with restless impatience."[11]

Life is not to be contemplated, but to be passionately lived.

And cast its atoms into a new mould ...

By his own strength he will produce

A new world which will do his pleasure.[12]

This call to impatient initiative is the chief revolution wrought by Iqbal in Islamic thought and consequently to the Muslims. He believed that this revolution in ideas is necessary, if Islam is to survive. Modern thinking must be dynamic, modern ethics must be positive and creative. Iqbal castigated as sinful the static pessimist ethics of resignation which had 'misled' the Muslims. For him this resignation is not only inherently bad, but also outmoded. It was appropriate to a pre-scientific society. It is bad to-day because it is anachronistic, outdated because modern technology has advanced life to a new level. He explained this by giving an example that in feudal days if an only son died of cholera the father could do nothing but to resign himself and accept the situation with dignity. There was no value in his ranting and raging, in cursing his Fate and in making both himself and his fellow villagers miserable. It was in any possible sense best that he should say "*Allah* be praised" and contemplates with courage and serenity the inscrutable working of God---i.e., of the universe. A religion which enabled him to do so was good.

Referring to the advancement in science he said that the situation is now radically changed. Iqbal believed that if a man bestir himself and have foresight, he can prevent his son's death from cholera by inoculation and hygiene. If a man co-operates with his fellow-countrymen, he can build up a new creative planned society based on science and large-scale industry and thereby he can banish disease and much other evil from new exuberant human life. Quiet resignation, therefore, which once was good, is now bad. Iqbal rendered a great service by his reiterated call to action in the name of Islam, his raising of action to be a virtue in itself, his bold insistence that a dynamic infidel is more righteous than a passive Muslim:

An infidel before his idol with wakeful heart

Is better than the religious man asleep in the mosque.[13]

He condemned the formalism of the pious, and despised those who are observance of a code above creative love and energy:

I have ascertained none of the ins and outs of the Law But this: that who denies love and passion is infidel and atheist.[14]

Iqbal rejected orthodox cleric's belief that those who deny God are infidels, for Iqbal believed that those who deny their selves or the joy of life are much worse than infidels. His activist reinterpretation of religion is well brought out in his treatment of the Adam myth, in his poem "The subjugation of nature" *(Taskhir i Fitrat)*[15]. According to this presentation, the "fall" of man was in reality "the first rung in the ladder of man's glory".[16] Iqbal differs from the accepted Islamic moral attitude. In his view, the goal of humanity is not submission but supremacy and the chief end of man is to be the Vicegerent of God on Earth. Thus, Iqbal wrought the most important and the most necessary revolution of modern times. He made God immanent, not transcendent. Iqbal's God is in the world, with us, facing our problems from within, creating a new and better world with us and through us. Religion is life, and life, this mundane material life, is religious. The present world, of matter, time, and space, is good. "All is holy ground."[17]

Iqbal endorsed this radial reversal of ascetic dualism with tradition: "As the prophet so beautifully puts it: 'The whole of this earth is a mosque'." The traditional remoteness of God is an error:

> We have strayed away from God; He is in quest of us;
>
> Like us He is humble and is a prisoner of desire...
>
> He is hidden in every atom, and yet is a stranger to us;
>
> He is revealed in the moonlight....[18]

God himself, and all the values, rewards ideals, and objectives of religion transferred to the empirical universe. Correspondingly, the will of God is not something imposed from without to be accepted resignedly, but surges within, is to be absorbed and acted upon:

> In his (i.e., the true Muslim's) will that which God wills become lost.[19]

Thus, Iqbal attempted to provide a systematic Islamic basis to the political ideas of the Indian Muslims in modern India. The major strand of his philosophy was Islam as practiced by the Prophet and the first four Caliphs. "I am afraid," he once reflected, "I have no philosophy to teach. As a matter of fact, I do not hate systems of philosophy nor do I trust principles or conclusions of philosophy. No man has condemned human intellect more than I, i.e., as applied to ultimate realities of religion. No doubts I talk of things which are matters of living experience and not philosophical reasoning."[20]

Iqbal considered Islam to be a perfect system. It can fulfill all the spiritual and material needs of modern man. It is an "ever vitalizing idea." It is neither rigid nor static but a dynamic system. Islam was from the very beginning "a civil society. Politics has its roots in the spiritual life of man.... Islam is not a matter of private opinion. It is a society or as you like, a civic church."[21] Though Islam is a superb form of spiritual idealism Iqbal believed that present day Islam needs emancipation from medieval fancies of theological and legists. "Spiritually we are living in a prison house of thoughts and emotions which during the course of centuries we have woven round ourselves."[22] Islam is law given by the Prophet, which "is realizable as arising from the very core of human conscience."[23] Iqbal believed that Islam is perfect and eternal as a guide for social and political life.

He was aware of the fact that the medieval spirit of Islam had rendered it useless to the modern man. He believed that this was not due to any inherent weakness of Islam; but to the fact that the people did not understand its true spirit. Iqbal threw all blame on the orthodox, narrow-minded and self-seeking *sufis*. To Iqbal medieval mysticism robs its followers of their healthy instincts and gives them only obscure thoughts in return. During the course of centuries, it has absorbed the best minds leaving the affairs of the state to mediocrities.[24] It "enervated the people and kept them steeped in all kinds of superstition."[25]

He believed that if true Islam is revived all the ills of the world would be cured. What is needed is a careful study of Islam which will give "a kind of insight onto its significance as a world-fact.[26] It has the potency of becoming a "living force."[27] The ideal society and the state which Iqbal visualized were based upon his view of Islam and will be established by the Muslims- chosen people of God, the deputies of God on earth. A Muslim is "the embodiment of God to the world." He is a perfectly sociable individual and possesses the qualities of "justice and benevolence." The Muslim is not a titan but a common man who possesses the traits of obedience to law and self-control and these make him capable of "Divine Viceregency."[28] Iqbal strongly believed that only by "self-affirmation, self-expression, and self-development can the Muslims once more become strong and free."[29] These three, according to Iqbal, are the stages towards achievement of uniqueness by the ego. This philosophy of 'egoism' or 'self' of Iqbal is also significant from the point of view of political ideas.

Political Ideas of Iqbal

Iqbal as an idealist-realist philosopher-thinker, penetrated deep into the conditions of his time, realized that the cherished goals of humanity—peace, security, prosperity, equality, justice, liberty, rule of law, harmony, and peaceful co-existence, once elaborated and practiced by Islam, were being destroyed by the communities of the modern world of both the East and the West. Instead of peace and harmony, one observes chaos and conflict.

On the eve of 1938, in his message broadcasted from the Lahore Station of the All-India Radio, Iqbal expressed his disenchantment with the modern dominant political tradition largely because of its irrational and illogical insistence on the denial of spirituality, acceptance of materialism, its ties to capitalist economics, and its lack of a meaningful conception of the so-called democratic community. He echoed, in fact, the view of Bertrand Russell and said that scientific civilization is, no doubt, a good civilization but it is by itself not sufficient; increase in knowledge and skills should be accompanied by an increase in wisdom. For Russell and Iqbal, wisdom means the right conception of the ends of life. Both believed that this is something which science in itself does not provide. They, therefore, concluded that the progress of science by itself is not enough to guarantee any genuine progress.[30] For Iqbal the conditions of his time manifested empirical evidence for this truth identified by Russell. He, therefore, made the following statement in the court of humanity:

The modern age prides itself on its progress in knowledge and its matchless scientific developments. No doubt, the pride is justified. Today space and time are being annihilated and man is achieving amazing successes in unveiling the secrets of nature and harnessing its forces to his own service. But in spite of all these developments, the tyranny of imperialism struts abroad, covering its face under the masks of Democracy, Nationalism, Communism, Fascism and heaven knows what else besides. Under these masks, in every corner of the earth, the spirit of freedom and the dignity of man are being trampled underfoot in a way to which not even the darkest period of human history presents a parallel. The so-called statesmen to whom government and leadership of men was entrusted have proved demons of bloodshed, tyranny and oppression. The rulers whose duty it was to protect and cherish those ideals which go to form a higher humanity, to prevent man's oppression of man and to elevate the moral and intellectual level of mankind, have in their hunger for dominion and imperial possessions, shed the blood of millions and reduced millions to servitude simply in order to pander to the greed and avarice of their own particular groups. After subjugating and establishing their dominion over weaker peoples, they have robbed them of their possessions, of their religions, their morals, of their cultural traditions and their literatures. Then they sowed divisions among them that they should shed one another's blood and go to sleep under the opiate of serfdom, so that the leech of imperialism might go on sucking their blood without interruption.[31]

Iqbal further continued saying:

As I look back on the year that has passed and as I look at the world in the midst of the New Year's rejoicings...the same misery prevails in every corner of man's earthly home, and hundreds of thousands of men are being butchered mercilessly. Engines of destruction created by science are wiping out the great landmarks of Man's cultural achievements. The governments which are not themselves engaged in this drama of fire and blood are sucking the blood of the weaker people economically.[32]

Iqbal raised a pertinent question:

Do you not see that the people of Spain, though they have the same common bond of one race, one nationality, one language and one religion, are cutting one another's throats and destroying their culture and civilization by their own hands owing to a difference in their economic creed?[33]

This single event Iqbal believed demonstrates clearly that 'national unity' is not a 'very durable force.' He asserted that only one unity is dependable, the unity of brotherhood of man, which stands above race, nationality, color or language.[34]

Hence, he argued that: as long as this so-called democracy, this accursed nationalism and this degraded imperialism are not shattered, so long as men do not demonstrate by their actions that they believe that the whole world is the family of God, so long as distinctions of race, color and geographical nationalities are not wiped out completely, they will never be able to lead a happy and contended life and the beautiful ideals of liberty, equality and fraternity will never materialize.[35]

Iqbal believed that the phenomena described above are only "premonitions of a coming storm, which is likely to sweep over the whole world." According to him it is the natural result of a "wholly political civilization" which has always perceived man as a "thing to be exploited and not as a personality to be developed and enlarged by purely cultural forces." He further asserted that the people of Asia, particularly, are bound to rise against the acquisitive economy which the West has developed and imposed on the nations of the East. The people of Asia, according to Iqbal, cannot comply with modern Western capitalism with its undisciplined individualism anymore.[36] He felt, therefore, that only faith which he himself represented recognizes the worth of the individual, and disciplines him to give away his all to the service of God and man. He maintained that its possibilities are not yet exhausted. It is a historic fact that in the beginning, faith played a revolutionary role in human societies by challenging, altering, and often smashing the old but irrational values, customs, habits, and opinions of the peoples. He believed that faith can still create a new world where the social rank of man is not determined by his caste or color, or the amount of dividend he earns, but by the kind of life he lives, where the poor tax the rich, where human society is founded not on the equality of stomachs but on the equality of spirits, where an Untouchable can marry the daughter of a king, where private ownership is a trust and where capita cannot be allowed to accumulate so as to dominate the real producer of wealth.[37]

Iqbal rejected the harshly critical argument of Marx who thought that faith was "the heart of the heartless world" and reasoned that by submitting to God, people were placing their creative power outside themselves, a tendency according to Marx that would only prolong their willingness to be dominated by each other and by capital. Iqbal held totally a different view. For him the essence of religion is faith, and faith which has a cognitive content is the source of creative energy.[38]

For humanity to be genuinely liberated, he maintained, there is no other way except to surrender itself to the faith, for faith in true God would induce in humanity the spirit of free man who is able to see himself as the sole, creative, and responsible power over world's affairs. He, therefore, reminded his people and told them that they should come forward to save humanity from the destruction of capitalism and liberalism. But they should not forget that at this stage of history what they needed first was to realize that the superb idealism of their own faith, however, needed emancipation from the medieval fancies of theologians and legists. Iqbal asserted that at the moment his people, spiritually, were still living in a prison house of thoughts and emotions, which during the course of centuries they had woven around themselves. And let it be further said to the shame of us—men of older generation—that we have failed to equip the younger generation for economic, political and even religious crisis that the present age is likely to bring. In this background, he argued that the whole community needed a complete overhauling of its present mentality in order that it might again become capable of feeling the urge of fresh desires and ideals. They have not recognized the inner force of their faith and they have long ceased to explore the depths of their own inner life. The result is that they have ceased to live in the full glow and color of life, and are consequently in danger of an unmanly compromise with forces which, they are made to think, they cannot vanquish in open conflict.[39]

Keeping these limitations of Muslims into consideration, Iqbal urged them to struggle to bring a constructive change in the society. He said: "He who desires to change an unfavorable environment must undergo a complete transformation of his inner being. God will not change the condition of a people until they themselves take the initiative to change their condition by constantly illuminating the zone of their daily activity in the light of a definite ideal. Nothing can be achieved without a firm faith in the independence of one's own inner life. This faith alone keeps a people's eye fixed on their goal and saves them from perpetual vacillation. The lesson that past experience has brought to you must be taken to heart. Expect nothing from any side. Concentrate your whole ego on yourself alone, and ripen your clay into real manhood if you wish to see your aspirations realized. Remember! The flame of life cannot be borrowed from others; it must be kindled in the temple of one's own soul."[40]

He, therefore, told Muslims that no obstacle should stop them from marching forward to save humanity from self-destruction. He said "I am quite sensible of the difficulties that lie in our way; all that I can say is that if we cannot get over our difficulties, the world will soon get rid of us."[41]

Iqbal wanted to liberate his people from intellectual slavery of the so-called modern scientific thought and ideologies and to create confidence among them on their own Islamic perspective to life and society by way of scrutinizing their own heritage and sources. He suggested a fundamental principle that so far as human thought is concerned it should be studied critically, and with regard to the understanding of the Divine sources, he was of the opinion that the Qur'an is the authentic Divine source. It should be understood based on the principles in the Qur'an, which have been identified by commentators of the Holy Book. Here, he was open for any alterations and modifications of knowledge. So far as the collection of Traditions is concerned, he was of the opinion that it should be approached critically. Iqbal further argued that for the understanding of the Divine sources or the Reality, we need to depend upon all possible ways and means. In this way he refuted the claims of rationality and empiricism as the only sources of knowledge respectively. His method was a combination of all those means which are useful for the understanding of Reality. He also did not discard personal inner experiences of individuals as a means of knowledge. He contended that all possible means of knowledge are in need of each other for they seek visions of the same Reality. Our reasons, senses, perceptions, intuitions, inspirations and mystic experiences all play a role according to their functions in our life.[42] Based on this Iqbal, therefore, decided to show them the sound spiritual and logical basis of Islamic thought by way of elaborating the logical weaknesses of the modern political thought and eradicating the dogmatic and fatalistic attitude of his own people. He argued that his convictions were the result of a comparative study of world religions and ideologies on one hand and the critical study of legacy of Islam on the other. He argued that a search for such spiritual principles which could be the basis of social organization must be based on a comparative and critical study of all currents of thoughts, philosophical and religious.

Iqbal displayed profound distrust of the west and of western civilization. To him, the west is the symbol of the values of materialism. It is the negation of all the high values of spiritualism or religiosity. The west stands for reason and discards love which constitutes the basis of the eastern civilization. This conflict of east and west, reason and love form a cardinal element of Iqbal's political thought. This led him to discuss the need for the creation of an ideal society. Iqbal was well aware of the achievement of the west and its shortcomings. All these defects are found in the structure and working of the system of society. The capitalist society is the typical product of this material civilization. To Iqbal society should exist for making the life of its members happy and good. There should be complete concord and harmony between the individual and collective interests. Every member should find enough opportunities for the development of his 'ego' and personality. The capitalist society, Iqbal believed, cannot secure the good of the people. Its basis is the profit of the few. Everything is made subordinate to the interests of the ruling life. Science, philosophy, democracy, constitution and the fundamental rights of equality and liberty are subservient to the exploiting class. The 'Triumphs' of this society are 'want' and unemployment. It lacks 'visionary light'. It is determined by steam and electricity. The machines crush all humanity. The hours of laboring class are grueling and it is condemned to eternal slavery. Man in this society has lost his individuality. In spite of all his so – called progress and learning 'he has lost count of good and ill'. Iqbal pointed out that "in the domain of thought he is living in open conflict with himself; and in the domain of economic and political life he is living in conflict with others. He finds himself unable to control his root less egoism hand his infinite gold-hunger which is gradually killing all higher striving in him and bringing him nothing but life weariness." The modern man finds himself helpless. He has lost control over his own creations. He is no more the master but has become the slave of the system.

Iqbal believed that this capitalist system was responsible for the emergence of the nation-state. Nationalism, he said, provides to such states, a psychological and political justification for existence. This Nationalism is based on the consideration of territory. It is not, however, merely an attachment to one's own country. Patriotism, according to Iqbal, is different from nationalism, patriotism is "a perfectly natural virtue and has a place in the moral life of man."[43]

Education

Iqbal was greatly disturbed by the complete overshadowing of Muslim history and culture, in the sphere of education, by its western counterparts. He perceived a threat both political and cultural not only from the west, but also from the majority community in India.

Iqbal's views on education were guided by the principle that "a living nation is living because it never forgets its dead." He felt that "a truly national education" should breed intimacy with one's "social and historical tradition", since only this could create that "healthy pride" which was "the very lifeblood of a truly national character." He therefore believed that every Muslim student should be familiar with the glories of Muslim civilization and history, the achievements of its leading figures and the extent of its influence over modern western civilization. He felt that the present western-oriented system of education in India on the other hand, by breaking away Muslims completely from their past, did not in the least do justice to their needs. He wrote in 1909 that if they did not develop their own educational institutions which would keep alive their social and historical traditions, their very survival would be threatened.[44]

Iqbal was not satisfied with Muslim educational efforts of the last fifty years, which he felt had been totally oblivious to long-term needs, concentrating only on immediate gains. He felt that the fears of the traditionalist followers of Islamic culture, who had disputed with Sir Sayyid about western education, had been proved true-that a shift in education would change hearts. He was convinced that no nation could abruptly break the link with its past and for Muslims, whose collective traditions were the lifeblood of their nationhood, it was all the more impossible to do so.

To Iqbal the modern Muslim appeared to be an intellectual slave of the west and devoid of that healthy self-respect which is born of a study of one's national history and literature. He felt that the present system of education was creating a new group of quasi-Muslims who, in being intoxicated by western literature and bereft of their national traditions, had moved far away from the Islamic center of gravity. He feared that due to the lack of a unifying center this group would someday lose its identity and he merged into some other, more vital community. In 1938, he reiterated that imperial powers not only subjugated weaker peoples but also robbed them of their religion, literature and cultural traditions.[45]

Faced with such a situation, Iqbal realized and reaffirmed the primacy of religious education in 1910. Significantly enough, he felt that those who had followed the principle that the education of every Muslim child should commence with lessons in the Qur'an, were wiser than modern Muslims. Having established that the solidarity of Muslims as a community lay in their grasp on the religious principle, he felt that the best way to tighten this hold and thus ensure the continuity of national life was to provide "sound religious education" to the Muslim woman-the "principal depositary of religion", and the virtual "maker of the community."[46]

Iqbal insisted that Islamic culture was an independent entity. While Muslims must keep abreast with the swift pace of modern sciences, their culture should be purely Islamic and for this they needed a national university run on thoroughly Islamic principles. Iqbal felt that Muslim preachers and scholars had a limited knowledge of Islamic history and sciences and emphasized that besides economics and sociology they should also have command over Muslim educational institutions could not satisfy these needs, a new exemplary university should be set up, whose overriding principle should be Islamic culture and in which the old and the new should be perfectly blended, even while he realized that this was not an easy task.[47] Iqbal was essentially a man of thought and developed his history of education more as a philosophical ideal. His pre-occupation with education was limited to the early period, politics becoming the field of his thought and action and the means of safeguarding the Muslims community in his later life.

Concept of Nationalism

Iqbal's political philosophy is deeply embedded in his broad and comprehensive Islamic conception of *tawhid*, the unity of God, the unity of life, the unity of the *ummah*, and the unity of humanity. His rejectionist approach toward secularism, materialism, western democracy, and nationalism is based upon his concept of *tawhid*. His philosophy of self-hood *(khudi)* and its related concepts like "man of belief" *(mard-i-momin)* "perfect man" *(mard-i-kamil)*, and his conception of the Islamic social order and divine vicegerency are not only related to each other, but also are steeped in his dynamic conception of *tawhid*. Hence, all of his concepts and ideas, which bear the message and mission of *tawhid*, are contrary to the ideology of nationalism, which is rooted in secularism and materialism. In his writings on Islam's social order, Iqbal states: "(Islam) "finds (that) the foundation of world-unity in the principle of *tawhid* and Islam, as a polity, is only a practical means of making this principle a living factor in the intellectual and emotional life of mankind."[48]

Two important points can be deduced from this statement: Islam is a practical means to make the principle of unity a reality in humanity's intellectual and emotional life, and *tawhid* supplies the foundational principle for world unity.

The first point forms the basis of his concept of *tawhid* and strikes the secular origin of nationalism. By portraying Islam as a practical means for making the principle of *tawhid* a living factor, Iqbal implies that Islam unites and integrates all aspects of life (e.g., intellectual, emotional, social, political, and others) into a unified whole. In other words, Islam totally disagrees with the artificial division or compartmentalization of life into "religious life" and "worldly life." This unified and holistic perception of life is "religious" domains. At several places, Iqbal elaborates upon Islam's unified approach to life. He writes:

That according to the law of Islam there is no distinction between the Church and the state. The state with us is not a combination of religious and secular authority, but it is a unit in which no such distinction exists.[49]

Iqbal's upholding of the unity of life and the unity of the spirit and matter can be seen in many of his statements. For example, he states: "All that is secular is therefore sacred in the roots of its being"[50] and "All this immensity of matter constitutes a scope for the self-realization of spirit."[51]

In other words, unlike Hegel, Iqbal did not have to make a synthesis of "reason" and "spirit" in order to form a state. For him, the state by itself is spiritual because all that is secular is spiritual in Islam. He writes: "The state according to Islam is only an effort to realize the spiritual in a human organization."[52]

The following is Shamloo's comment on Iqbal:

Now Islam is not a cult. It is a whole philosophy of life and political philosophy is an essential and indispensable part of it. He (Iqbal) could not, therefore, avoid being a political thinker as well. Indeed, it is his special merit which distinguishes him from most other Muslim thinkers in history, that he took a comprehensive and sympathetic view of Islam and treated it as a completely integrated unity.[53]

Iqbal also expressed his Islamic concept of the unity of life through his philosophy of *faqr*. As explicated by Muhammad Manawwar, Iqbal defined *faqr* as "a state of spiritual elevation and loftiness."[54]

He further points out that *faqr*, in Iqbal's poetry, "creates in man dignity of detachment, a godly state of being free of wants."[55]

Iqbal writes:

Of those men of God, the Arab cavaliers of note!

The bearers of excellent conduct,

Truthful, men of strong conviction.

Their manner of rule made clear the wonderful mystery.

That the government by the lovers (of God) is through

Faqr and not through kingship.[56]

Elsewhere, Iqbal said:

What is caliphate?

Faqr accompanied by crown and throne.[57]

The foregoing clearly shows that not only are matter and spirit fused in the caliphate but also in the lovers of God, who run the government and rule through *faqr*, a state of being free from material enslavement. However, it is important to note that Iqbal is not one of those thinkers who advises Muslims to abandon matter altogether in order to lead them to a narrow and spiritual:

Forgiveness, dominance, holiness and forcefulness –

These four make a Muslim of a human being ...

His intentions are the measure of destiny.

He is like a balance, both in this life and in the hereafter.[58]

In reality, the underlying purpose behind the unity of matter and spirit, as well as the unity of the "religious" and "worldly" realms, is nothing but the success in this world and the Hereafter. Thus, Iqbal asserts that Islam, unlike secularism and nationalism, provides a balance in life by joining matter and spirit into a harmonious entity for a great success here and in the Hereafter. The sheet anchor of *tawhid* is one's ultimate loyalty to God. Since Islam makes no division between state and mosque, it demands ultimate loyalty to God and implies that His laws prevail in all spheres of life, including the political, which further implies the *Shari'ah's* supremacy. Iqbal writes:

It (Islam) demands loyalty to God, not to thrones. And since God is the ultimate spiritual basis of all life, loyalty to God virtually amounts to man's loyalty to his own ideal nature.[59]. Contrary to this loyalty, nationalism demands supreme loyalty to the Nation state. Since nationalism is basically secular, behind its division of life into "religious" and "worldly" realms lies the division of loyalty: one to the state and another to God. Moreover, in the case of a clash between loyalty to God and loyalty to the state, nationalism says that loyalty to the state must prevail. The rationale for such a view is that nationalism, being a political concept, demands political loyalty to the state and would like to see the state's laws prevail over all other laws.

Iqbal therefore writes:

In the present-day political literature, however, the idea of nation is not merely geopolitical: it is rather a principle of human society and, as such, it is a political concept. Since Islam also is a law of human society, the word "country," when used as a political concept, comes into conflict with Islam.[60] This clearly shows that political principles and the laws of a nation state would clash with Islamic principles and laws, because Islam would like to see its own principles and laws work and prevail in all of a society's institutions, including political institutions. Iqbal further elaborated this point by saying:

In its principles of human association, Islam admits of no Modus Vivendi and is not prepared to compromise with any other law regulating human society. Indeed, it declares that every code of law other than that of Islam is inadequate and unacceptable.[61] Iqbal was fully aware of the fact that the nation-state that would emerge from the secular ideology of nationalism would clash with Islamic law and would become an "idol" to be obeyed fully and worshipped by the people.

Tracing the origin of nationalism to Machiavelli's views, Iqbal referred to him as: "That Florentine worshipper of Untruth." Iqbal points out that Machiavelli blinded the eyes of the people and wrote a new code of guidance for rulers, thereby sowing the seeds of war and conflict:

His mind fashioned new patterns (of principle)!

His religion made the state into a deity.

And presented what was evil as God!

He kissed the feet of this deity.

And tested truth on the criterion of profit! [62]

Iqbal forcefully explained these divisive and mischief making characteristics of nationalism in the context of the Indian subcontinent and in general terms. He pointed out that if nationalism was accepted in the sub-continent, Muslims would have two wrong ways before them: "The Muslims as a nation can be other than what they are as a *'millat'*[63] and "Muslims would have to forget Islam as a complete system of life." [64]

Iqbal pointed out how the leaders of the Hindu majority community persuade Muslims to believe that religion is a private affair. According to those leaders, Muslims "should not regard themselves as a separate nation: they should rather lose themselves in the majority." [65]

Iqbal asserted that accepting such a viewpoint would reduce Islam to a private affair, and that this would have dangerous implications for the subcontinent's Muslim community.[66]

Thus, according to Iqbal, Nationalism, is a political concept and is not in consonance with the true spirit of Islam. The *Qur'an (Sura 49: 10)* also instructs that all the believers are brethren. If nationalism is accepted as an Ideal, Islam will cease to be a living factor. Nationalism "comes into conflict with Islam only when it begins to play the role of the political concept, and claims to be a principle of human solidarity demanding that Islam should recede to the background of a more private opinion and cease to be a living factor in the national life."[67]

Muslim Nationhood

Iqbal's fully worked out, complex and rich philosophy of the concept of Muslim nationhood is outlined in his various articles, speeches and notes between 1909 and 1911. In an article published in 1909 he wrote that the basis of nationhood for Muslims was Islam itself, which besides being a religion, was also "a community a nation", whose membership was not based on birth or naturalization, but on identity of belief. He even said that since Islam was above time and space, phrases such as "Indian Muhamadan" although convenient, were actually a contradiction in terms. Nationality for Muslims was a pure idea, without any geographical basis-its material center if any, was the holy town of *Makkah*. The basis of Muslim nationality thus combined the real and the ideal, the concrete and the abstract.[68]

Iqbal in the early years of his life stood for composite Indian nationalism. His Urdu poetry before 1906 and specifically poems such as 'The New Temple' and 'The Indian Anthem' bear ample testimony to this fact. His visit to Europe was a turning point and his thoughts altered from composite Indian Nationalism to Muslim Nationalism.

It was during his stay that he was able to closely observe the political developments in Europe. He made a deep observation to explore the basis of their political models. In this exercise he highlighted the inherent flaws which were responsible for creating tensions between countries. It was nationalism based on love for land i.e. territorial nationalism. It was prime factor to provoke selfishness among the countries to protect their national interests. Iqbal concluded that territorial nationalism was of gross misuse. According to Iqbal it was, for instance, a weapon of European Imperialism which destroyed the unity of Muslim world: [69] After his return to Europe Iqbal's abandoned the concept of composite Indian nationalism and adopted Muslim Nationalism. He carved out his views on Islamic universalism. He believed that European concept of nationalism cannot be applied to India. He asserted that according to European notion India is not a land with one nation. Because two major communities living in India i.e., Hindus and Muslims do not share common language, common culture, common history which is the basis of nationalism. Rather Muslims posses separate identity with their own religious and cultural values. These views were expressed in his poem 'The Anthem of the Islamic Community.'[70]

Iqbal considered territorial nationalism and Islam as contradictory and irreconcilable. He reasoned that mission of Islam was to demolish idolatry, it could not approve of patriotism (born out of nationalism), which was nothing but "a subtle form of idolatry".[71]

He wrote a poem 'Territorial Nationalism'[72] and in one its couplet said:

Country is the supreme among all the contemporary idols.

Its cloak is the shroud of Islam.

Territorial nationalism creates division in the Muslims community. He said that:

God's creation is divided into nations by territorial nationalism.

The roots of Islamic nationality are destroyed by it.

Iqbal advocated that Muslims have their own basis of nationalism whose origins lie in Islam. Islam did not follow the confined scope of nationalism. Its membership would not be determined by birth or domicile, it did not consider the natural, historical and cultural differences of different races but it is based on common faith. Muslims living in different parts of the world with variant socio-cultural backgrounds, ethnic divisions and cultural values constitute a single Muslim nation i.e. *ummah*. It was Islamic universalism which was a basis of Muslim nationalism.

Iqbal opposed the economic and political system that creates institutions which enslave the individual. He believed that it undermines not only religion but all the ethical principles. Iqbal, therefore, offers a higher ideal worth living and dying for. It will create self-consciousness amongst the people. Obedience and discipline are essential to keep the "ego" within proper limits. It will ultimately lead to the Vicergency of God. Iqbal believed that the mission will be fulfilled by the Muslims who are guided by the Book of Wisdom- the *Qur'an*. I have been repudiating the concept of nationalism since the time when it was not well-known in India and the Muslim world. At the very start it had become clear to me from the writings of European authors that the imperialistic designs of Europe were in great need of this effective weapon—the propagation of the European conception of nationalism in Muslim countries—to shatter the religious unity of Islam to pieces. And the plan did succeed during the Great War. It has now reached its climax inasmuch as some of the religious leaders in India lend their support to this conception. Strange, indeed, are the vicissitudes of time. Formerly, the half-Westernized educated Muslims were under the spell of Europe: now the curse has descended upon religious leaders. Perhaps modern conceptions of Europe seem attractive to them but alas!

"All the material of the building of Kaaba, won't become new,
if the idols to put in it are imported from England!" [73]

Iqbal differentiated between the terms 'nation' and 'country'. He said that since remote past nations have been associated with countries and countries with nations. We are all Indians and are so called because we live in that part of the world which is known by the name of India. So, with the Chinese, the Arabs, the Japanese, the Iranians, etc. the word "country" used in this statement is merely a geographical term and as such, does not clash with Islam. Its boundaries change with time. Till recently those living in Burma were Indians: at present they are Burmese. In this sense every human being loves the land of his birth, and according to his capacity remains prepared to make sacrifices for it. Some unthinking persons support this by the saying.

"Love of one's native country is a part of one's Faith." which they think is a Tradition of the Prophet, but this is hardly necessary. Love of one's native land is a natural instinct and requires no impressions to nourish it. In the present-day political literature, however, the idea of "nation" is not merely geographical: it is rather a principle of human society and as such, it is a political concept. Since Islam also is a law of human society, the word "country", when used as a political concept, comes into conflict with Islam.

Experience also proves the truth of the above-mentioned claim of Islam. First, if the purpose of human society is to ensure peace and security for the nations and to transform their present social organism into a single social order, then one cannot think of any other social order than that of Islam. This is so because, according to my reading of the *Qur'an*, Islam does not aim at the moral reformation of the individual alone; it also aims at a gradual but fundamental revolution in the social life of mankind, which should altogether change its national and racial viewpoint and create in its place a purely human consciousness. The history of religion was national as in the case of Egyptians, Greeks and Iranians. Later on, it became racial as that of the Jews. Christianity taught that religion is an individual and private affair. Religion having become synonymous with private beliefs; Europe began to think that the State alone was responsible for the social life of man. It was Islam and Islam alone which, for the first time, gave the message to mankind that religion was neither national and racial, nor individual and private, but purely human and that its purpose was to unite and organize mankind, despite all its natural distinctions. Such a system cannot be built on beliefs alone. And this is the only way in which harmony and concord can be introduced in the sentiments and thoughts of mankind. This harmony is essential for the formation and preservation of a community.

As Maulana Roomi said:

"Mutual love and unity is much better

than merely speaking the same language." [74]

Any other way will be irreligious and contrary to human dignity. The example of Europe is before the world. When the religious unity of Europe got shattered and the nations of that continent became disunited, Europeans began to search for the basis of national life. Obviously, Christianity could not be such a basis. The Europeans found this basis in the idea of nationality. But what has been the end of their choice? The reformation of Luther, the period of unsound rationalism, and separation—indeed war—between the principles of religion and state. Where did these forces drive Europe to? to irreligiousness, religious skepticism and economic conflicts.

Iqbal said that in the present-day world people think land is the necessary basis of a nation. No doubt, this is the general feeling these days, but it is also evident that this basis is by itself inadequate. There are a number of other forces also which are necessary for the formation of a nation. For instance, indifference towards religion, absorption in the day-to-day political issues, and so on. Besides, there are also other factor which statesmen think out for themselves as means for maintaining unity and harmony in that nation. The Maulana ignores the fact that if such a nation comprises with different religions and communities, the communities generally die away and the only common factor that remains in the individuals of that nation, is irreligiousness. Not even a layman, let alone religious leaders, who think that religion is a necessary factor for human life, desires that such a state of affairs should be brought about in India. So far as the Muslims are concerned, it is a pity that, simple-minded as they are, they are not fully aware of the consequences for this view of nationalism. If some Muslims have fallen into the error that religion and nationalism can go hand in hand as a political concept, then I want to give a timely warning to the Muslims that this course will ultimately lead to irreligiousness. And if this does happen, Islam will be reduced to an ethical idea with indifference to its social order as an inevitable consequence.

Iqbal knew the evils of irreligiousness. He firmly held that irreligiousness will create a corrupt society. He did not have any idea of 'secular ethics. Therefore, he could not visualize a moral state without a religious basis. Absence of religion will lead to selfishness, petty materialism, worldliness and disregard for the interests of others. "I am opposed to it" Iqbal observed, "because I see in it the germs of atheistic materialism which I look upon as the greatest danger to modern humanity.[75]

Iqbal, however, was not opposed to that type of nationalism which has all the potentialities of uniting the people of a particular country for the achievement of freedom. This, according to him, was not inconsistent with the spirit of Islam. But what could more effectively unite the people is religion and not nationalism.[76] The westerners wanted to use nationalism "to shatter the religious unity of Islam to pieces.[77] And so although Iqbal viewed nationalism as a disturbing element in politics but he was not opposed to the freedom movement. He thought that the growth of nationalism tantamount to the weakening of attachment towards Islam. What really matters is "man's faith, his culture, his historical traditions."

The ultimate goal of Muslims according to Iqbal should be the strengthening of Muslim nationalism for the attainment of Islamic universalism. For this purpose, Muslims should be concerned with the problem of survival and protection of their separate identity. Iqbal believed that Muslims of India have their separate identity. Muslims are not just the community but a separate cultural entity. Attainment of political power was essential to retain uniqueness of Muslims. He envisioned an ideal state which works for the creation of Muslim *ummah*. It should be designed on divine law of Islam, and free of all artificial distinctions between men.

Iqbal did not only attack western nationalism, but was also afraid of its growth in India. He started with the premises that India is not a nation. Firstly, because the Muslims in India are in minority. Therefore, Islam and nationalism are not practically identical. In those countries where the Muslims are in a majority Islam has accommodated nationalism. Muslims in India constitute a separate cultural unit. The Muslims form a community. The Qur'an refers to the community as a 'party of men and this party can come into being......upon the bases of tribe, race, color, language, land and ethical code. *Millat*, will carve out of different parties a new common party. In other words *Millat* or *Ummat* embraces nations but cannot be merged in them. He believes that the Muslims are "bound together not by racial, linguistic or geographical ties, but by their communal brotherhood."[78] Iqbal thus concluded that India is not a single nation. He believed in diversity. The idea of one nationhood implies the obliteration of this diversity and this, according to him, would be most undesirable. Moreover, nationalism according to Renan's definition i.e., presence of moral consciousness, is not present in India.

But it does not mean that Iqbal was not in favour of United India. "A United India," he said "would have to be built on the foundation of concrete facts i.e., this distinct existence of more than one people in the country. The sooner Indian leaders forget the idea of a unitary Indian nation based on something like a biological fusion of the communities the better for all concerned.[79] Iqbal had in mind the failure of the mission of Nanak and Kabir in the past. History also bears witness to the futility of attempts to secure the fusion of the communities. Now in the 20th century unity should not be "sought in the negation, but in the mutual harmony and co-operation of many. Iqbal had realized that the people as well as the leader's clarity of thought and insight regarding the unity of India. He, therefore, characterized all talk of one nation as "futile" and likely to continue so for a long time to come.[80] Iqbal's insistence on the maintenance of the distinct communities by recognizing them as separate entities, gave rise to what is described as Muslim Nationalism. This has also directly or indirectly has made him the father of the idea of Pakistan.

Some may think that the Muslim League carried Iqbal's concept of Muslim Nationalism to its logical end. But this does not appear to be valid. Firstly, Iqbal never thought of partitioning the country. The politics especially in the Punjab and generally in India, the emergence of Hindu militant groups, communal riots, general conditions of Muslims and lack of discipline and organization amongst them led him to remark that "the problem in India is international and not national" He also suggested the idea of a separate Muslim State in the North in his Presidential Address to the Muslim League in 1928. This demand was only for "a state within the state", and not for an altogether separate state. No question of partition was involved. Probably he would have been satisfied with the establishment of a true federation in which full internal autonomy is guaranteed to the constituent units.

Edward Thompson states that Iqbal was disillusioned with his idea of 'a state within the state' regarding it as disastrous to the British, to the Hindus as well as to the Muslim community. Thus, Iqbal's scheme has no relation to the League demand for partition. Jinnah and the others of the League were closer to Choudhary Rahmat Ali than to Iqbal regarding the concept and scheme of partition. There were others who had also advocated such schemes before Iqbal. But the League leadership exploited Iqbal's name to give strength and sanctity to the demand for Pakistan.

Secondly, Jinnah and many other Muslim leaders in the forties were rallying anti-Hindu forces under the guise of Two Nation Theory. Here, too, the League was more profoundly inspired by Rehmat Ali than by Iqbal. Iqbal had great respect for the non-Muslim communities.[81]

He believed that no religion teaches hatred of others religious communities. Iqbal is reported to have said to Ranjee G. Shahani "I am sprung from the same stock; India is older than Hinduism and Islam, and will remain when we and our creeds have become one with Yesterday's Seven thousand years…"

"It is wrong to utter a bad word;
To infidel as well as the faithful is God's creations;
Humanity consists in respect for man
So acquaint thyself with the dignity of man."

-Translated by S.A.Vahid

Iqbal would never have agreed to the demand of Pakistan, because he felt "that Islam in its pure form had a contribution to make towards the building of new India". This reflects that Iqbal was very much opposed to sectarian and narrow nationalism inside and outside India as the basis of polity. The nature of opposition was more Islamic than political. By attacking nationalism, he never wanted to create obstacles in the way of Independence of the country. On the contrary he had a passion for India's freedom. He sounded a note of warning that nationalism, the product of the west, will be anachronistic and dangerous to the interests of humanity. His aim was to expose the game of the west and explode the myth of nationalism. Iqbal thought that a government based on the concept of One God (*Tawheed*) will be more stable and better than democracy of the western type. The principle of unity of God is a "living factor in the intellectual and emotional life of mankind."[82] The other cardinal principles of Islamic democracy will be 'obedience of law', [83] 'tolerance'[84] 'universalism.'[85] Iqbal in his book 'Reconstruction of Religious Thought in Islam' refers to the democratic development in Muslim countries. He "approved of a growth of republican spirit in Muslim countries, which he regarded as a return to the original purity of Islam."[86]

Iqbal appreciated the adoption of democratic institutions in the Muslim countries. But they should be in conformity with the basic principle of Islam. He was also aware of the necessity of reform and a proper change in religious instruction. Thus *Ijtehad* (Independent enquiry) can be used to re-interpret the law "in the light of modern experience and the altered conditions of the modern life."

Iqbal adopted the same attitude towards democracy in India. He was of the opinion that the western institutions of democracy did not suit Indian conditions and the genius of our people. He held that the Indian Muslim was not essentially opposed to the democratic ideal. But he has reason "to be afraid of communal oligarchy in the garb of democracy in India. He wants to ensure the substance of democracy even at the expense of its conventional form." Therefore, he pleaded for a modification of the democratic institutions. He said that the "minorities of India can ill-afford to accept the principle of Western democracy until it is properly modified to meet the actual conditions of life in India."

The discussion reflects that Iqbal rejected capitalism, nationalism and democracy on religious grounds. He believed that their character is un-Islamic. Iqbal's object was the "exposition of Islam's message and main features of its ethical code" as the basis for the unity of mankind.

Iqbal's political philosophy had two aspects- critical and constructive. The constructive aspect of Iqbal's political thought consisted in his recommendation of the principles of social, political and economic order as a remedy for the existing strife and conflicts. In one of his lectures Iqbal had pointed out that "humanity needs three things today- a spiritual interpretation of Universe, spiritual emancipation of the individual and basic principles of universal importance directing the evolution of human society on a spiritual basis." Here Iqbal attempts to show what the modern age lacks. The crisis is produced by the materialism of modern science which discards spiritual values. In 1938 he said, "So long as this so-called democracy, this accursed nationalism and degraded imperialism are not shattered so long as men do not demonstrate by their action that they believe that the whole world is the family of God, so long as distinctions of race, color, and geographical nationality are not wiped out completely, they will never be able to lead a happy and contended life and the beautiful ideals of liberty, equality and fraternity will never materialize."[87]

Iqbal believed that these ideals will be materialized in the spiritual democracy which is the ultimate aim of Islam. He knew that Islam will act as a regulator of society as well as a psychologically integrative force. Iqbal, however, was not guided by " a false reverence for past history and its artificial resurrection because he knew that they constitute no remedy for a people's decay," But he could not at the same time ignore the Islamic past. The origin of his ideal Society can be traced to the glorious period of the Rashidin Caliphs which "was a model of sociological excellence." Iqbal advocated the revival of that society "to bring about a rapprochement between knowledge, and vision which is fruit of love and intuition." This rapprochement is necessary because power without vision tends to become destructive and inhuman. Therefore, this unity is essential for the "spiritual expansion of humanity."

One fundamental principle of the Islamic community is the recognition of Prophethood. The belief in the finality of the Prophet is vital to the existence and survival of society.

After the establishment of Pakistan, he came to be considered as "the spiritual founder of Pakistan."[88] The conflicting interpretation of a few of these writers critical of Iqbal do not also help to understand his philosophy. Iqbal described himself as a "Visionary idealist" in the Presidential Address of All India Muslim Conference. He complained that no one knew him well and no one understood his message too.

References

1. *(Bang-i-Dra-163)* ,Tule -e-Islam.

2. Iqbal, Mohammed, *Six lectures on the Reconstruction of Religious thought in Islam,* Lahore: Sang-i Mil Publications, 2004

3. Iqbal, Allama, Dr. Sir Muhammad (1930). *Reconstruction of Religious Thought in Islam,* Lahore: Shaikh Muhammad Ashraf, 1982, p. 6

4. Schimmel, Annemarie 1987. *Gabriel's Wings* Urdu Translation by Muhammad Riaz, titled, *"Shahapar-i-Jibreel"*, Lahore: Globe Publishers, Lahore (F.E.), 1987, p.393.

5. Quraishi, Ishtiaque Hussain, *The Psychological Sources of Iqbal's Philosophy, Annual Iqbal's lecture,* Lahore: Punjab University, 1966

6. Enver, Ishrat Hasan, *The Metaphysics of Iqbal*, Lahore: Muhammad Ashraf, 1944, p. 7-8.

7. Extracts from Presidential Remarks by Professor Dr. Sayyid Zafarul Hassan on *"The Six Lectures"*, delivered by Iqbal at the Muslim University, Aligarh, 1929, p. 7.

8. Iqbal, Allama, Dr. Sir Muhammad (1930). *Reconstruction of Religious Thought in Islam,* Lahore: Sheikh Muhammad Ashraf, 1982, pp. 100 -101.

9. Iqbal, Mohammed, *The Secrets of the Self: Asrar-i Khudi,* translated by Reynold A. Nicholson, London: Macmillan, 1920, line 88.

10. Chaudhary, Muzzaffar Hussain, *"Khutbath ka Asal Mauzu"* (The main Theme of Lectures by Iqbal), *Iqbaliyyat* (Iqbal Review) (January–March,1997), p. 35.

11. Iqbal, Mohammed, *The Secrets of the Self: Asrar-i Khudi,* translated by Reynold A. Nicholson, London: Macmillan, 1920, line 1019-1030, 1033.

12. *Javid Nama,* The book of eternity, Lahore, 1932, p. 40

13. *Zabur i 'Ajam'*, The Psalms of Persia, Lahore, 1927, p. 160.

14. *Payam I Mashriq,* The Message of the East, Lahore, 1923 p.85.

15. Ali, Sheikh Akbar, *Iqbal, His Poetry and Message*, New Delhi: Deep & Deep Publications, 1932, p.265.

16. Iqbal, Mohammed, *The Secrets of the Self: Asrar-i Khudi,* translated by Reynold A. Nicholson, London: Macmillan, 1920, line 1325.

17. *Zabur i 'Ajam', The Psalms of Persia,* Lahore, 1927, p. 132.

18. Iqbal, Mohammed, *The Secrets of the Self: Asrar-i Khudi,* translated by Reynold A. Nicholson, London: Macmillan, 1920, line 1325.

19. *ibid.,* line 1325.

20. *ibid.,* line 1325.

21. Natesan, G.A., *Emminent Mussalmans,* Madras: G. A. Natesan & Company Publishers, 1926, p. 397.

22. Shamloo (compiled by), *Speeches and Statements of Iqbal,* Lahore: Hamidullah Khan for al-Manar Academy, 1944, p. 38.

23. *ibid.,* p. 55.

24. *ibid.,* p. 120

25. *ibid..* p. 129.

26. *ibid.,* p.133.

27. *ibid.,* p. 3

28. Iqbal, Sir Mohammed, *The Mysteries of Selflessness,* A Philosophical Poem, translated, with Introduction and Notes by A. J. Arberry, London: John Murray, 1953, p. 70

29. Nicholson, Reynold Alleyne, Sir Muhammad Iqbal; *The Secrets of the Self (Asrár-i Khudí)* a Philosophical Poem, Biblio Bazaar, 2010, p. XXVII.

30. Bertrand Russell, *The Scientific Outlook,* London: Routledge, 2001, p. XXIX.

31. Iqbal, Mohammad, *Thoughts and Reflections of Iqbal,* edited by Sayyid Abdul Vahid, Lahore: Sh. Muhammad Ashraf Publishers, 1992, pp. 373-374.

32. *ibid.,* p. 374.

33. *ibid.,* p. 375.

34. *ibid.*

35. *ibid.*

36. *ibid.,* p. 212.

37. *ibid.,* p. 213

38. Iqbal, Mohammed, *Six lectures on the Reconstruction of Religious thought in Islam,* Lahore: Sang-i Mil Publications, 2004, p. 1

39. Iqbal, Mohammad, *Thoughts and Reflections of Iqbal,* edited by Sayyid Abdul Vahid, Lahore: Sh. Muhammad Ashraf Publishers, 1992, p. 213.

40. *ibid.,* pp. 213-214.

41. *ibid.,* p. 46.

42. Iqbal, Mohammed, *Six lectures on the Reconstruction of Religious thought in Islam,* Lahore: Sang-i Mil Publications, 2004, p. 3.

43. Safia, Amir, *Muslim Nationhood in India, Perceptions of Seven Eminent Thinkers,* New Delhi: Kanishka Publishers and distributors, 2000, p. 70

44. Vahid, Sayed Abdul (ed.), *Thoughts and Reflections of Islam,* Lahore, 1973, pp. 44-46.

45. *ibid.,* pp.373-74

46. as quoted in Safia, Amir, *Muslim Nationhood in India, Perceptions of Seven Eminent Thinkers,* New Delhi: Kanishka Publishers and distributors, 2000, p.65

47. Tasdiq, Husayn Taj (ed.), *Madamin-i-Iqbal,* Hyderabad: Dakkan, 1941, Pp. 98-100 ; Safia, Amir, *Muslim Nationhood in India, Perceptions of Seven Eminent Thinkers,* New Delhi: Kanishka Publishers and distributors, 2000, p. 65.

48. Muhammad, Iqbal, *The Reconstruction of Religious Thought in Islam,* New Delhi: Kitab Bhawan, 1994, p. 147.

49. Vahid, Sayyid Abdul (ed.), *Thoughts and Reflections of Iqbal* (Lahore: Sh.Mohammed Ashraf, 1992), pp. 60-61. This book is comprised of the original lectures and speeches delivered by Iqbal. Sayyid Abdul Vahid compiled them and wrote an introduction.

50. Muhammad, Iqbal, *The Reconstruction of Religious Thought in Islam,* New Delhi: Kitab Bhawan, 1994, p. 155

51. *ibid.*

52. *ibid.*

53. Shamloo (ed.), Speeches and Statements of Iqbal, Lahore: Al-Manar Academy, 1948, p. IV.

54. Muhammad, Munawwar, Iqbal and Qur'anic Wisdom, Delhi : Noor Publishing House, 1986, p. 28.

55. *ibid,* 29.

56. *"Bal-i-Jibril,"* 133, quoted in *ibid.,* p. 35.

57. *"Armughan-i-Hijaz,"* 50, quoted in *ibid.*

58. *"Dharb-i-Kalim,"* 60, quoted in *ibid.,* p. 20.

59. Muhammad, Iqbal, *The Reconstruction of Religious Thought in Islam,* New Delhi: Kitab Bhawan, 1994, p. 147

60. Shamloo (compiled by), *Speeches and Statements of Iqbal,* Lahore: Hamidullah Khan for al-Manar Academy, 1944, p. 225.

61. *ibid.*

62. *ibid.*, 134.

63. Shamloo (compiled by), *Speeches and Statements of Iqbal*, Lahore: Hamidullah Khan for al-Manar Academy, 1944, P. 229

64. *ibid.*

65. *ibid.*

66. ibid.

67. Safia, Amir, *Muslim Nationhood in India, Perceptions of Seven Eminent Thinkers,* New Delhi: Kanishka Publishers and distributors, 2000, p.19

68. Vahid, Sayed Abdul (ed.), Thoughts and Reflections of Iqbal, Lahore, 1973, p. 20

69. Shamloo (ed.), *Speeches and Statements of Iqbal,* 224 quoted by Riaz Hussain, *The Politics of Iqbal: A Study of His Political Thoughts and Actions,* Lahore: Islamic Book Service, 1977.

70. Rashida Malik, Iqbal: *The Spiritual Father of Pakistan,* Lahore: Sang-e-Meel Publications, 2003, p.17

71. Amir, Safia, *Muslim Nationhood in India, Perceptions of Seven Eminent Thinkers,* New Delhi: Kanishka Publishers and distributors, 2000. ISBN-81-7391-335-8, p. 70

72. *ibid.*, p. 19

73. i.e., the Kaaba was built for the worship of One God only, and idols are contrary to its purpose! In other words, the Muslims should be faithful to monotheism and to their own traditions, without being affected by Western culture!

74. i.e., then being people of the same country!

75. Shamloo (compiled by), *Speeches and Statements of Iqbal*, Lahore, Hamidullah Khan for al-Manar Academy, 1944, p. 141.

76. *ibid.*, p. 205.

77. *ibid.*, p. 204.

78. *ibid.*, p. 204.

79. Spann, Richard Neville (ed.), Dr. Javed Iqbal Quoted in *Constitutionalism in Asia,* New Delhi: Asia Publishing House, 1963, p. 137.

80. Shamloo (compiled by), *Speeches and Statements of Iqbal*, Lahore: Hamidullah Khan for al-Manar Academy, 1944, p. 194.

81. *ibid.*, p. 71

82. Daryabadi, Abdul Majid: *Mazamine Abdul Majid*, P. 52.

83. Iqbal, M., *Six Lectures on the Reconstruction of Religious Thought in Islam*, Lahore: Kapur Art Printing Works, 1930, p. 142.

84. Bilgrami, H.H., *Glimpses of Iqbal's Mind and Thought: Brief Lectures on Iqbal Delivered at London*, Cambridge and Oxford, Sh. Muhammad Ashraf, 1966, p.102.

85. *ibid.*, p.108.

86. *ibid.*, p.109.

87. Sadiq, Muhammad, *A history of Urdu Literature*, Delhi: Oxford University Press, 1995, p. 371.

88. Shamloo (compiled by), Speeches and Statements of Iqbal, Lahore: Hamidullah Khan for al-Manar Academy, 1944, p. 203.

INTELLECTUAL FERVOUR TO REVIVALISM:
DR. ZAKIR HUSSAIN

"My message to you is this: have your character-building program me in your own hands. Develop all its elements by self-control and selfless service. Build good character, and making it an instrument of high and absolute values, elevate it to the level of faithful man *(banda-e-momin)* and struggling man *(mard-e-mujahid)*. It is a difficult job and it is a lifelong job, but you get life only by working for it. How can it be achieved by sitting idle? Life itself should be invested in it."

"India is my country and all the people inhabiting it are my family," said Zakir Hussain at the time of taking oath as the President of India and he lived every word of it. Dr. Zakir Hussain was an ardent patriot and eminent statesmen who adorned many high positions in the country including the highest with great dignity and grace. He was not only merely a scholar of repute and an intellectual par- excellence, but above all he was a humanist who in his own life reflected the synthesis of different cultures. A deeply devoted man, Zakir Hussain believed that humanism was the highest form of religion and showed the same reverence and respect for all the religions of the world. His personality was happy blend of a political visionary who foresaw a social order free from injustice and inequality and an educationist, who sought through education, emancipation of men and his adherence to the highest human values.

A shining star on the firmament of Indian intellectualism and nationalism, Zakir Hussain believed that the goal of mankind is knowledge, and not pleasure. He wanted to make India free from the colonial shackles imposed on the educational sector and to bring the Muslim community into the mainstream of national life. His patriotic fervor in the struggle for freedom, his intense love to identify himself with the hopes and aspirations of the people, and his stewardship as the President of the nation, all entitle him to rank as one of the most creative thinkers and statesmen of modern India. The gentleness of his mature mind, the compassion and love for mankind, the humanism and liberalism of his inner soul, and the simplicity, sincerity, purity and nobility of his life, mark him out as one of the finest flowers of Indian renaissance.

Dr. Zakir Hussain chose teaching as a profession. His mission was to evolve a system of education suited to the genius of people in Independent India. He was a firm believer in the dictum that knowledge can be made the basis of moral life and the manner in which it can be applied to the ethical reorganization of society. His significantly contributed to the promotion of new attitudes and values in the society, to the enhancement of knowledge and culture among all segments of the land and to the pursuit of excellence in the finer aspects of life. He struggled all his life to bring about a creative integration of that composite culture which is the hall-mark of this great country, and which finds expression in unity in diversity and identity in multiplicity. He strived to inculcate in Indians, a sense of social responsibility, a sense of hope, faith and pride in the future of this country and to inspire in them a sense of urgency to live harmoniously and graciously with their fellowmen.

Throughout his distinguished career, education had been very dear to Dr. Zakir Hussain's heart- its dissemination and spread, its philosophy and thought, its planning and implementation, its latest methodology and skills and above all, his efforts for according it a pivotal role in national life.

Zakir Hussain (1897-1969), son of Fida Hussain Khan, was born on 8th February 1897 in Hyderabad where his father was a much-respected legal practitioner. Zakir Husssain belonged to a well-known family of Afghans domiciled for many centuries in Qaimganj, a small town in Farrukhabad District (U.P.) Zakir Hussain returned to Qaimganj along with his mother after the death of his father in 1907.The responsibility of Zakir Hussain's upbringing was devolved on his mother who gave him the best possible education. His mother's influence made him conscious of his duties towards his countrymen, irrespective of any consideration of caste, creed or religion. His mother passed away in 1911. His uncle Uta Hussain Khan, then took care of him.[1]

During the days of his early his education in a school at Etawah, he was influenced by Sayyid Altaf Husain, headmaster and a fine man, who had a hand in the early orientation of his mind. He awakened in Zakir a sense of social awareness which helped him in molding his future course of life and created in him a lasting interest in national and international problems. Zakir Hussain was also influenced by a Sufi Saint Hasan Shah who became his spiritual teacher. It was his influence that instilled in Zakir Hussain great simplicity, modesty, humility, tranquility, patience, love and service. It was his impact that Zakir lived like a recluse even in Raj Bhawan and Rashtrapati Bhawan. The Sufi element in Zakir Hussain made him conform to poet Sa'di's dictum that the head that wears a crown should have a heart that throbs in a saint. During the years spent in Islamia High School, Etawah, Zakir Hussain had the opportunity to acquire all the high qualities of leadership. He believed in the Aristotelian dictum that happiness does not exist in the possession of inmate objects but in the right use of one's own energy for a purpose. At the age of 13 years, he wrote an article entitled *Talibilm ki Zindagi, i.e.,* Life of a student.[2] This article is well reflective of his sincerity and keenness to learn from teachers and the view that only an earnest student can become a teacher.

He did his matriculation with distinction, joined M.A.O. College at Aligarh and graduation in 1918. He did Masters in Economics with a course of Law in 1920. He was a popular student leader in Aligarh, held several responsible positions and won laurels for his speeches at debating contests. Later on, he was appointed as a lecturer in the same college.

October, 1920 marked a turning point in Zakir Hussain's life when after the end of World War I, there was a storm on the political scene of the country. The victory of the Allies in the war was followed by Khilafat movement and the Raj's atrocities in Punjab agitated and moved the whole country. Mahatma

Gandhi, called upon the countrymen to non-cooperate with the British government. Spelling out his seven points non-violent, non-cooperation program me, he asked the students of the country to come out of such institutions which were owned, aided or controlled by the government, and help establishing national institutions instead.

Mahatma Gandhi along with Ali brothers visited Aligarh College and advised the students and teachers to leave the institution run by the British government. On October 12, 1920, Gandhiji addressed the students inspiring them to join the national scene. While speaking to the students Mahatma explained why Indians should boycott educational institutions controlled by British government and should develop centers of national education instead. Gandhi asked that if the Hindus and Muslims were to unite, what remained of the British? But the appeal of Mahatma Gandhi fell on deaf ears and a majority of Aligarh boys did not wish to disappoint Principal Beck who had exhorted the boys in such words:

"Should ever the necessity arise, the stone heart and strong arms of the students bred in the College, trained in cricket and football fields, would be ready facing the enemy, to render to government such assistance as would prove that the *Mussalmans* of India, with their martial spirit burning as of old, were ready to face the bullets and bayonets in the defense of the glorious empire to which it was their privilege to belong."[3]

Mahatma Gandhi appealed to the students of Aligarh to boycott the institution, but the students did not respond to this idea. Zakir Hussain was in Delhi due to his illness. On his return journey to Aligarh that evening, Zakir Hussain heard humiliating comments about Gandhi made by some students at the station platform. The coarseness of some of the remarks made by a group of the strolling students and the fact that others seemed to enjoy them filled Zakir with a "deepest shame" and a conviction that atonement was called for.

Ali Brothers, Shauket Ali and Muhammad Ali who were also in Aligarh for the same purpose came to meet the student union next day. They were informed that they had failed in rousing the young students. With regret and tears in their eyes bid farewell and went away with a broken heart. This was a reference to the apparently successful efforts of the pro Raj elements on the campus to frustrate the effort of Gandhi and the Ali brothers. The disappointment of the brothers was so transparent that many students including Zakir Hussain also began to weep.

Witness to the frustration and disappointment of Ali Brothers, Zakir stood up and spoke vehemently and implored that the future should not be lost for the flimsy gains of the present. He said that country's honor and self-respect are more important than degrees and diplomas; a life of liberty and misery should be preferred to a life of comfort in slavery.

Zakir joined the movement and mobilized his friends to accept Mahatma Gandhi's appeal. To his dismay, many students laughed, mocked and ridiculed the movement the Trustees agents also opposed it. Zakir was accused as a hypocrite, of having the appearance of a nationalist and yet protecting his salary as a lecturer. Responding to such comments Zakir Hussain immediately resigned from his job and inspired others also to do the same. Ibn-e-Hasan and a few others resigned from their jobs.

Thus, Zakir Hussain left his Alma Mater to join the band of Muslim Nationalists. He was lured by Dr. Ziauddin, the then Vice-Chancellor, with lucrative jobs if he desisted from joining the non-cooperation movement.[4] But he preferred to serve the cause of the Nation, and emerged as the soul of the new movement. When he left the college nearly three hundred students followed him. Zakir Hussain was eager that these students should receive proper education. With this objective in view, he helped in building the Jamia Millia Islamia.

Zakir Hussain, met Hakim Ajmal Khan, Dr. Ansari, Maulana Muhammad Ali and other leaders in Delhi and assured them that there were quite a few in Aligarh who sincerely believed in the righteousness of the national cause and are prepared to make all sacrifice for the establishment of a national center of learning. This section in Aligarh is prepared to leave the college, and enter into the mainstream provided speedy arrangements were made for setting up a national centre. The leaders were pleased to know the sincere intentions of these promising young men, jumped at the idea and thus Zakir Hussain became the pioneer of a new venture.

Revivalism through Education

Zakir Hussain conceived education as an instrument to reform society at all levels, to bring a social change and to remove ignorance from the land.

Jamia was established against the background of the Muslim psyche which had never been reconciled to their children being educated in foreign tongue, learning foreign morals and manners. Aligarh College had earned a peculiar image of a highly controversial image. People were disappointed see that Aligarh College which was considered to be a seat of learning to produce good scholars had become a place of refuge of mischievous undesirable elements. Sayyid Ahmad Khan's initiative of Aligarh to promote Islamic ethos and culture was unfortunately converted into a centre where western thinking had diluted the pristine Islamic values and principles. Unfortunately, an institution which was a hope for the community to bring about social solidarity had converted into an arena generating disruptive forces by dividing the community into small camps. Aligarh College failed to foster a new economic, political and intellectual order and became merely a factory to produce "Babus" to man the administrative machinery of the colonials. The discouraging situations at Aligarh College contributed in the establishment of Jamia as a National center of Islamic Education backed by Indians.

Although Sir Sayyid had started Aligarh movement for the regeneration of the community and to remove Muslim ignorance, but we can see a difference in the objectives. Zakir's Jamia movement was to remove the vanity and restore the pride of the Muslims, whereas Ahmad Khan was a reformer with a restricted task of rescuing the drowning Muslim community. He preached the Muslims to prefer modernism to traditionalism. Sir Sayyid asked the Muslims to be loyal to the English, whereas Zakir Hussain asked the Muslims to be loyal to the country. Sir Sayyid condemned vernacular languages in strong terms as "there is but very little difference between a man ignorant of English and a beast", but Zakir Hussain installed Urdu on a high pedestal and made that the medium of instruction in Jamia.[5] Sir Sayyid had kept the Muslims away from the mainstream of Indian nationalism, Zakir Hussain was knee deep in it, and desired that his community too should fall in line with their compatriots. Thus, they differed on the on view that politics should be kept away from education. Ahmad wanted to keep the students away from politics whereas Zakir believed that a genuine and broad-based national renaissance could not be ushered in through the narrow gate of politics-it must have its moorings in, and draw its inspiration from a renascent education and culture.

But the services rendered to the Muslim community by Sir Sayyid Ahmad Khan cannot be ignored because without his help the community would have reduced to drawers of water and hewers of wood. The self-respect he gave to the members of the community, the solidarity he injected in them, the spark of learning he ignited in their heart, and the direction he showed them for the march, though controversial, were all suited to the exigencies of the time. Zakir Hussain acknowledged Sir Sayyid's great services to the community, and became complimentary, to finish the task he had commenced. Zakir helped his community through education, and to remove their poverty, apathy, superstition and degradation.

Articles written by Zakir Hussain had a great impact on the young minds of his fellow men. His thought-provoking article entitled "Eternity or Toy" published in March- August 1920 issue of Aligarh Magazine was reflective of awareness and need for a total change in the thinking of the community to meet the demands of the time. He said that education will be of a great help to improve the economic conditions of people and likewise good education was not possible until economic conditions were improved.

In the same essay Zakir Hussain emphasized on the need for moral education. For him morality and ethics were closely interconnected with religion. Religion has two aspects; one is faith and other is righteous deeds. The two together would make a man truly religious. A good Muslim could also be a good nationalist because he would exhibit fine qualities such as generosity, action, love and service. At Aligarh he was disappointed to see only formalism, and complete absence of true religious zeal and spirit. And so, he aspired a thorough review of the entire educational philosophy of Aligarh with a purpose to bring about renaissance among the Muslims. He wanted to examine the causes of the failure of Aligarh so that corrective measures may be suggested. At the end of the essay Zakir puts a question, who would purchase a moment's pleasure in return for a week's misery, and who would prefer a toy in bargain for eternity? He warned the responsible people that they should not commit this blunder again.[6]

In his view, man is an organic whole, and one cannot compartmentalize him into different units saying that one unit is independent of the other. Social, cultural, educational, economic and political affairs are all inter-related, and one would not understand them better if a comprehensive outlook was not developed. For him the established pattern of English education is soulless-its ideals were limited, its methods stereotyped its contact with currents of national life vague and remote.

Nurturing Jamia Millia Islamia

The foundation of Jamia Millia Islamia was laid on 29 October 1920 by Maulana Muhamudul Hasan. Maulana Mohamed Ali was appointed as Vice- Chancellor. Jamia – was inspired by a new ideology. Zakir Hussain, with a national spirit and an intellectual vision, made Jamia the educational front of the struggle for freedom and dedicated himself to the service of the institution as a coworker. Jamia represented a new and promising adventure in education. For the inaugural ceremony of Jamia, a deeply venerated and enlightened religious leader, Shaikh-ul-Hind Maulana Mahmood Hasan, was present. In his speech which was read by his disciple, he said that the education of the Muslims must be in the hands of the Muslims and the foreigners should not meddle with it, both in respect of religious thought, moral values and practical deeds. The college should not be allowed to produce cheap servants. Instead, they should become a model of what had existed earlier in Bagdad or Cordova which had made the whole of Europe their students, and not become the students of Europe.[7] From the very beginning its first Vice-Chancellor Mohammad Ali stressed the teaching of Islamic history and Qur'an and ensured that the teaching day began with a full hour devoted to the rapid exegesis of the *Qur'an* based on the preaching of prominent Deobandi Ulema. It was registered under Society Registration Act in 1939 as a traditional religious institution and recognized as deemed university in late sixties and finally granted the status of a central university in 1988.[8]

To nurture Jamia in the spirit it was conceived was a herculean task for Zakir Hussain. Jamia was shifted to Karol Bagh, Delhi in 1925. He joined Jamia as a Vice- Chancellor, in 1926. The economic condition of the institution was so bad that it was about to be closed. It somehow survived with the help of Hakim Ajmal Khan who passed away in 1927.

The shifting of Jamia from Aligarh to Delhi was a landmark in the history of this institution with great potential. Starved with economic crunch, it gained the protection of loving people of Delhi. It was Zakir's dedication to the cause of Jamia, that it was revived once again and Jamia's reputation spread far and wide in the country. Considering the financial constraints Dr. Zakir Hussain persuaded his colleagues to work on a meagre salary of Rs 150 per month. He himself drew only Rs 75 to 95 per month. While on a tour of the country with a begging bowl he succeeded in collecting a fund amounting to Rs 2 crore. With the funds' raised land was purchased near Okhla and buildings of school and colleges came up soon. The Jamia then was shifted to its present place in 1935. As the real founder of the Jamia Millia Islamia, he instilled the values of nationalism, patriotism and other human values in Muslims so as to enable them to join the freedom struggle and contribute in the progress of the country. He wanted to make Jamia an institution where a nationalist could take pride in being a Muslim and a Muslim would be proud of his being a nationalist.[9] With great pride Jamia was introduced as an Islamic institution to the country.

In his speech of 1933, he said:

"The Jamia is an Islamic institution and its main objective is to provide education for Indian Muslims. Islam and Islamic culture are the basis of education at the Jamia. Islam signifies in this context the faith which frees one from the worship of anyone other than Allah. It binds one to serve the One True God and thus lays the foundation of a universal brotherhood and fraternity. Islamic culture stands here for the role model set by Prophet Muhammad (Peace and blessings be upon him). In recognition of the local culture and conditions, we may pursue some other objectives as well, as for example, a keen desire to attain our independence and to serve the cause of Urdu."[10]

In August 1937 while addressing a gathering of *Hamdard-i-Jamia* he said, "The biggest objective of Jamia Millia is to prepare a roadmap for the future lives of Indian Muslims with the religion of Islam at its core ...."[11] If the objective of this university is rooted to the core of a religion, can it not be called a movement for Islamic revivalism?

In his speech delivered at the flag hoisting ceremony at the educational meet in 1944, elucidating the Jamia motto he remarked:

"Do you know what the meaning of this symbol is? Look, there is a star at the top and inscribed in it is "Allah Akbar". On a dark night a lonely traveler who has lost his way is guided to his destination by the stars. This loadstar for the Jamia community is the star engraved with Allah Akbar. Their eyes will be focused on it. It guides them in the darkness of this world. For it reminds them Allah is the greatest to whom everyone should surrender. Whosoever surrenders himself to Him is guided on a true, meaningful life. One who turns subservient to Him cannot surrender before anyone. Below this shining star is a book on which is inscribed "*Allamma al Insana Ma Lam Ya'lam*" (He taught man which he did not know). The book stands for the blessed Qur'an. It is through this book that Allah has made His will be known to His servants. It informs what Allah demands of man. The ideal of brotherhood, by removing the barriers between the rich and the poor and the discrimination arising out color and status, we can become good, true servants of Allah. The Qur'an has guided mankind from darkness into light. It showed the model through his conduct, through his example and through his efforts trained a band of pious persons who put an end to all evils in the world and established a genuine fraternity of Allah's servants. This motto is flanked by date palm trees on both sides. What is their significance? These symbolize the land where the final Messenger of Allah was born. These refer to the arid valley where the divine faith made its appearance. Those who feel dispirited by adverse circumstances should draw comfort from this symbol that a county where nothing was grown except a palm tree became the fountain and source of all guidance. It offered spiritual and religious sustenance to millions of hearts. One should not therefore despair, if the circumstances are not apparently favorable.

At the bottom is the crescent on which is inscribed "Jamia Millia Islamia". Of course, it is only a crescent. As we know, crescent grows into the full moon. By the same analogy, the Jamia work which in its infancy would grow into a bright, full moon, which would please the beholders.[11] Referring to the Jamia flag as the symbol of the aspirations of the Jamia community, Dr. Zakir Hussain said:

"For realizing our ideals, we will have to make the Jamia the centre of Muslims, assuring them of bright future. Outwardly this flag is made of inexpensive cloth, yet it is valuable in terms of ideology, ideals and aspirations associated with it. He turned then to expounding the reality which underlies the Islamic culture, rather every great culture in that it invests life with beauty and meaning. He exclaimed:

This flag symbolizes the reality that life cannot be led with a mere verbal recital of some beliefs. Rather it is upon contingent, sincere, hard work. Life does not stand for material losses or gains. Rather, it stands out as an opportunity for achieving certain objectives. Life is not built upon the axis of material comforts and happiness. Rather, it revolves round the fundamental principle of progress and evolution. Our flag represents hard work, rather than mere verbal profession of some ideal. Likewise, it stands for constant striving and hard work instead of any indolence or self-complacency. It represents also help, firmness, cleanliness and beauty which would replace disease, weakness, filth and ugliness. Health stands for both a sound body and a pure soul and a clean mind. Likewise, firmness includes both that of body and of the resolve. Likewise, we believe in the cleanliness of both body and soul. If our resolution, our achievements and our constancy correspond to this flag, the latter, though outwardly a piece of ordinary cloth, would be an invaluable asset, more precious than all he worldly possessions and it would ensure honor and dignity for us in the country.[12]

On the Silver Jubilee of Jamia, in 1946, Zakir Hussain recalled the great inauguration day of Jamia. Zakir said,

"I remember the time when in the Aligarh Mosque a saintly soul was seated, leaning against a wall. He could not even address the gathering as he was so weak, and his message was read by his student Maulana Shabbir Ahmad Usmani. Gentlemen, please remember that the support of the wall against which he was leaning was not just made of bricks and stones. It was of solid faith, and as a result of that faith, a mighty national wall of the past had been erected. On that day, no foundation stone of any building was laid, nor was there any inauguration of any construction. No announcement of any donation was made and yet a caravan set out without any of the required needs. It was bargaining immediate loss against immediate gains. It preferred lasting value to fleeting things. It was in this atmosphere that Jamia came into existence."[13]

Jamia was the outcome of Zakir's sincere attempt to blend Islamic trends with Indian nationalism. While describing the aims of the institute, the great Turkish publicist Edib said:

The institution has two purposes. Firstly, to train the Muslim youth with a definite idea of their rights and duties as Indian citizen and secondly, to coordinate Islamic thought and behavior with Hindus.... It is nearer to the Gandhian movement than any Islamic Institution I have come across."[14]

The purpose of Jamia was to inject nationalist feelings amongst the youth and to restructure the courses according to the "cultural goods" of the country. Zakir Hussain injected the finest elements of the Islamic culture into the courses. Zakir Hussain had the firm faith that principles of could well be integrated with the main trends of Indian culture, which are unity in diversity, identity in multiplicity, continuity and adaptability, and humanism and tolerance. Once the Islamic ethos of the unity of God and the unity of man merged with the Indian trends, they would enrich the total heritage of mankind. Little brooks join the bigger streams to flow into mighty seas.[15] Zakir Hussain believed that national education as an instrument of Indian renaissance can bring great social change affecting all sections of the society. He emphasized on the "cultural goods" and wanted them to act as a searchlight to illumine the dark patches of nation life. He said that 'cultivation of mind', 'culture of mind' or education is possible 'only by means of cultural goods,' which he meaningfully designates 'objectification of human mind'. This constituted the bedrock of his philosophy of education-in-operation. Zakir Hussain applies his view of culture/ cultural goods, while defining culture as 'the vital system of ideas of a period' and identified with the cultivation of mind.

Through Jamia Zakir spread a message that a true Muslim is a true patriot as well. It was wrong to think that the religion of the Muslims stood in the way of a speedy march towards freedom. During the time when the country was ablaze with misgivings and misunderstandings, Zakir Hussain tried to remove this cobweb of confusion. He argued that the true understanding of Islam by the Muslims would promote the national cause.[16] No one was in greater need to understand the spirit of Islam than the Muslims themselves, who have become the prime factor for making the Islam the most misunderstood religion of the whole world.[17]

To understand the religion of Islam in true sense, and to eradicate misunderstanding about it, Zakir concentrated on Islamic Studies in Jamia. He emphasized that far from being a stumbling block, Islam is a cementing force for national unity, harmony and solidarity. It is not a divisive force. Zakir wanted that Islam should be understood in its true spirit, and not by surface manifestations as reflected by its own votaries whose Islam had not touched the chin of their beard. Through Jamia Zakir wanted Islam to penetrate the souls of those who professed Islam, and impart to them its true value. He tried to excite in Muslims true patriotism, to make them love and know their land and serve their land. Zakir propagated that true patriotism is a true sentiment of good faith which regards all humanity as one family. The first lesson of the holy *Qur'an* says that the entire creation of the family is God.

A pehla sabaq tha kitab-e-Huda ka,

Ke makhlooh sari ha kunba Khuda ka.

Jamia, being a center of learning and an agent of social change, had its publication programs also. A literary magazine-*The Jamia* was brought out in 1923. The purpose was to educate the children, to stir their imagination regarding the treasure of knowledge that was hidden in own culture, and to tell people about the progress made by other nations in all fields. *Payam-e-Talim*, a periodical for children became a classic in children's literature. The greatest service Jamia did to the community was through *Maktab-e-Jamia*. It established an Urdu Academy with the distinguished scholar Abid Saheb as its secretary. The Academy, apart from producing course books, brought out numerous useful works which earned Jamia the credit of being a unique institution which linked education with the heritage of people.

A night school for Adult Education was started in the Jamia premises in 1926 which attracted a large number of students. Besides formal literacy: the adults were made aware of the social responsibility, civic consciousness value of good habits and general awareness of what one should do to lead a healthy, happy, peaceful and civilized life. The dedicated teachers of Jamia night school contributed greatly in the well-being of the adult students.

Primary or elementary education is the foundation on which decides the future of the child. Jamia's experiment in basic education was highly appreciated nationwide. Zakir Hussain's said, "our entire educational structure was weak only because of the neglect of the primary education. Our tertiary level is weak, because our elementary education is not sound, and the reason for that is traced to primary and preprimary education." Jamia's experiment to improve matters were so good that it attracted the attention of Gandhiji, who entrusted the job of preparing a report to Zakir Hussain in 1937, which came to be known as the Wardha Scheme of Basic Education.

Zakir Hussain had evinced keen interest in German Kreischensteiner's Activity school, whose two basic tools were "work ethics" and "cultural goods". He experimented on those principles in Jamia. Zakir Hussain improved his model by being benefitted by two more thinkers, Dewey and Gandhiji. The finest elements of German, American and Indian mind found a fertile field in the Islamic brain of Zakir Hussain, who produced a new idea of giving physical input the status of intellectual output. Zakir Hussain thought that any unapplied knowledge is shorn of meaning. Thus, the history of Jamia became a fascinating story of a great man, Dr, Zakir Hussain, who played a key role in revolutionizing the thought process of his community. He made Jamia a centre, dedicated to the preservation, promotion and dissemination of knowledge which should help to integrate the best of the past with the finest of the present to build a brilliant tomorrow.

Zakir Hussain insisted on the use of the mother tongue as the medium of instruction. English language had created a cleavage among Indians: a new elite class was emerging which was denying the common man the great advantages of modern science and knowledge. Primary and elementary education should be given in the mother-tongue of the child. He advocated a character-building education where determination, perseverance and sincerity of purpose would mold the character of the child, promote creative vision, logical reasoning and clarity of thought. A little sensitivity to feel for others would also be required. If reasoning is the quality of the mind, sensitivity is the quality of the heart. "Someone listens to all that to which others are deaf; he sees the colors which are invisible to the eyes of others; he smells that which others cannot; he tastes that which others cannot; he touches and feels that which others cannot. Painters, musicians, jewelers, blacksmiths, scientists in their laboratory, all these would put humanity in wonder by the intensive sensitivity."[18] Equanimity in temperament, sobriety and moderation would immensely help a man in building up his fine character.

Zakir Hussain laid emphasis on 'self-education' as a pre-requisite for personality development of the Muslim brethren. Self-education according to him meant elevation of the self to a higher level of behavior. It is an upward movement; giving up bad habits, evil desires, wrong ideas and putting oneself in the right direction. Sincerity of purpose and unity of thought would excite moral courage and those values of life which are essential for a refined culture. He said, "My message to you is this: have your character-building program me in your own hands. Develop all its elements by self-control and selfless service. Build good character, and making it an instrument of high and absolute values, elevate it to the level of faithful man *(banda-e-momin)* and struggling man *(mard-e-mujahid)*. It is a difficult job and it is a lifelong job, but you get life only by working for it. How can it be achieved by sitting idle? Life itself should be invested in it."

In short, with education as the base, he desired to change the total personality of man for the better. He believed in education as saints believed in God. He emphasized that Man's intellect was to be fully used to make his body function in an organic way so that each part yielded the best results it was meant for. Not merely the mind but also the heart, the hands, the eyes, the ears, the tongue, the nose, the feet, every organ of the body should work in unison so as to move fast towards that destiny whose ideal is perfect man. He said that Nations are made by thinkers, philosophers, workers, artists, saints and scientists and by the struggling masses of men and women. Zakir explained to them that it is the realm of knowledge, skill, wisdom and understanding which holds the key to national development and man's mind is the seat of his sublimity of thought. Zakir Hussain's aim was that man should gradually move towards his ideal which was the perfect man *(insan-e-kamil)*.

A Reformist: Igniting Minds

Zakir Hussain was not a religious. political or a social reformer like Marx Rousseau or Lenin, but an intellectual reformer whose main job was the change of man's mind. Zakir Hussain had a clear vision about what he wanted others to do. He wanted see a positive change not only in the child's mind, but also in all those who were directly or indirectly connected with the child – his parents, his associates, his environment, his playfield, his health, his body, his nutrition, his psychology, his habits, his thoughts, his feelings and so on and so he ventured a change in his own area of activity, namely education.

He adopted various techniques to reform the society. Absorption of assimilated ideas to an overflowing degree, experimentation through educational reforms, discourse or debates, for dissemination of his ideas all over the country. The educational addresses in Urdu, which have been published as *Talim-i-Khutbat* are a veritable treasury of his thoughts on how he wanted to reform a society from the grassroots level.

Zakir Hussain emphasized on the "cultural goods" and wanted them to act as a searchlight to illumine the dark patches of nation life. He propagated that 'culture of mind' could be equipped only by means of "cultural goods", which constitute the mental food. The cultural goods (material, equipment, science, literature, art, philosophy, technique, religion, customs moral and legal code, social forms, personality of the surrounding society) are 'objectification of the human mind with a significance, objective externalized with a meaning' Man's growing mind according to Zakir 'takes hold of these external goods and uses them for its development' for growing into the cultured mind'. Thus, it is the culture which supplies the mental food and acts as a spring- board in the process of evolution of culture. The cultural goods which society inherits from the past human endeavors is neither static and nor worthy of its preservance in its entirety. At times, it needs cleansing of 'decaying material'. It has to be continuously replenished, developed and furnished with 'fresher and richer acquisitions' by every generation who is simultaneously under the obligation of its preservance. Zakir Hussain applies his view of culture/ cultural goods, while defining culture as 'the vital system of ideas of a period' and identified with the cultivation of mind. This constituted the bedrock of his philosophy of education-in-operation.

Zakir Hussain considered Man as a Moral Being, an ethical identity, distinctly differed from a 'social animal'. 'Moral advance' is the 'justification and destiny of Man'. He possesses a 'cultivated mind' and in the ultimate analysis he is 'ultimate morally changed' 'cultural entity,'.[19] To him, Man is not a lonely individual, living exclusively for himself but also a 'fraction of the national arbiter' citizen 'charged with the duty and privilege of shaping society'. He helps his society to grow more and more in the direction of a moral society. He is a Universal Being and so understands the 'physical scheme of the world', 'fundamental themes of organic life', 'historical processes of the human species', structure and functioning of 'social life' and the 'plan of the universe'. The Man of Zakir Hussain's vision, is essentially a man of the universe, a global being who is placed at the 'height of times' and is familiar with the 'vital ideas' of the universe'.

To preach the Muslim brethren, that 'work is worship' the terms Zakir used were *riyazot* and *ibadot*. He built up an entirely new philosophy wherein he perceived the inner relationship among man's mind, culture and destiny. To him mind was the source of intellect that linked the individual to society; society was the generating force that produced a culture; 'culture' is a bundle of values the totality of which would give new meaning to man's life; and this new meaning is man's destiny which is the purpose of life.

Thus, Zakir Hussain's social philosophy of life centered around man's intellect which he believed found expression in the wider society. Society needs values and education to build up institutions whose vitality would be known by the nature of its high moral values. Zakir Hussain said:

"For the individual who desires to develop within himself qualities of perfection, it is inevitable for him to develop the same qualities in the society as well. A philosopher of life like Plato had to find all the finer elements of an individual only in the entire structure and development of the society."[20]

Composite Culture

Indian culture was woven into the texture of Zakir Hussain's thought and as a true embodiment of humane-Indianity, represented the great composite culture of India. He believed that 'Providence has destined India to be the laboratory in which the greatest experiment of cultural synthesis will be undertaken and successfully completed'. It seemed to him that 'India's mission in world history' was to evolve 'a distinct type of humanity, combining and harmonizing in itself the virtues of diverse types which history has produced, all blended together to form a new type that might evolve a characteristic and, perhaps, more satisfactory pattern of civilized existence than those in vogue.' He was well aware of the fact also that the composite culture has yet to cover a long distance for reaching its destination due to certain inherent problems of Indian society.

Zakir Hussain's wisdom highlighted the beauty hidden in diversities prevailing in India. He said that 'there are a thousand strands of culture that make of the cultural life of our people a variegated pattern of exquisite beauty and richness'. Speaking in the words of Rabindranath Tagore, he wished to bring to life the "streams of ideals that originated in the summit of our past, flowing underground in the depth of India's soul, the ideals of simplicity of life, clarity of spiritual vision, purity of heart, harmony with the universe and consciousness of the infinite personality in all creation" and the urge to bring these 'to the surface for our daily use and purification'. He thought that such a grand dream could perhaps be materialize 'by implanting in every Indian breast the love and esteem' of their past achievements, from time immemorial down to our own day.

Zakir Hussain's culture stretched from 'home' to cover geo-political boundaries of India, its past and the present. He viewed 'home' as the main unit of country. So, when the 'home expands' it becomes the country. It grows to be India. And, then, it is the expanded homes that 'becomes the Himalayas and the Vindyachal, the Ganges...the Cauvery; it becomes Badrinath and Rameshwaram...it grows to be Rama and Laxman, the Buddha and Shankracharya, Moinudhin Ajmeri and Jalaluddin Akbar; it becomes Nanak and Kabir, Surdas, Tukaram and Mirabai; it becomes Kalidas and Tulsidas; it becomes Mir, Ghalib and Anis; it becomes Vallathol and Tagore; it becomes

Gandhi and Abul Kalam, Vinoba and Nehru. This is what he treated culture, his culture, Indian culture housed in the home of 'the mother's affectionate lap' Cultural heritage is the collective inheritance of all.[21]

This inheritance comprised both the old and the new, and contributions of different cultural groups. He asserted that 'in the rich treasure of our history nothing is good or bad because it is new or old...Hindu, Muslim, Sikh, Christian or Parsi'. He suggested that 'genuine' heritage as different from 'spurious' and the one 'that helps' as different from 'that hampers' should be distinguished and accordingly adopted. He advised with a caution that 'nothing is rejected or accepted because of the label some people seek to put on it'.[22]

He believed that Indians have inherited from the precious past is humanism, love, devotion, reason and creative of things beautiful. Pursuit of truth by the sages of the past has been the hallmark of his country. Philosophy has been its soul; religion has been its symbol; tolerance has been its technique; *bhakti* (devotion) has been its spirit; God has been the center of its thought; beauty has been the object of worship; good traditions have been its assets; all branches of knowledge, whether literature, drama, medicine or mathematics, have been the source of its joy; and humanism has been its pride. Modern science and technology, Zakir Hussain regretted, had pushed all our cultural goods to the background. As a revivalist he strived to give a new life to all these values.

Zakir Hussain's speech at Kashi Vidhyapeeth on August 14, 1935, was a volume on national consciousness when he touched the vital issues of national reconstruction in his address. On this occasion he spoke on behalf of the Muslims. He pleaded fervently not to wound the Muslim psyche by cutting its umbilical cord of culture. He went to the extent of saying that it was an issue on which no compromise could be made. The Muslims should have the right to fashion their education in the framework of their culture. He became a crusader to fight for the just demands of the Muslims that if they were to be denied the privilege to protecting their culture and educating their children in the light of that culture, all would not be well with the nation. That was a warning he sounded in 1935, but nobody listened to him. He made it very clear that the Muslims considered their religious traditions, their history and their cultural heritage as precious not only to themselves but also to the country.[23]

Zakir Husain's conviction was that because the Muslims love this land, they would not be a party to any situation which involved their cultural extinction. He wanted them to be good Indians and good Muslims, and there was no contradiction between the two. "No Muslim would be ashamed of his being an Indian, and no Indian would point a finger at him for being a Muslim". He wanted Islam not to be an excuse for not being an Indian, but to be an agent to impose a sense of duty on them. Islam should not be a source of defeat but a point of pride. He said that once the Muslims join the mainstream of national life, the question of their separate existence and other disputes would also disappear. A reformer fights for a righteous cause. This is what Zakir Hussain did to advocate the Muslim's rights for cultural identity.

Addressing the graduates of Kashi Vidyapeeth, he said:

"The country you are going into is a country of great misfortune. It is a country of slaves, a country of ignorant people, a country of hard heartedness, a country of cruel customs, a country of indifferent priests, a country of hatred between brother and brother, a country of sickness, a country of laziness, a country of poverty and helplessness, a country of hunger and sufferings, in short, a country of great misfortune. But what should be done. It is your and our country. We have to live in it, and die in it. Therefore, it is a country which would test your courage, your strength and your love."[24]

Afraid of a few weaknesses which society suffered from, Zakir Hussain put in all his energies to eradicate them. The weaknesses listed by him were: social, political, economic, psychological and cultural. Hunger, poverty, injustice, ignorance, cruelty, laziness, helplessness, hopelessness was all there. He said that these weaknesses implied a few more such as jealousy, fanaticism, short-sightedness, selfishness, snobbishness, acquisitiveness, haughtiness and arrogance, which had resulted in the monopoly of privileges by a few, in the feeling of self-centeredness in many, and in disregard of human values by all. He believed that a reformer should not merely sing a song of a hopeless situation, but would think of a remedy too. And in a true revivalist spirit he suggested what should be done. He said,

"Our country does not need warm blood oozing out from our necks, but it needs the sweat of our brow that would flow twelve months in a year. The need is great for work, sincere work, and serious work. Our future would be made or marred by the broken hut of the farmer, by the dark roof of the artisan, and by the straw-covered school of a village. It is possible to settle the disputes of a day or two in political strife in conferences and congresses, but those places which I have indicated have been for centuries the centers of our destiny. Work in these areas requires patience and perseverance. It tries you much and it is thankless too; it does not yield quick result; but yes, if someone holds on for long, it would give him sweet fruit."[25]

Zakir Hussain suggested the remedy – industry and integrity. He said Man is a miracle of genius because he is a sincere worker. Duty at all times and in all circumstances is the highest form of human culture. He said, the sweat of a person would decide his destiny. He further said, fate rotates at the three converging points of a triangle: the labour of a poor peasant in a farm, the skill of a neglected artisan at his workshop, and the intellect of an ignored teacher in a rustic school. The fitter, the farmer and the teacher are the three sides of triangle, the three angles who would feed mind, body and soul of a person. They are also, head, heart and hands. Take care of them and all will be well. Thus, as a reformer Zakir Hussain instilled a new life in Muslim community.

For strengthening the composite culture in India Zakir Hussain pinned great hopes on the youth. He shared with them, the currents of his thoughts, which he had picked up from the wisdom of India, from the *Sufi* saints, from the *'bhakti'* teachers and from the Western philosophers. He fermented them all in the churning process of his reflective thought to result in the system of his social philosophy, whose implementation effort was his great reform.

Zakir Hussain wanted that the Indian Muslims should draw their spiritual inspiration from their religion of Islam. The elements of Indian and world culture should be integrated into it in such a manner as to result in a common human culture. Its basic elements would be sincere love of the land, a healthy nationalism, and the unshaken faith that all true religions teach only selfless service, unbounded love, national integration and world peace. For Zakir Hussain knowledge is not merely for earning one's daily bread but knowledge is for building life itself. Knowledge, thus, embracing within its fold all aspects of human culture, whether religion, wisdom, philosophy or art will make an excellent model for all humanity.

Zakir believed that Science and Technology are the indicators of progress and change in any nation. He desired that India should master science and technologies because to solve its problems. He cautioned the youth in the Students Federation Conference on September 27, 1941, at Agra by explaining to them the meaning of 'change' and 'progress'

"During the last few years, we have been constantly told that we are living in a rapidly changing world, and shall be cast away as wreckage if we do not change along with it". In this context he pleaded to be alive to "to our problems and our needs, and we must meet the new situations not with the mental equipment that was old and rusty fifty years ago, but with the new weapons progress has forged". Zakir Hussain does not spurn studying other countries and their solution to resolving this urgent problem. But he cautioned that while America, Russia, or England may serve as good models for furnishing certain answers, "But these will be details that must fit into a scheme of things in our life that are "permanent and immutable," before we join the mad race for complete and abrupt changes. He said that "Change itself may have little meaning and no substance." He explained that Change does not mean a complete break away from the past and opting for everything new. "Such change", he said, "deprives life of all stability, undermines national character and confuses minds".[26]

Zakir Hussain desired that the spirit of science should be the pursuit of truth, zest for enquiry, thirst for knowledge, and search for excellence. Science should aim at the conquest of nature for the benefit of man, and not to find faults with faith. Zakir believed that Man cannot live without faith in some Supreme and Sublime one, some Creator and Protector. Inspite of all the advancement of science, man has not been able to unravel the mystery of life and death, creativity and destruction. With all the wonders at his command, he cannot make a single blade of grass, a single drop of water or a single grain of sand, unless he finds them gifted to him in nature by God. Even a scientist of the order of James Jeans says, "God is a mathematical necessity". and accepted the role of God. Science as such has not disproved the existence of a Conscious Creative Will behind the visible manifestation of this whole physical universe. Life is a mixture of both physical and spiritual elements. Zakir Hussain had faith in this line of argument. To this he was a spiritualist, but he had tempered his spiritualism with a scientific outlook wherein superstition was excluded.[27]

Nationalism: Zakir's dream of United India

Zakir Husain was a great nationalist Muslim. He was among those enlightened leaders whose nationalism transcended the accepted norms in order to know the land, to serve the land, and to love the land. His nationalism was an aspect of his intellectualism which went beyond the realms of time, space and boundaries to touch humanity as a whole. It was based on his rationalism and humanism with an ideal to love all mankind. It was an off-shoot of his educational and social philosophy which first aimed at unifying all our people into one homogenous whole, and then making them an integrated part of a bigger family of the entire humanity. His nationalism eschews negative aspects as intolerance, bigotry shortsightedness, self-centeredness, despotism and tyranny.

Zakir Husain's nationalism was the outcome of his intellectual exercise. He knew that the Muslim leadership, under the guise of protecting Muslim interests, was not progressive enough to think of what was in the larger interest of the community in the long term. He believed in the Congress ideology that stood for democracy, nationalism, secularism, which were all modern concepts with potentially to serve the interests of all communities. Congress did not deny the Muslims their due, but was not willing to give more than their due also. He favoured Congress which was anxious to remove the colonials first and then sort out the internal problems of mutual adjustments. Zakir liked the national character Congress, which desired to evolve a secular, democratic and united India. It was Zakir Husain's strong conviction that the colonials should be first eliminated from our land. This idea had agitated his mind ever since he was a student of Aligarh in the second decade of this century. That was the reason why he wrote a very thought provoking easy early in 1920, "Eternity or Toy" in which he was critical of the political thinking associated with Aligarh movement.

From 1884 to 1947, nationalism entered so deep into the heart, mind and conscience of the people that the whole history of this period is nothing but the struggle for freedom, being excited by some leaders of world stature, who were all dedicated to the national movement. Once nationalism was ignited in the soul of India it became a wild flame consuming towns and villages, the rich and poor, the youth and old, men and women, the enlightened and ignorant, even the peasants and the common man. Irrespective of caste, creed or class, region, language or culture, all were charged with a new current which excited the people to suffer and sacrifice for the freedom of the land, and to sing the songs of national fervor. But divide and rule was an age-old accepted policy of the British to blunt the blow of nationalism on them. They were superb in this game of chess, and the pawn they played was the Muslim community. Zakir Husain a staunch nationalist and a committed secularist, chose a new path, under which his intellectualism, conviction and patriotism forced him to resist the torrents of Muslim thought which swept the flow into a different direction from the mainstream.

The debate was whether should Muslims join the mainstream of Indian nationalism and fight with others to remove the colonialists first, and then sort out their problems with majority community, or stand aloof for a while from the main political struggle, in order to reconstruct and improve their economic, social, cultural and educational situation and bring it on par with that of the majority? The whole of the nineteenth century witnessed two powerful streams of Indian renaissance, one of social reforms, new awakening, and cultural rejuvenation, both among Hindus and Muslims, and the other of nationalism, which was the product of the first. When the Brahmo Samaj, Arya Samaj, Prarthana Samaj and a host of other cultural movements quickened a new consciousness among the Hindus, the Muslims, though late by half a century, did not lag behind. Their recovery centered around on the Aligarh movement under Sir Sayyid Ahmad Khan, whose two powerful weapons to beat Muslim backwardness was western education and compromise with the British. The first was not a dangerous weapon. In fact, it was a healing balm, the only safety valve to survive as a dignified segment of a society. But the second was a double-edged sword. The concept of compromise with the British was the original sin, the temptation of touching the forbidden fruit in the Garden of Eden, whose retribution the nation had to suffer in 1947. India was never again the same after those tiny seeds of separatism were sown in the minds of the Muslims masses, and thereafter, Zakir Husain despite insurmountable obstacles on the way never compromised his principle of nationalism.

The study the Muslim psychology in the scenario of the late 19th century and thereafter until 1947 reflected that the Muslims had a strong sense of history having a positive and a negative factor. They had not forgotten their past in India wherein they had contributed much in the political sphere. They had brought to India their rich experience of how to build large states, how to expand them and how to consolidate them. They had given the concept of a strong, centralized and unified Government. They had injected the idea of a new social order which had reduced the rigidity of the caste system, and had excited interest in an egalitarian society in the wake of the *bhakti* movement. In the economic domain, their presence had led to the growth of urban life, to the promotion of art, craft and industry, and to the linkage of India with the outside world for trade, commerce and business. They had made significant contributions to art, architecture, language, literature, morals, manners, religion, philosophy and such other aspects which go by the name of "cultural goods". Palaces, tombs, mosques, gardens, forts, foundations, roads, bridges, and a host of other creative and constructive things came under that label of "cultural goods". The Muslims felt proud of having made these contributions.

The Muslims knew that all this had happened because of one powerful factor: their political hegemony in the land. They clung fast to the memory of the past. That was their comfort, solace and joy. But its negative element soon depressed them. Would they be able to repeat their performance in future? Was it all a dream they had in their mind? What is the reality of the situation? It is good to know they were once rulers, but what are they now? History began to sting their conscience. They became lifeless. Utter dejection seized them. Future prospects made them more miserable. In this confusion, they lost their balance. They judged things from a lower logic, not a higher one. They felt that for so long they had been British subjects; tomorrow they would become Hindu subjects. They did not think that freedom meant freedom for all: that they would also be partners in the concern; they would also be sharers of the joys and sorrows; they would be members of the same family.

This higher logic was not taught to them; on the other hand, their leaders misguided them. They glorified the past with the hope that they could revive the past. They forgot the fact that history is more often linear than cyclical. It does not repeat itself exactly in the way people expect. It moves along the line making progress. Therefore, the situations they have left behind in the journey would not be seen again unless they returned from where they started, which was not possible. It was only Zakir Husain, Maulana Azad, Ajmal Khan, Ansari and Maulana Muhammad Ali and such other nationalists who knew what was in the best interest of the Muslims. But they were in a minority in the minority community of the Muslims, whose majority was fired by a different concept. The Muslim masses were excited by wrong psychology. They were not enlightened with the right principles of nationalism. They were not reminded of the Montesquieu dictum, "Don't cut a tree to get at the fruit". They were not told Sartre's saying that sacrifice is the seed of a new life. They were not taught the Sufi teachings that you have to kill yourself in order to live in God. For short-term benefits, they sacrificed the future.

On the intellectual plane, Islam was opposed to nationalism because the concept simply does not exist in Islam. What exists is merely the unity of God and unity of man. Unity of God is the faith part of the religion, but the unity of man is more relevant for political life. Islam had claimed that all people of the races and of all countries, whether Semetic, Hamitic, Negro, Iberian, Caucasian, Iranian, Turanian or Indian, were members of the same family, and should be treated as such on the basis of the faith. Islam does not insist on the habitation of a people within defined geographical limits to recognize them as shares of common political life. Therefore, the Islamic concept of the unity of man created problems for Indian Muslims to come under the umbrella of nationalism. On the other hand, like history and psychology, this factor from the cultural ethos relieved the Muslims from the obligations of national limits. Interested groups made much of this liberty to release Muslims from any control. Poets sang the song that a Muslim was neither an Indian, nor a Turk, nor an Afghan, nor a Persian, nor an Arab; he was just a man in the mighty ocean of humanity. However high this human ideal of weaving the whole of humanity into a common pool of brotherhood might be, in the reality of the day, it would not work. The whole world had gone mad after nationalism, and a single swallow like Allama Iqbal singing a song of common humanity would not carry the conviction too far. But to the Muslims, this escapist tendency from the required rights and obligations of nationalism was a God-sent opportunity to relax in a make-shift world of their own, while others were taking rapid strides on the path of progress. Zakir Husain realized this serious flaw in Muslim thinking, and he attempted to rectify it to the best of his ability. His difficulty was that he was not a political activist. He was only a thinker, a teacher and a philosopher and these areas did not possess sanctions to impose his will or ideas on others.

The politics of the time had also much to do in alienating the Muslims. The Muslims got a feeling that the Hindus wanted to do away with everything that remained of the Muslim rule. Small issues had become pin-pricks. High caste Hindus never regarded Muslims as equals in the social set-up; they were called *mlechas* or impure, and the *Shuddhi* and *Sanghatan* movement to convert Muslim into Hindus was started. The Muslims answered them soon by their *Tabligh* and *Tanzim* movement. A few enthusiasts became over-zealous about the Hindu Rashtra. Raj Narain Bose said in 1872, "I see in my mind the noble and puissant Hindu nation rousing her after sleep and rushing headlong towards progress with divine prowess. I see this rejuvenated nation illumining the world by her knowledge, spirituality and culture and the glory of the Hindu nation again spreading over the whole world"[28]

Bankim Chandra Chatterjee depicted the Muslim in such dark colors in his novel *Anandmath* which the Muslims could hardly resist to retaliate. Both Hindus and Muslims were trading their polemics so vehemently at each other that the atmosphere became uncongenial for nationalism to grow in India.

Zakir Husain's nationalism envisaged that the country should gain not only political freedom but usher in a cultural renaissance, which should transform our people into really enlightened souls. Such a renaissance would involve social reforms, a rational outlook, refined manners and morals, liberal education, dignity of labour, development of personality, and appreciation of our cultural heritage. This cultural renaissance should be fortified with moral and spiritual strength to liberate the land and set up democratic institutions. But Muslims were steeped in traditionalism, and nationalism was a concept of modernity. Ever since the time of Sir Sayyid, a serious debate had been going on between 'modernity' and 'traditionalism'. These were two concepts that affected the basic life of man in modern times. Even in such an area as religion, faith and belief, they played a vital role. Every religion, in every age, has its modernists and traditionalists. Modernism relates to rationalism and scientific method. It discards dogmas and supernaturalism. It filters all things on the screen of truth. Modernity insists on the fully integrated human personality. It makes a distinction between intrinsic and instrumental values. It promotes ceaseless creativity of values rather than conservation of values. Zakir Husain's nationalism leaned more on this kind of modernity in his thought process.

Zakir Husain's nationalism was not a rejection of old values but creation of new values. The creation of new values needed an apparatus, and nationalism would fulfil that need. For the effective preservation and promotion of those new values, some agency was required. Secularism was the answer to the requirement. These new values must have a purpose to serve. Humanism was the purpose for which these values were to be created. Thus, Zakir Husain would link nationalism, secularism and humanism in one chain as different units of his new value system. Eternal and intelligent vigilance was required to draw the best out of these new values, which were a mixture of modernism and traditionalism.

Zakir Husain wanted to help the Muslims find a place in Indian nationalism. Many did not respond to his call. But he was very clear that an integrated personality was required to appreciate nationalism. He was sure that the angularities and imbalances which were quite a few in the Muslim society could be corrected only by enlightened nationalism which was emerging in India, but the Muslims were turning their back on it. The push of science and the pull of reason, and the love of the land were arousing a new spirit in all, but the Muslims were living in the midst of pulsating events in an illusion of their own.

Zakir Hussain did his best to open the eyes of the Muslims but he could not give them new eyes to see the light which was so apparent to him. He warned the Muslims again and again that their survival depended only on fulfilling their obligations to the nation that the Muslims possessed the same rights and privileges as other and they should not demand more, that the community had to discharge the same duties and responsibilities, or else it would have no right to live in India.[29]

Zakir Hussain's nationalism is reflected in his educational thought also. A Muslim would not be a good Muslim unless he was a true Indian. Being a true Indian he would not cease to be a good Muslim. Islam does not stand in the way of its followers becoming good Indians. Whatever a good Indian has to do is permissible under Islam. A good Muslim can accept all the principles and perform all the functions that were necessary for national development. The social ethics of Islam and the guiding principles of nationalism were identical. Therefore, there was no conflict between Islam and nationalism, according to Zakir Husain. Both were concepts of service, loyalty, faith and devotion to a higher cause of human solidarity.

Thus, he spared no labor, time and energy in teaching Muslims the elementary principle of nationalism. He asked, "Is Islamic polity just this policy of playing safe and begging for what one wants? Does Islam enjoin this indifference towards the social environment and social aims for the pursuit of personal interest which we have cultivated through our efforts to educate? No, a thousand times No!"[30]

Zakir Husain's nationalism had to answer one more serious problem of the Muslims – their economic backwardness. Zakir was worried about Muslim poverty which was increasing in proportion to their population. They were multiplying very fast. Their number of 50 million in 1850 had become 100 million in 1940. Poverty, ignorance, superstition and ill-health had added to their misery. All the reforms of the British until the end of the

19th century had helped only the Hindus. Sartre's law of nihilism came into force here. An ignorant man in such a situation becomes more depressed. He curses himself, suffers the sorrow and blames God for the misery. But an enlightened man would think of a remedy, would act fast to come out of the darkness, and would help himself and help others from drowning. This required enlightenment Dr. Zakir Hussain said could be achieved only through education and therefore he pleaded that education plays a vital role. Education would give knowledge and wisdom to run from darkness to light, and seek shelter under good deeds. In a crisis, one has to think fast and act fast.

Zakir Hussain's linked nationalism with some 'ideal'. What should be the ideas and ideals of the Muslims, he explained in his address at the All-India Muslim Educational Conference at Aligarh in March 1937. He said:

"Our way of the life must be changed. The old way is bad, because it differs from the ways of a highly favored, dominant nation. Since it is not evident why (The Muslim) community should possess political power in order to further individual ambition for the advancement and elevation of status, politics should be avoided....Religion, for centuries the focal point of the community's life, could not be given up; it had to be maintained, but in such a way as not to come into conflict with the worldly aims, or become an obstacle in the path of progress."[31] Not the religion as such, but the religion as practiced by Muslims needed to be changed.

One issue on which Zakir Husain's nationalism was not in tune with the nationalism of the majority community, and that was Urdu. Zakir Husain felt unhappy that the issue of language which should have been a unifying force was needlessly made a divisive one. Urdu was attributed as a language of the Muslims, whereas, it was not. It was understood, spoken and used by both Hindus and Muslims. Over the years, a common culture of the upper strata of Hindus and Muslims had acquired a Muslim bias.

Urdu was the result. It had its base in Persian in which both Hindus and Muslims had gained great proficiency. Persian was for a long time the court language, and Hindus had learnt it both as source of employment and knowledge, just as they learnt English later. Takchand Bahar was a great Persian lexicographer. Many Hindus had enriched Urdu. Daya Shankar Nassem, Prem Chand, Firaq Gorakhpuri, Ram Babu Saksena, Daya Narayan Nigam, Trilok Chand Mahroom, , Krishan Chander were eminent Urdu writers or poets. As earlier stated in my study an agitation was started early as 1867, to remove Urdu from Government offices and law courts. It was this agitation that made Sir Sayyid advocate that Muslims be firm in protecting their culture heritage. Nobody listened to Gandhiji's suggestion to adopt Hindustani in both *Nagari* and Persian scripts. That would have solved the problem. The Muslims were keen to protect Urdu because it was their cultural link with the past. All their fine literature was either in Urdu or in the script of Urdu. Persian had been for a long time not only a source of knowledge in India but also over a great part of the Islamic world. Zakir Husain was very keen that Urdu should be preserved, protected and promoted because that was the key to the cultural goods of the Muslims in India, and that was the test whether Muslim identity would be respected in free India. Speaking on the status of Urdu in the future setup in India at Kashi Vidyapith in 1935, he observed

"Will a national system of education give or not give to the Muslims the right to make their cultural life a means to their education? You know how crucial this question is in our national life. It is possible that some well-intentioned but extremist persons conceive of an Indian Nationalism in which giving the Muslims this right would be a source of weakness and an obstacle to progress. But if experienced educators with goodwill create a system of education for the country, I am sure they will gladly accede to the desire of the Muslims to have their education on their culture, as this is what sound educational principle and political policy require us to do. You will forgive me if I state frankly before this august assembly that while selfish personal ambition, narrow- mindedness and inability to form a correct picture of the country are reasons that keep on drawing the Muslims away from the idea of a common Indian nationhood, there is also the deep suspicion that under a national government there would be fear of cultural identity of the Muslims being obliterated. This is a price Muslims are not willing to pay under any circumstances. I, not only as a Muslim but also as a sincere Indian, am happy that they are not willing to pay this price."[32]

Zakir Hussain is very explicit here. Here he defends Urdu without taking the name of Urdu. He uses his professional vocabulary of protecting the cultural goods, but he is very emphatic that the Muslims would not compromise on this principle.

Thus, to sum up, Zakir Husain's nationalism can be viewed in the context of his intellectualism. He was not an activist in the political arena to translate his thoughts into deeds. He was not a theorist of any particular brand to inject into nationalism any specific line of action, like extremism or modernism, revolution or peaceful methods, democracy or theocracy, conservatism or liberalism. His nationalism had a value system of its own. Its basis was rationalism. Its spirit was humanism. Its objective was social good. Its operational method was educative. Its ideal was enlightenment. Its source of strength was unity, harmony, solidarity and cooperation. Its weakness was intolerance, bigotry, narrow-mindedness and self-centeredness. Its allies were liberalism, secularism, socialism, universalism and democracy; and its enemies were tyranny, despotism, dictatorship, revivalism and fundamentalism.

Nationalism was the product of his mature thought. The main aim of Zakir Hussain's nationalism is protection of human civilization. He had pitched his ideal as high as humanity, and not "this nation or that nation". He taught that nationalism was too sacred a sentiment to be taken lightly. It should be a cementing bond to unite all the people together. It should be a healing balm to remove any malady. It should be a unifying and pacifying force to regard everyone in the land as a member of the same family. Every nation has to add something to the world culture. Zakir Hussain felt that India too had the potential to contribute something substantial and great. Europe had given nationalism. France had gifted socialism; Britain had added Democracy and constitutionalism. Russia had experimented with capitalism; America was proud of its capitalism and free enterprise. Zakir Hussain was keen like Pandit Nehru, that India should contribute Secularism, Humanism, Universalism and an exquisite model of composite culture. India had a culture that was five thousand years old with a breath-taking record of several luminaries on the horizon of humanity.

Being a rationalist, and educationist, a thinker and a philosopher, he had reflected deeply on this concept, had analyzed all its aspects, and had formed his own views after careful consideration of all its implications. Therefore, his was not a blind acceptance of an idea. Nationalism formed an important principle of his philosophy. He thought that loyalty to the land was the first duty an individual owed to himself as the citizen of the country he belonged to. He proudly declared, "It is out of the earth of this country that we were fashioned and it is to this earth that we shall return".[33]

Zakir Hussain served the nation until he breathed his last. He was the epitome of T.S. Eliot's saying, action is suffering and suffering is action. Nothing great could ever be achieved without suffering. Whether in the case of individuals or nations, self sacrifice and unselfishness are the only unfailing guides to freedom and happiness. He built a philosophy of humanism which fixed man's destiny as universal brotherhood. He regarded education as the key for the welfare and the progress of man and an agent of social change whereby the youth should be engaged in the quest of new humanism and in the pursuit of creative integration of culture where truth and beauty, virtue and honour, justice and courage which would act as precious gems in the crown of man's character.

Zakir Hussain was a nationalist Muslim. He was a child of the national movement which took a romantic turn in the twenties of the Twentieth century. He was not active in politics, but he attempted in his own way to wean the Muslims away from the Muslim League, and to make them join the mainstream of national life. Zakir Hussain's patriotic zeal and nationalist outlook compelled him to work for Hindu-Muslim unity and for national integration. He stood for all his life for a united India, where Hindus and Muslims would live like brother and members of the same family. He was a humanist with a passionate love for mankind, with an intense desire to serve fellow beings, and with an unlimited compassion for all loving creatures. He was an optimist and dreamer of a happy world who like a mother, would not lose hope for a better tomorrow. He came very close to the Aristotlelian concept of a perfect man. (*Insan-e-Kamil*)

Soft while speaking but hard while striving,

Whether battlefield or fellowship, noble of soul and pure of mind

A speaker and writer of outstanding eminence, Zakir Hussain had a distinctive style of his own and an effortless artistry which remained not only unsurpassed but almost unmatched. Apart from address and stray essays, some of which have been published under the title 'Dynamic University' and Patel Memorial lectures on 'Educational Reconstruction in India'. Most of his published writings are in Urdu, which include his translations of Plato's 'Republic' and 'List's

National Economics' and some delightful books for children under an unsuspended *nom-de-plume*.

References

1. Mujeeb, Mohammad, *Dr.Zakir Hussain: A Biography*, New Delhi: National Book Trust, 1972, p.8.

2. B. Sheikh Ali, p. 51.

3. Singh, K.R.P., *Educating India's Masses, A study of Dr. Zakir Hussain's Educational Thought*, Delhi: Unique Publications, 1987, p.29.

4. Sayyid, Abid Hussain, "Zaki, Sahab", *Nuquoosh: Shakhsiat Number, 1955*, p. 269.

5. Mujeeb, Mohammad, *Dr.Zakir Hussain : A Biography*, New Delhi : National Book Trust, 1972, p. 36.

6. *Aligarh Institute Gazattee*, 30 December, 1882, p. 1430.

7. Rao, P. Rajeshwar, *The Great Indian Patriots*, Vol II, New Delhi : Mittal Publications, 1991, p. 101.

8. Hasan, *Mushirul* and Jalil, Rakshanda, *Partners in Freedom*: *Jamia Millia Islamia, Delhi*: *Niyogi Books, 2006*, p. 92   9. http://www.eurasiareview.com/27122011-jamia-milia-islamia-its-history-and-current-trends-analysis/21.1.2015

10. Noorani, A.G., *President Zakir Husain: a Quest for Excellence*, Bombay: Papular Prakashan, 1967, Pp 28-32.

11. *Mudholi, Abdul Ghaffar, Jamia ki Kahani*, New *Delhi*: Maktaba Jamia, *1965*, pp. 182-183.

12. ibid., 268-269.

13. Mujeeb, Mohammad, *Dr.Zakir Hussain : A Biography*, New Delhi : National Book Trust, 1972, pp. 36-37.

14. *Mudholi, Abdul Ghaffar, Jamia ki Kahani*, New *Delhi*: Maktaba Jamia, *1965*, pp. 360-361.

15. Diwakar, R.R, *Bravery and Insight as quoted in the Book* ed. Dr. Zakir Hussain As I Saw Him, p.33.

16. Ali, B. Sheikh, *Zakir Hussain: Life and Times*, New Delhi: Vikas Publishing House Pvt. Ltd., 1991, p. 149.

17. Farooqi, Zia-ul-Hasan, *Shaheed-e-Justuju*, New *Delhi* : Maktaba Jamia, *1988,* p.294.

18 Hussain, Zakir, *Talimi Khutbat,* New Delhi: Maktaba Jamia Ltd., 1982, p. 2

19. Ali, B. Sheikh, *Zakir Hussain: Life and Times*, New Delhi : Vikas Publishing House Pvt. Ltd., 1991, p. 151.

20. Hussain, Zakir, *Talimi Khutbat,* New Delhi: Maktaba Jamia Ltd., 1982, pp.139-40

21. Khan, Dr. Shaukat Ullah, *Culture- the Gravitational Force of Dr. Zakir Hussain's Thought,* in, Ruhela, S.P. and Dr. Ikram Ahmad (ed.) *Uniqueness of Dr. Zakir Hussain and His Contributions* New Delhi: Regency Publications, 1997. pp. 22-23

22. *ibid.,* p.25

23. *ibid.,* p.26

24. Hussai.n, Zakir, *Talimi Khutbat,* New Delhi: Maktaba Jamia Ltd., 1982, pp. 20-21.

25. *ibid.,* p. 24.

26. Farooqi, Zia-ul-Hasan, *Shaheed-e-Justuju*, New *Delhi*: Maktaba Jamia, *1988*, p. 238.

27. Pal, Rajendra Singh, *Zakir Hussain: Dynamics of Indigenous Education,* New Delhi : Sterling Publishers Pvt Ltd., 1968, pp. 82-83

28. Ali, B. Sheikh, *Zakir Hussain: Life and Times*, New Delhi : Vikas Publishing House Pvt. Ltd., 1991, p. 426.

29. Majumdar, R.C., *History of the Freedom Movement in India*, Vol. 1, Calcutta: Firma K.L. Mukhopadhyay, 1971, p. 333.

30. Mujeeb, Mohammad, *Dr.Zakir Hussain*: A Biography, New Delhi : National Book Trust, 1972, pp. 83-84

31. Mujeeb, Mohammad, *Dr. Zakir Hussain* : A Biography, New Delhi: National Book Trust, 1972, pp. 82-83

32. Zakir, Hussain, *Talimi Khutbat*, pp. 42-45

33. as quoted in Ali, B. Sheikh, *Zakir Hussain: Life and Times*, New Delhi: Vikas Publishing House Pvt. Ltd., p. 378.

THE PROPONENT OF NATIONALISM:
MAULANA ABUL KALAM AZAD

"If today an angel descending from the clouds were to declare from the top of the Qutub Minar in Delhi, 'Discard Hind-Muslim unity and within twenty-four hours swaraj is yours,' I would prefer to sacrifice swaraj rather than Hindu-Muslim unity, for delay in the attainment of swaraj will be a loss to India alone, but if our unity disappears it will be a loss to the whole world of humanity."

Maulana Azad stands among the great men of India. Perhaps few could excel him in the fertility and brilliance of his mind, in the force of his powerful writings and speeches, in the depth of his Islamic scholarship, in the intensity of his national fervour, and in his sharp perception of men and affairs. Maulana Azad was a brilliant debater, as indicated by his name, Abul Kalam, which literally means "lord of dialogue". He adopted the pen name 'Azad' as a mark of his mental emancipation from a narrow view of religion and life.

An outstanding Muslim intellectual of modern India, the range of his mind was encyclopedic and was a unique synthesis of the East and West. He tried to reconcile religion with reason without injuring either. In Azad we can see the confluence of tradition and the forces of change. He served as a bridge between the new and the old worlds of thought.

To understand the Muslim revivalism of 19th century, it is essential to examine Azad's thoughts. Azad was a complex personality. Taciturn and reserved, he was strictly a private person who would not easily reveal his thoughts. Three passions dominated Azad's life: the freedom of India from British rule, the promotion of Hindu-Muslim unity and passion for learning. As an intellectual nothing mattered to him more than the life of mind which he cultivated unobtrusively like Voltaire's *Candide*. He threw boundless energy and passionate zeal into the cause of India's freedom from British rule but he was pushed into this arena by the sheer pressure of circumstances. Both the intellectual and political spheres of his activity impinged on each other and produced a sharp conflict in his life. He made a desperate effort to reconcile these two diverse trends in his personality.

Influences and Rationalism

Abul Kalam Ghulam Muhiyuddin Ahmad was born at Mecca in 1888 in a most conservative family of a famous Muslim *Pir* who had lacs of followers. Azad had an extraordinary family background. He had roots in Mughal India. His forefathers had migrated to India from Heart in Babur's time, and settled first in Agra and moved later to Delhi.[1] Azad's father was a reputed Arabic Scholar, known throughout the Islamic world, a religious divine and a *sufi* of the Quadriya school. Khairuddin stayed in Mecca for about thirty years before returning to India. While Azad did not fully share their orthodoxy nor supported their reactionary political role, he appreciated their erudition and their courage in defying political authority. They could utter truth in a downright manner before the kings with a courageous disregard of consequences.

The early education imparted to Maulana Azad was of traditional type. Azad's father had a strong prejudice against English education and therefore Azad's course of studies consisted of old categories *Ulum-e-diniya* (religious sciences) including grammar, logic, philosophy and mathematics. Azad believed that the various courses that he followed were all '*nakis*' (worthless)[2] The object of this Muslim mode of learning according to Azad, was to produce a squadron of well-versed likeminded theologians. He felt that Muslim scholasticism diverted man's attention from more useful scholarly pursuits.

Under the rigid guidance of his father, he learned Arabic from his mother, Persian and Urdu from his father and Islamic theology from an old Arab teacher. Azad's father who believed in the old ways of life, guarded the young Azad against anything which might deviate him from the path of his pious father. So as a boy he was locked in corners of the *Khankah* and was not allowed to read any books not prescribed by his illustrious father. He did not have any formal education. Later on his father appointed one of his trusted disciples to take up his education. A genius, Azad mastered all the subjects taught to him within a few years. His logical bent of mind, infinite vastness of knowledge, and command over expression, led him to discussions with notable theologians like Abdul Haq Haqqani and Maulana Abdulla Taunki.

Azad was known by several names like His father called him Firoze Bakht, Gulam Mohiyuddin Azad, Abul Kalam Azad Dehlavi but in Indian politics he is known as "Maulana Abul Kalam Azad" which is the one to go down in history.[3]

Maulana Azad had a proverbial fertility of mind that prompted Sarojini Naidu to remark that he was forty at the time he was born. Maulana's range of activities were quite diversified, as he intended to bring about a social change in the Muslim community, inject a new trend in the politics of the country, activate a reformation in religion, and enrich the area of Urdu language and literature. He fought against the domination of a foreign power, against the traditional values of his own family, against the political alignment of his own community, against the reactionary forces of his own land, and against the partition policy of his own party.

Mental Crisis and Understanding Islam

Azad had to go through a period of mental crisis during his formative years. The conflict between reason and religion disturbed and he decided to edit Al Hilal at the young age of twenty-five. Born in a family, which was deeply immersed in religious traditions and superstitions incited a spirit of revolt in Azad against the old order. His own study of the affairs of the wider world, particularly of the French, caused radical changes in him and he was bent upon a new adventure of ideas. He wanted to move out of the family orbit and chalk out his own path. Puzzled by the exhibition of differences among the different sects of Muslims and the needless disputations of the *Ulema*, Azad strived to present Islam in its correct perspective but it was a difficult journey necessitating many hard decisions.

Azad was against monasticism and found it unrealistic, unreasonable and unhelpful. Azad believed that there might have been some need in the Middle Ages for mysticism when Sufis were real saints, but in the modern days of science and technology when the world had undergone a sea-change, to revive practices of monasticism which in many cases were superstitious was to put the clock back.

Azad was against *pir muridi* also. He thought that the whole exercise of *pir muridi* was a "unsavory ordeal performed as ritual which signified nothing." He thought that he was an ordinary man like his father's disciples and done nothing to deserve the honor they tried to give him. On the first death anniversary of his father quite a number of influential people approached Azad and tried to persuade him to assume the role of a *Pir* like his father but he firmly repudiated the suggestion. This was the first sign of revolt in Azad against the family traditions which his father wanted to maintain at all costs.

At the age of fourteen, three questions confronted him:

Firstly, does God exist, and if so, what is the evidence of his wisdom and power in Creation?

Secondly, if reality is one, why are there different religions professed in the world by various communities and why are there differences in the world among communities concerning belief, traditions, religious practices and laws etc.? Azad said,. differences among the orthodox schools began to raise doubts in my mind concerning religion itself. If religion expresses a universal truth why should there be such differences and conflicts among men professing different religions? Why should each religion claim to be the sole repository of truth and condemn all others?[4] He said that Islam alone was not at fault. All religions indulged in polemics. Religion had become a divisive force causing dissensions in society. What was meant to know higher truth had degenerated to gross ignorance.

Thirdly, if religions promote peace and tranquility, why does it lead to religious controversies and sectarian intolerance between Christians and Jews, Muslims and Hindus and *Shias* and *Sunnis*? He realized that religion itself, which was supposed to create a spirit of harmony, was the greatest cause of strife in the social history of man. There cannot be either multiplicity or contradiction in truth. Where there is opposition and dispute, there is no truth.[5]

To search answers to the above questions was a great mental anguish. Azad gave up *namaz*[6] and abandoned *Id*. His quest was to know the very purpose of human existence and meaning of Life. He posed philosophical questions 'The beginning and end of life', 'how to apprehend reality and truth' and 'how do we determine that the method of finding Truth is valid?'[7] During this period of mental his studied different religions and modern philosophy and some branches of science available in Urdu and Arabic translations but instead of providing any remedy to his spiritual-intellectual agony, they further increased his doubts and dissatisfaction in regard to religion and religious beliefs.

During this stage of uncertainty and almost disbelief, Azad found a new world before him in the writings of Sir Sayyid Ahmad. Through Sayyid Ahmad Khan's religious writings Azad understood the true spirit of Islam which has been obscured by the juristic sects and meaningless controversies raised by the contentious *Ulema* in the interpretation of *Qur'an*.[8] Sayyaid Ahmad Khan had subjected the *Qur'an* to rational criticism and rejected all that was opposed to logic and nature. Now he was not enslaved to *taqlid* and common law. The impact of Sayyaid Ahmad Khan's writing's resulted in the repudiation of his family's traditional orthodoxy and a complete refocusing of his ideas about Islam.[9] Under the influence of Sir Sayyid, he realized that a person has no claims to be called "educated in the modern world unless he studied modern science, philosophy and literature." Education in English, according to him produced "great mental crisis"[10] while the knowledge of modern science revolutionized faith and many old customs and values become outmoded and unnecessary. He realized that modern science and technology has rocked the foundations of religion every old value need not be useful and relevant to the modern age. Sir Sayyaid's conception of Islam transcended the narrow considerations of the *Sunni* and *Shia* cults[11] and so Azad endeavored to follow and employ Sir Sayyaid's rational technique. Azad was intoxicated with Sir Sayyaid Ahmad Khan's writings which opened a new vista of thought for him.[12]

In his own words, I was worshipping Sir Sayyid as an idol.[13] Sir Sayyid's literature made him depart from traditions and Agnostic trends attracted his attention. He was so shaken in his faith and belief that religion itself had no meaning to him. He was irresistibly drawn towards materialism and rationalism and turned a full-fledged agnostic.[14]

But Sayyid Ahmad Khan's intellectual influence on Azad was short lived. When he came into contact with the writings of Rasheed Raza of Egypt, Azad deviated from Sir Sayyid. He found that the application of rationalism results first in skepticism and leads to the negation of religion. Sir Sayyid had no answer to questions like existence of God, attributes of God, eternity of soul, divine revelation, Prophethood etc.[15] This led him to think that Sir Sayyid's approach to religion was faulty and unconvincing.[16] It was inadequate and illogical. The theological deviations from Sayyid Ahmad Khan now became the basis of the differences in political approach as well. He was convinced that the political lead given to the Muslims by Sir Sayyid was misdirected and "a blunder",[17] because the Aligarh movement led by Sayyid Ahmad Khan was confined only to the problems of Indian Muslims. Azad firmly believed that a universal movement in the Islamic world is required for the benefit of the Muslims rather than a local or national movement. And that if the object of the Aligarh movement is to impart only higher education of the Muslims, then it was of no use.

Azad's intellectual doubts carried him to a stage of insatiable curiosity where he suspended all religion and experienced the spiritual agony that emanates from the total loss of faith. He questioned the entire basis of religion and its place in life. Puzzled over the fact that every person adherent of religion thinks his own brand to be best he found it difficult to understand how differences between one religion and the other could be explained.

During the years of great mental tension Azad battled with his own self and indulged in self- introspection to probe deeper into the state of mind. This crisis did not last long he at last found a solution. The light came to him from the life of the Prophet, that prompted him to go to the revealed Book, the Qur'an. In Qur'an he found the answers to all his questions. Faith in God dispelled all his doubts. He could see Divinity in the whole universe. He realized that search for higher truth should be the sole concern of man and that the Supreme and the Sublime could be detected even in tiny atoms. Concentration on things of beauty would make a man a part of that beauty and purity of heart would make Divinity reflect in it. He found the *Qur'an*, the best witness to God's truth, which invited man to show its light in his life. When these thoughts dawned on him, he became a different man thereafter. The spiritual light resolved his mental crisis and thereafter he started his mission of sharing his experiences through his journal Al Hilal.

In 1908, during his trip to Iran and Egypt, he found that the Arab and Turkish nationalists expressed their surprise on the fact that the Indian Muslims had not joined the nationalist movement, but were acting as mere camp- followers of the British. Azad was then convinced, that Indian Muslims should work for the political liberation of the country. Before this visit Azad was primarily concerned with religion and literature, but after it he began to take active interest in nationalism and politics also.

Thus Abul Kalam Azad, with constant introspection and critical self-examination started his career of politician and activist as a revivalist Muslim and as an upholder of pure Islam. His career from 1906 to 1920 was influenced by his religious teachings. During this period Azad firmly believed that the Muslims were the leaders of the world. In his writings and speeches which appeared in his journal Al-Hilal, Azad talked about the superiority of Muslims over the followers of other religions and called for an "Islamic Way" to independence. In these writings he appeared as a Muslim fundamentalist who is in favor of a linkage between politics and religion. His response to a correspondent of *Al-Hilal* in the issue of December 29, 1921 characterizes his fundamentalist tone,

"You have suggested separation of politics from religion", underlines Azad in his article. "But if we do this what, then, is left with us? We have developed our political thinking from religion...We believe that every thought which draws inspiration from any institution (including politics) other than the Qur'an is *Kufr* (infidelity)." [18]

Revivalism through Journalism

Azad rendered a great service to Islam through his journalism. Using breathtaking language, the journal simultaneously preached 'pure' Islam and Indian independence. Through his particular interpretation of Islam, Azad sought to bring Indian Muslims onto the platform of the freedom movement and to work in cooperation with Hindus who were already there. Despite his earlier admiration for Sir Sayyid, Azad was a harsh critic of the loyalist politics of Aligarh University.

Azad's journalist career can be divided into two parts- first from 1900 to pre *al- Hilal* period, and his starting of *al- Hilal* in 1912 to its renewal in 1927 when he made his best effort then to publish it.

In the pre *Al-Hilal* period, Azad was highly influenced by Sayyaid Ahmad Khan, Altaf Hussain Hali and Shibli Numani for acquiring an attitude towards Muslim society, religion and literature, a subject to be still explored. As previously discussed, Azad owed to Syyaid Ahmad Khan his quest for modern knowledge as a key for emancipating Muslim society from the fetters of bigotry, superstition and obsolete customs. Sayyaid Ahmad's writing provoked Azad to rationalize the Qur'an and challenge Muslim orthodoxy and dogmatism.

Looking to the need for social advancement of Muslims, Azad absorbed the elements of Hali's thinking and transformed them. Influenced by Hali, Azad criticized the old notion of lauding literary works and emphasized the need for using modern canons of literacy criticism in reviewing books. [19]

Azad launched his first literary journal *al-Misbah*, modeled on the Egyptian *Misbah-Al-Sharq*, towards the end of 1901, when he was about thirteen years old [20] The first article published by him was on *Id* festival. The journal contained pieces on '*Imam-e-Ghazali*', 'Newton and the Law of Gravity,' and '*Khakani Sherwani*'.[21] It was a ten-page piece on the life and poetry of *Hakim Khakani Sherwani*. The purpose of this article was to produce an anthology of the lives of some famous Persian poets by discarding old techniques and adopting the autobiographical mode of delineation. The journal lasted for three months or so.

Azad wrote a provocative article on 'Islam and Muharram' *(Ahsan-al-Akbar,* weekly published in 1902) which raised a storm among the local *Shias* because of the scanting criticism it made of some of the rituals connected with the festival[22] The *Shias* were outraged and held out a threat to Azad's life. The journal lasted only two to three months. In exchange of this journal, the office of *Ahsan-al-Akbar* received Egyptian and Arab journals and newspapers including the Cairo periodical, *Al-Hilal, al-Maqtataf* , and *al-Manar*. Azad contributed religious articles to *Tufa-e-Ahmadiya* published and edited by Maulvi Ahmad Hussain Fatehpuri from Calcutta.

Makhzan was one of the leading Urdu literary magazines of the day which was published from Lahore and edited by Shaikh Abdul Qadir. Azad contributed in May, 1902 an interesting article on the 'Art of Newspaper writing' in which he discussed the utility of newspapers as an instrument of molding public opinion. He showed how the newspapers in Europe and U.S.A. had brought about a change in social thinking. Azad wrote an article on 'Modern Knowledge in Islam' in *Maraqq-e-Alam* in January 1902, in which he suggested the editor to improve the contents of the articles on scientific themes.

Reformation through Education

Lisan-al-Sidq (Voice of Truth)

Azad launched his own journal *Lisan-al-Sidq* (Voice of Truth) at the age of fifteen. This journal established him as a writer and editor and brought him fame. It was supposed to be a sixteen- page weekly but its pages increased sometimes running to forty- and sixty. With Shibli's recommendations, *Lisan al-Sidq* became an organ of the *Anjuman-e-Tarakki-e-Urdu*(Society for the advancement of the Urdu). His contributors included celebrities like Shibli, Persian and Arabic scholar and historian Maulvi Muhammad Zakakullah, and Abdul Halim Sharar.

The *Lisan al-Sidq* was a literary journal in which excluded politics and poetry. In its issue of August- September, 1904 Azad set the aims of the journal which were to

i. promote social reforms by discarding social abuses;

ii. popularize literary criticism through review of books for improving the quality of literature;

iii. cultivate taste for literature among the reading public, particularly in Bengal.

Azad was deeply committed to the cause of reforming Muslim community. These aims intended to arouse social conscience, to refine literary taste, and to stimulate thought among the educated classes. He believed that Muslims were intellectually and socially backward because of their poverty, lack of education and social practices involving wasteful expenditure beyond their means on marriage and religious ceremonies. In the journal he emphasized that such wasteful expenditure leads to the ruination of a large number of families. [23]. To create awareness in the area of science among Muslims he bought out articles on scientific themes.

Azad believed that education is a key to all improvements and pleaded for the promotion of education among Muslims. According to him, education awakened the mind through the diffusion of knowledge. Like Becon he too believed that knowledge is power. Books being a storehouse of knowledge, he made a distinction between good and bad books and wanted proper books to be made available to the public. He promoted those books which contained modern knowledge and were free from puerile fables and idle fancies. He protested against the publication by *Anjuman-e-Taraqqui-e-Urdu* of books dealing with trite themes. Thus in *Lisan al-Sidq* Azad showed his firm faith in the liberating role of education and deplored the common tendency of adopting passive attitude towards the acquisition of knowledge. He represented a true spirit of Renaissance spirit by his emphasis on science, modernity and dignity of man. Education, he regarded a powerful means for the regeneration of Muslim society. Azad assumed the role of a regenerator of his times at a young age although unfortunately *Lisan al-Sidq* was closed due to shortage of funds.

Understanding Islamic History and Theology

al-Nadwa

The *Nadwa madrarssa Dar-ul-Ulum* was established in 1858 to provide instruction in Islamic studies and western learning (including English and Mathematics) and to create a new type of modernized *Ulema* who besides Islam and its history, should be acquainted with trends of contemporary thought. *Nadwat-ul- Ulema,* an association of *Ulema* was founded in 1893 with the objective of bridging the gulf between the old and new ideas.

As the editor of *al-Nadwa* from October 1905 to March 1906 Azad wrote articles on 'The Muslims', 'Treasure of Knowledge' and the 'Guardianship of Europe'. The article appeared in two parts. In the first part, Azad showed how the European interest in Arabic language and literature arose and in the second, he provided a list of works dealing with this theme.[24] A regular feature of *al-Nadwa* was 'Scientific News' under which Azad published an article illustrating the efforts made in Europe to evolve a common language known as Esperanto.[25]

Azad produced an entire issue of *al-Nadwa* on 'The Judiciary in Islam' which he dealt with the administration of Justice in Islamic history.[26] The article was divided into three parts dealing with the – duties of the plaintiff and defendant in the court of law, method of prosecution and the principles of evidence. Azad believed that Islam provides sound guidelines to the legislators and judges. He wrote:

The materialistic law of the universe has no hold on the heart or conscience of the judge to ensure that he follows its dictation. Islam does with its spiritual and divine power which materialistic law can never do. …. Islam gives to the judge the benefit of rules and with its spiritual premises, tends to sway his heart to do right.[27]

In his article titles as *"Nadwat-ul- 'Ulema' ka Ijlas-i-Delhi aur Qaum ki Shahrah-i-Maqsud* (The Delhi Session of the *Nadwat-ul-'Ulema'* and the Goal of the *Quam)* he wrote that English education among Muslims, for the urgent need of which so much hue and cry was raised as if it was the only panacea for all the ills of Muslims society, had failed to yield any such revolutionary results as were expected from the so-called sound system of education. It had proved, he further said, a hopeless venture as it could only produce job-hunters who were to serve the administrative machinery of the British bureaucracy. He also mentioned the sad plight of the existing class of the *'ulema'*. He said that the *'ulema'* who were considered as the natural leaders of the community were morally degenerated, and the product of the *madarsas* which pursued the traditional courses of study could not be of a better quality. *Nadwah,* he said wanted to introduce a radical change in the situation. [28]

At the young age of seventeen Azad's association with *al-Nadwa* deepened his understanding of Islamic history and theology and widened his interest in European learning and sciences. While working with *al-Nadwa*, Azad edited the prestigious newspaper, *Wakil*. The *al-Nadwa* was meant exclusively for the *Ulema* whereas the *Wakil* dealt with serious matters with national and international importance. As an editor of *Wakil* Azad expanded the editorial to two to four columns and increased the number of articles on literary and historical themes. Within a few months the circulation of the paper increased to over one and half times of what it was at the time of his taking over as editor. This was a clear-cut reflection of Azad's tremendous influence on the Indian Muslims and their faith shown in his revivalist movement.

Azad's visit to Islamic countries including Iraq, Syria, Egypt and Turkey and also France in 1908 had a profound impact on his political thinking. Azad was able to crystallize his thoughts on the neo-colonialists who were exploiting these countries and how India could help them. He found a new world astir with ideas of liberty, progress and revolutionary Islam. Earlier Azad had read a great deal and inspired from the Egyptian and Turkish literature including the writings of Abduh (the great reformer of Islam and the chief Mufti of Egypt) and Rashid Rida of *al-Minar*. His Middle East experience motivated

Azad to plunge into the journalistic venture of *Al-Hilal* and *al-Balagh*.

Political Strategy al- Hilal (Rise of the Crescent)

He convinced the Muslims that their loyalty towards British was no remedy to their ills, as it would not pay them in the long run. It would be better if Muslims join hands with their countrymen, and first remove the foreigners so that the resources of the land could rationally and equitably be distributed among all. He made efforts to dispel the notion that the colonials were the benefactors of the Muslims. He emphasized that the aliens were only using the Muslim shoulders to shoot at the Hindus, and that they would not hesitate to use the Hindu shoulders to shoot at the Muslims, if that were to serve their purpose. Azad brought to the notice of his fellowmen how the Government had once passed orders that no Muslim should rise above the level of a 'chaprasi' which is on record also. In Al-Hilal Azad used rational, religious and historical arguments to draw the Muslims to the main stream.

Azad was very much displeased by the piteous spectacle of the Muslim community in India which Azad thought had 'no religion' and 'no politics. To him the Muslim League founded in 1906 to safeguard the interest of the Muslims was completely a servile creature of the British Government of India. He got disturbed by the revocation of the partition of Bengal in1911 and found Muslim politics at low ebb. He was greatly impressed by the educational and social advancement of the Hindus. He wanted a similar spirit to be generated among the Muslims. On the international scene Italy had conquered the province of Tripoli in 1911. The Balkan states were determined to dismember Turkey. The background of these happenings on the international plane lent a new urgency to the cry of 'Regeneration of Muslim community.[29] The impact of the plight of Muslim countries and the degrading condition of Muslim in India moved Azad to launch *al- Hilal* and *al- Balagh*.

The conditions of the Islamic world disturbed Azad's mind . The colonials had imposed uninterruptedly their political will on the Muslim world. Islamic decline became more apparent from the eighteenth century when the French Revolution gave new concepts of democracy and nationalism to Europe, and the Muslims were left far behind in every walk of life. Their intellectual decline led to the decay of a civilization, which had continuously flourished for over a thousand years in the major areas of three continents, Asia, Europe and Africa. Even their political authority was seriously challenged by the British in India, the Dutch in Indonesia, the French in Africa, and the Russians in Central Asia.

Azad's journal "Al Hilal" had the broad objective of awakening the Muslims of India to their political, social and educational potential. He sought to fulfill this objective with a fusion of nationalism, pan-Islamism, social revolution and Hindu-Muslim unity . He thought that if ever there is a threat to the universal truth of God, it is none other than from the British Government. Therefore, it is obligatory on the part of the Indian Muslims, that keeping in mind the injunctions of the *Shariah,* keeping before them the beautiful conduct of the Prophet... that they tie the knot of truth and love with the Hindus of India and become one nation.

In the December1912 issue of Al Hilal, the Maulana wrote:

"For the Hindus, struggle for the independence of the country is a sign of love for the land. But for the Musalmans it is a religious obligation and equivalent to jihad in the way of God. And the meaning of jihad includes every effort made to establish justice and truth and human rights and the removal of servitude".

Al-Hilal and *Al-Balagh,* the classics in Urdu journalism, thus aimed at evolving a harmonious society based on moral and spiritual values. The object was to bring back Muslims to the main stream of national struggle through an appeal to their higher conscience. Azad's new technique of an exhaustive use of the Qur'anic verses was employed to bring home to his people that 'patriotism' was a virtue and 'loyalism' would lead the Muslims nowhere. His purpose was to remove the built-in inhibitions of the community towards the Congress, which was looked upon as a hindrance in the way of the social and economic progress of a people who were just recovering from a long spell of backwardness.

Azad was aware of the fact that a new crusade seemed to bestow uniform success to the Cross and consistent defeat to the Crescent, and the word Crusade was substituted by a new word Colonialism, which used not religious teeth to bite but gun-boat diplomacy to destroy. The military superiority of the West unnerved the Muslims. It was not a clash between Islam and Christianity as religions, but a clash between two cultures, between the highly industrialized and vastly superior military might of the West and extremely backward feudalistic states of the Islamic world. The clash was for raw materials for their industry, new markets for their goods, new areas to spread their culture and new zones to impose their political will.

Another danger was that the West regarded Islam as an archaic, conservative, rigid, dogmatic and primitive order which they wanted to change through the secular traditions of Voltaire and Tom Paine, and through the thought process of Greco-Roman culture, and not in the tradition of Palestinian-Biblical order. The idea was not to convert Muslims to Christianity, but to inject into them Western secularism as a positive system of values, based on the western ideals of justice, order, reason and humanism.

This was a war on the Islamic system of ideas, which Azad wanted to challenge through quoting profusely Qur'anic verses in his Al-Hilal. Azad was fully aware of the Islamic mind since the time of Shah Waliyullah how Islam had responded to the

West. The continuous enjoyment of political power by the Muslims for over a thousand years had given them self-confidence which was based on faith, *Iman,* which they believed would never let them down, as in all confrontations in the past it had never done.

Azad was perturbed by the very fact that Muslims were highly influenced by the West. At a time when the West was aggressive, the Muslims became willing victims to its onslaught. Instead of remaining firm on Islamic values and ideals, some leaders were inclined to appreciate Western culture. Muhammad Ali of Egypt, Sir Sayyid of India and Mustafa Kamal of Turkey openly advocated Westernization and modernization. Although, a few other leaders such as Sheikh Muhammad Abduhu, Mehdi of Sudan, Rashid Raza, Shakeeb Arsalan, Abdul Qadir of Algiers, Mustafa Kamil of Egypt, Bu Hamara of Morocco, Shamil of Central Asia and Jamaluddin Afghani had all attempted to revive the Islamic spirit, none had used Qur'an as the main source for a new life among Muslims. Al-Hilal was nothing but the Qur'anic version of the code of conduct the Muslims had to follow for their betterment. Two other intellectual giants, apart from Azad, who were thus engaged in Islamic resurgence in India, were Allama Iqbal and Muahmmad Ali Jauhar.

"The subject of the revival of the *Millat* was quite obvious, which was to remove the Muslims from the present degradation and lift them to the position of dignity and honour. What should be the means that are to be adopted, and what line of action was to be taken for this purpose?" Three different views were envisaged in this regard, which the reformers of India, Egypt, Turkey, Iran, Tunis, Central Asia and Caucasia had planned to adopt.

The first view was called 'westernization'. Nineteenth century proclaimed the emergence of European culture and the rise of industrial revolution... When the dazzling glare of the

European culture cast its shadow over the Islamic world, its impact caused the formation of two groups; the major part was immersed in apathy and inertia and took no notice of the events, but the wise and the sensitive suddenly felt the change... the first group was captivated by its charm; sentiments of acceptance and adoption of its culture were excited in it instead of resistance and challenge. Sir Sayyid Ahmad Khan and his followers were the votaries of this group in India.

The second school of thought believed in 'Political Reforms'. It thought that the immediate need was political reformation. The most powerful spokesman of this view in the Islamic world was Sayyid Jamaluddin Asad-Abadi.

The third school of thought was of the 'religious reformation'. Although the propagators of this school were relatively smaller in number than in the past, in reality it was this group of true guidance that illumined the righteous path... The times increasingly accepted its call and came closer to its message. Al-Hilal was started in 1912 in order to carry and disseminate the principles of this last group. [30]

The purpose of Al-Hilal was quite evident- the resurgence of Muslims through Qur'an and Sunnah. The intention was to remind the Qur'anic lessons which had been forgotten by the Muslims so that they make these lessons their own guiding principles. Azad quoted profusely from the Qur'an which said,

Let their arise out of you a band of people Inviting to all that is good Enjoining what is right, and Forbidding what is wrong: They are the ones to attain felicity. [31]

Again, the Qur'an has repeatedly reminded the people to carry out these injunctions. It said, Ye are the best of Peoples, evolved for mankind, enjoining what is right, forbidding what is wrong, and believing in God, if only the people of the Book had faith, it was best for them. [32] Maulana Azad clarified this point stating that the presence of a party among you is always needed which would invite you to do good and prevent you from doing bad, so that those who are misled either because of ignorance or because of fear or greed are brought back to right path. When the Muslims ignored this injunction and turned indifferent towards their obligatory duties, they fell into bad days. The Qur'an called the Muslims 'The Best of Peoples' only when they would carry out their stipulated duties.

Azad pinpointed the Qur'anic verses, which enjoined righteousness.

The Believers, men and women, are protectors one of another; they enjoin what is just, and forbid what is evil; they observe regular prayers, practice regular charity, and obey God and His Apostle. On them will God pour His mercy. [33]

In Al-Hilal the thrust of his message was also on the positive aspect of the obligatory duties (*Al-Mauruf*) and prohibition of the forbidden deeds. He wrote three articles in Al-Hilal on these injunctions. While discussing these he said:

"In fact action on good and rejection of bad could be done only by he who is firm and constant in his faith in Allah. This is possible only when he does everything for the love of God and gives up everything for the sake of God. Nothing of self-love is involved in this, nor of any personal enmity; neither for his personal interest he cultivates friendship nor for his personal sake he incurs any hostility. He loves everything that is loveable in the eye of God, and sees his foes only from the eye of God. Nothing is of his own, neither his existence nor his life, nor his call. When he walks, he walks on God's feet, when he listens, he listens with God's ears, and when he speaks, it is God's sound that comes out of his vocal cords. [34]

Azad inferred the idea of *Jehad* from the concept of doing good and avoiding bad. The literal meaning of *Jehad* is 'intensive effort'. It was applied as a defensive measure to resist any aggression. Azad reminded the Muslims this religious duty of *Jehad,* was to fight against the enemy, who were no other than the colonials. Azad's idea was to make the Muslims join Hindus at least in the name of *Jehad,* a religious term, sensitive enough for Muslims to respect.

It was the call of *Jehad* only that had excited the Muslims to rise in revolt in 1857 and the English were about to lose all that they had gained. When they managed to crush the revolt they took such vengeance on Muslims that it was a holocaust. Those who escaped death lost all their properties. The disaster was of such a magnitude that they were reduced to a miserable position.

Sir Sayyid played an important role to the rescue his community who was utterly demoralized, dejected and bereft of all its past glory. To bring the Muslims out of their cocoon Sir Sayyid had adopted a double policy. To the Muslims he said that they should take to Western education, and to the British he said the Muslims were not opposed to them. He exhorted the Muslims to be loyal to the Government, as they were no match to the might of the English; and he asked the English to be friendly towards the Muslims, as they may need their help to improve their general conditions. In other words, his policy was 'loyalism in politics' and 'modernism in institutions'. In return he expected the British to help the Muslims in reconstructing their educational, social and cultural life.

Sir Sayyid fought on two fronts to bring about a change, a change both in the Muslims and in the English. The Mutiny was quite fresh in the minds of both. The English would not forget the inciting of the *Imams* that the Muslims should end the foreign rule through open revolt or *Jehad.* W. W. Hunter cornered the Muslims on this issue of *Jehad.* Sir Sayyid tried hard to convince the English that *Jehad* did not mean fighting with the sword but 'to work hard to achieve an object'. Finally Sir Sayyid was able to win over both his community and the Government.

But Maulana Azad had different views. He agreed with Sir Sayyid's educational policy that the Muslims should take to western learning, but differed from his political policy. His argument was that God alone was sovereign in all matters and the colonials had no right to rule over them. A Muslim cannot be a subordinate to any authority other than God. He would not bow his head before anyone. He is vice-regent of God on earth. For this purpose *Jehad* is necessary. Azad quoted The Qu'ran which says,

"And strive in His cause as ye ought to strive."[35]

Al-Hilal played a remarkable role in changing the mind of the Muslims. Azad used this powerful medium to touch the conscience of the Muslims. He assumed the leadership of a very difficult sort of people. Of all the Indians the Muslims were the most rigid folks who always attempted to sail against the current. They would become desperate and desolate, but would not change their stand. When the British were invincible, they made the futile attempts to overpower them. It was the skill, wisdom and perseverance of Sir Sayyid that he could bring about the change, when they were on the verge of collapse. When they accepted his word of loyalism with great difficulty, they took it as gospel guidance. They would not budge from that loyalty, even if the country had undergone a sea change. They would not see the writings on the wall that the nation had chosen a different path. They preferred the immediate gains to long time benefits. The nation was wide-awake to win liberty, and they had forgotten their own old lesson which Tipu had taught that the life of a lion for a day was far better than the life of a jackal for a hundred years. When they disliked the British, they regarded them as worse than Satan, and when they liked the British they took them to be angels.

Azad had to deal with such an excitable people. He resorted to appeal them through the only effective and sensitive weapon, which could have some impact on them the Qu'ranic injunctions where *Jehad* against foreign foes was permissible. Their own compatriots were already there deep in that *Jehad* or struggle for their rights, but the Muslims were giving an impression that they had a hand in glove with the foes.

With great efforts Azad successfully changed this trend. Azad carried on a campaign against Sir Sayyid's policy of loyalism which was totally against the teachings of Islam. Azad used his journalistic skills to put the Muslims on national track. The time was of Balkan Wars. The colonial powers aimed at dismembering Turkey. Fierce fighting was going on in the east of Europe and Tripoli was also under attack. Azad got the pictures of the campaigns, and started publishing them regularly. He was giving full details of the war campaigns along with the photos of the Generals. The idea was to excite the Indian Muslims against the colonials, and to tell them how their brethren were engaged in *Jehad* elsewhere. Azad took up the slogan of *Jehad* forcefully and consistently and yielded the desired effect.

The *Ulemas* woke up from their slumber. They appreciated his Islamic spirit, and were impressed by the depth of his Qur'anic knowledge. The *Ulemas* always held a hold over the Muslim public. When Azad's voice was reverberated from the pulpit, *Jehad* became a sacred term, which had once chilled the spine of the English.

Sir Sayyid had wiped it off from the dictionary, and Azad put it back where it belonged to. It was a great achievement of Maulana Azad.

The clarion call came from Deoband where Sheikh-ul-Hind Maulana Mahmood-ul-Hasan took the lead for *Jehad*. It was on his initiative a provisional government had been set up in Afghanistan under Raja Mahendra Pratap. It was he who had inaugurated the Silk-Kerchief Movement. Once Sheikh-ul-Hind was asked why he glanced Al-Hilal which carried pictures, knowing very well that Azad was not an orthodox Muslim, the Sheikh quoted an Urdu verse,

'None got up from the gang of the pious and the holy; if something was done, it was only by those who came out from the pub..'

The Sheikh added:. Why should I not read al-Hilal? It is the first journal that taught us the lesson of *Jehad* which was our obligatory duty, and we had forgotten all about it.

Thus the services of al-Hilal for Muslim revivalism were memorable. It annulled the policy of loyalism. It advocated Hindu-Muslim unity. It brought the Muslims closer to the main stream of national struggle. [36] When a few opposed this policy on the ground that Hindus were in majority, and that in a democracy where majority rule would prevail, Muslims would be ruled by Hindu, Azad quoted the Qur'an:

God forbids you not with regard to those who fight you not for (your) Faith, Nor drive you out of your homes from dealing kindly and justly with them; For God loves those who are just. God only forbids you with regard to those who fight you for (your) Faith, and drive you out of your homes, and support (others) in driving you out, From turning to them (For friendship and protection).

It is such as turn to them (In those circumstances) that do wrong. [37]

The implications of these verses were clear. The Hindus and Muslims have lived together as brothers for centuries. They belong to the same country, the same race, the same language and culture. The aliens, who had come from seven seas across who had enslaved the whole population, and had reduced the people to utter poverty and ignorance, had no right to deserve sympathy. It was strange how short was the Muslim memory when all that the English had done to them in 1857 and before 1857 was totally forgotten.

Azad elaborated this point in one of his lectures:

The Qu'ran has classified all non-Muslims into two groups... One is that which does not attack the Muslims, does not destroy Muslim Governments and the Khilafat. Such groups who have neither attacked Muslims, nor invaded Muslim towns or villages or population are not prevented by the Qu'ran to be made Muslim allies, and be treated on friendly terms. On the other hand, such nations that make war on Muslims, destroy the towns and habitations are required by the Qur'an to be boycotted.[38]

Azad proceeded to stress that the British aggression in Egypt, Iraq, Turkey and even on India deserved them to be declared enemies of the Muslim world, and it became the duty of all Muslims to fight against them. The Muslims never had a better chance to distress the English as their compatriots had already launched a campaign against them. The Muslims did not succeed in the past because they had to fight all alone. Now that the whole country was up against them, Muslims would do well not to miss the opportunity.

He went to the extent of saying that any sign of friendship or goodwill towards the English would be heresy, and those who were in favour of remaining loyal to them would no longer be Muslims.[39]

In the very first issue of *Al-Hilal*, Azad advocated Hindu Muslim unity and stated very clearly that the Hindu-Muslim unity was the only way to solve the Indian problem. He quoted Qu'ran to convince the Muslims that it was permissible for them to join non-Muslims, if it was beneficial to both. He said that the Prophet also entered into a convention called *Meesaq- e-Medina* with the Jews to establish a secular state. The injunctions of the Qu'ran and the traditions of the Prophet permit the Muslims to enter into an agreement with the Hindus to cooperate, with each other to win the common objective, which was to end the foreign domination. Azad did not spoke of expediency or rationality or diplomacy in asking Muslims to cooperate with the Hindus but used religious terminology to bring the two together. He said:

If the seven crores Muslims were to join twenty two crores of Hindus, they would be one (powerful) nation. I would like now to tell my Muslim brothers that after the word of God, the most powerful word is of the Prophet Muhammad who entered into an agreement in which he used the term One Nation. He called all tribes who lived around Medina, and concluded a Treaty of Peace to form one Nation.[40]

This Treaty is of great significance in the history of Islam. Similarly, the Muslims who have ever to live in amity and peace with the Hindus would be wise if they were to follow the precept of the Prophet whose *Meesaq* is a historical document of great significance. If the Jews and the Arabs and other non-Muslims could form a nation according to the Agreement, what prevented the Muslims of India to enter into a similar deal?[41]

al- Hilal served as a whip for the dead hearts to integrate the *millat* through the message of Islam. Islam meant to Azad very different from what it would mean generally to the people. Islam for him was pure and simple as laid down by Qur'an and not as interpreted by medieval interpreters. Through *al-Hilal* Azad strived to achieve two things which he considered absolutely necessary for the Muslim community: first, recovery of lost faith in the spirit of Islam and second, the diffusion of western learning and sciences among them. Being a regular reader of the Egyptian papers, he acquired technical knowledge necessary for production of good journals. It is important to note Urdu was a popular language but in Calcutta the readership of Urdu papers was somewhat limited. In the guise of teaching the basic tenets of Islam, Azad ingeniously hid the meaning of liberty which he expounded in an oratorical style heavily loaded with Arabic and Persian diction and enriched by glittering similes and metaphors. Through his discussion of the plight of Turkey and the portraits of the prominent Egyptian and Afghan personalities, he propagated the revolutionary idea of liberty. *Al-Hilal's* appeal to the Muslims of Calcutta was instant. The combination of style and subject matter was electrifying. His initial circle of readership included the *murids* of his father, who had always valued the word of their young *Pirzada (*son of the teacher).

Al-Hilal's appearance was duly noted by the government. In his weekly report dated 24 September 1912, the Secretary, Home Affairs, the Director of Criminal Intelligence wrote:

In Calcutta, the newspaper *al-Hilal* replaced the *Comrade* as the leading Pan Islamist organ. It contained on September 8, an article in which passages from the Qur'an were quoted to show that no government which was not democratic in form, could be acceptable to the followers of Muhammad.

Thus, Azad succeeded in building up the confidence of Muslim community not by any new philosophy but by reviving the philosophy of Islam which has been forgotten by the Muslims. He firmly believed that Islamic revivalism could bring about their moral and spiritual uplift. That is why *al-Hilal* and *al-Balagh* were thickly sown with Qur'anic verses. In fact Qur'an provided the substance and structure of these two weeklies.

Azad attacked the *Ulemas* also. In the very first issue of *al-Hilal*,(1912) Azad stated his views about the state sponsored *Ulema,* the so called custodians of religion:

It is a strange phenomenon that the very same priests who at the birth of a new faith are agents of uplift and reform, became the instruments of vice and depravity, once the movement has peaked. Rarely has any group caused as much harm to a religion as its own perpetrators and servants. This unscrupulous and dogmatic peak has been a curse of Allah for an orderly, principled and peaceful race. Since the beginning, the history of Islam has been interested by the superstition and communalism of this group. Whenever the call for truth has been given, the devil has used the *Ulemas* as his agents. Islam's great achievement was to rid the world of the domination of this gang.....but much to the world's surprise, in a very short while, Islam played right back into their hands and today, its controls are firmly held in the dark gasp of their soiled hands.

As a scholar of Islamic history, he knew the force and influence of the Ulema in Muslim society. Azad believed that to reform *Ulema*, most important is the diffusion of new ideas among them and on the use of critical methods in history as done by the German historian Ranke. It was the Ulema that had first to be educated in the real sense so that they could later exercise the right kind of influence on a wide segment of Muslim society through the propagation of their ideas. Through the pages of *al- Hilal* and *al- Balagh,* Azad built up a strong constituency of a dedicated set of Ulema to carry the message of Islam to the wider public.[42]

For the western educated Indian Muslims who in their adulation of western civilization were forgetting their cultural roots he firmly believed that only Islam could save them from losing their cultural moorings. Azad vindicated and rehabilitated the true spirit of Islam by reconciling the old with the new. Influenced by Shibli, Azad set high value on rationality for understanding literature, religion and society. Azad used Urdu as a vehicle for his scholarly contributions. His audience constituted the *Ulema* and the Western educated Muslims for whom *al- Hilal* and *al- Balagh* carried a special message.

About these two classes, the *Ulema* and the western educated , Azad wrote as follows:

It drives me mad to see the deplorable sight that today among the Muslims there are only two kinds of leaders, first the traditionalists that are the Ulema and the modernist group, the western educated intellectuals. Both are ignorant of religion and both are paralyzed limbs of the community. They have no idea of their destination .... the one is unable to set a boat. The other too cannot find the shore. The first group beset by religious superstitions or prejudice is stagnating while the other is caught up in atheism, imitation of the West and love of power and position. [43]

In the pages of *al-Hilal* and *al-Balagh* he emphasized that the greatest thing for a Muslim is to build up his character and the Islamic framework could be used by him to liberate himself from the present state of degradation. Islam thus was the guiding star of Azad's thought in *al- Hilal* and *al-Balagh*. He firmly believed that Islam alone can produce a change in the Muslim mind which is entangled in mundane interests behind a cloak of religious pretensions. [44]

To conclude, Azad was not only concerned about the Muslims of his own country but about but Muslims of the entire world. He emerged in *al-Hilal* and *al-Balagh* as a firm and convinced Pan-Islamist who conceived the idea of universal brotherhood of Muslims all over the world bound by common faith, beliefs and traditions.

Nationalism

Azad welcomed the manifestation of ardent nationalism which he regarded as a great force for gaining political independence. Azad declared that the history of thirteen centuries of Islamic heritage showed that Islam and nationalism were not incompatible. It is against political servitude that his strictures are directed in *Al- Hilal* and it is to liberty that his views are firmly dedicated. In the light of his historical analysis Azad saw the certainty of the triumph of liberty. He declared that no country can remain a slave any longer in the twentieth century.⁴⁵ While saying this he anticipated the future course of history.

By quoting verses from Koran, Azad showed in the pages of *Al-Hilal* that Islam stands for liberty and rejects every type of servitude. Thus, he emerged from *Al- Hilal* as a champion if liberty. It was difficult to give a call for liberty in those days but Azad had the courage to do so in his paper. In his Presidential Address to the Khilafat Conference in August 1921 Azad said that in the very first number of *Al-Hilal* he had tried to convince Muslims that according to the *Shari'at* their real enemy was British government which was wiping out the whole of the east. He then proceeded to remind them of the example of the Prophet (*Phuh*), who while making peace with the people of Medina had signed a treaty stating that Muslims would henceforth join with them to form "a single nation" (*ummah wahidah*). He inferred from this that it was the religious duty of Indian Muslims to not only nurture ties of true friendship with the Hindus, but also to join with them to form a single "nation"; the motive in both cases being to combat the threat to Islam posed by its enemies. ⁴⁶

In his Congress Presidential Address of December 1923 Azad remarked that the dormant spirit of Indian nationalism (*qawmiyyat*) had been aroused in the field of action and struggle, thus heralding a revolution in that it had marched from the initial period of debate and theorizing into the "life of action". In an article that he wrote in June 1924 soon after the death of C.R. Das, he noted with satisfaction the manner in which all of India, despite its disparities of religion and race, united completely in mourning the loss. He felt this was significant as a measure of the strength of the spirit of "nationalism", and the degree to which it had developed. Paying tribute to Das' patriotism and "nationalism" as being completely free of any taint divisive sentiments, he felt that in this quality lay the greatest trial of any Indian leader, and without it true patriotism and "nationalism" could never develop in a country like India. He was not surprised at the description of Das as an "idealist" by an Anglo-Indian newspaper, since for those who had passed the remark, the aim of Indian "nationalism" and freedom was nothing more than an impractical ideal.[47]

In his Congress Presidential Address of 1940 Azad dwelt on the fact that India was home to many races, cultures and religions which had settled here, the last of these being the Muslims. He believed that their arrival led, according to nature's law, to a merging of two different culture-currents-a new India began to be fashioned by the Hindus and Muslims sharing their precious heritage. In a thousand years of common history they enriched India with their common achievement, every aspect of their life and cultures bearing the stamp of their joint endeavour - their languages were different but they grew to use a common language, and their dissimilar manners and customs acted and reached on each other to produce a new synthesis.[48]

Azad was the first Indian thinker to publicly propagate the inclusive character of Indian nationalism shunning the prevalent path of exclusivist of the extremist Hindu Congress and Muslim League leaders. He reasserted the idea of inclusive nationalism which was conceptualized by the moderate Congress leaders and worked for India's freedom on this principle before the arrival of Gandhi on the national scene when it was unconventional. Gandhi defined this nationalism as composite nationalism and made it the mainstream of nationalist thought and behavior during the Non-Cooperation- Khilafat Movement. The fiasco of the Hijrat movement further convinced Azad that territorial national identity is the only justifiable collective identity for Muslim like others all over the world. He knew that the Islamic religious collectivity of the *Ummah* and the territorial collectivity of the nation may be compatible in many situations but may not be compatible in every case. He took upon himself to make it compatible in the Indian context.

His aspiration to become Imaul Hind and a front rank leader of the Indian national movement at the same time was an endeavour to make the *Ummah* and nation compatible. [49]

Muslim Politics

Azad made a debut in politics when the British Government partitioned Bengal in 1905 on religious grounds. The Muslim middle classes supported the partition but Azad rejected it outright. He took active part in the agitation, joined the secret societies and revolutionary organization, came in contact with Sri Aurobindo Ghosh and Shyam Sundar Chakravarty. He stood for a unified India and never deviated from his stand. He writes in his famous book 'India Wins Freedom':

'It is one of the greatest frauds on the people to suggest that religious affinity can unite areas which are geographically, economically and culturally different'.

It is a fact of history that while other Congress leaders accepted the partition in 1947, Maulana stood steadfast. His famous statement on Hindu-Muslim unity stands out as Magna Carta of his faith: "If an angel were to descend from the heavens and proclaim from the heights of Qutab Minar: Discard Hindu-Muslim unity and within 24 hours Swaraj is yours, I will refuse the preferred Swaraj but shall not budge an inch from my stand. The refusal of Swaraj will affect only India while the end of our unity will be the loss of our entire human world."

Azad exhorted his coreligionists to come out openly and joined politics. He pleads with them, cajoles them, and tickles them, expostulates with them, warns them, thunders at them and evokes the memory of the past to stir them to action . The following is a typical passage in *al-Hilal* in which Azad made a stirring appeal to his coreligionists-

Whatever is destined for a nation cannot be averted. Surely a day will come when India's political revolution will dawn. The chains of slavery which she tied on her feet will vanish all at once with the touch of the sword of liberty in the twentieth century. Suppose at that moment the history of the progressive stages of India's national life is to be written, then do you know what will be written about seven crore Muslims?

It will be written that when India was fighting for freedom, the Hindus sacrificed themselves bravely for the cause of liberty, but the poor Muslims chose to hide themselves in caves. It is a fact that the Hindus battled for freedom and in no case did they became silent spectators. Swayed by the noble passion they declared themselves as rebels in the cause of liberty.

The future historian will write that a law of determination operates in history. No country can remain a slave any longer in the twentieth century. But the world will remember unfortunately that all these revolutionary changes came about without any contributions made by Muslims of India. How will the Muslims take that verdict? [50]

The pages of *Al- Hilal* were also replete with strong criticism of the Muslim League. Azad believed that the government had distracted Muslims with a new toy-the Muslim League-which deceptively appeared as politics, although it was neither born of a political awakening and nor did it have any national (*mulki*) or *milli* strength. Muslims were made to believe that the factors for their abstinence from politics thirty years ago (lack of education, fewer numbers, pressure of the majority in the race for advantages etc.) still hold good, and therefore politics for them signified first securing their rights against those who had usurped them i.e., the Hindus. Consequently, whereas the demand for rights should have been targeted at the government, it was turned towards Hindu neighbors, and thus the political awakening of Muslims posed no danger to the government. However, he did not blame the government for this situation, for it had never prevented anyone from demanding their rights. Rather he felt that the fault lay with the leaders of the community, who did not give it an opportunity to tackle the real issues by engaging it first in higher education, then in the spell of the League, and finally in the movement of the Muslim University, at a time when the country was undergoing great upheavals.[51]

In an article of December 1912 Azad criticized Muslim leaders not only for advocating complete trust and loyalty for the British government, but also for never giving the Muslim nation (*qawm*) a chance to exercise its judgment. They believed that since it lacked education it should content itself with conformism, and must obey without protest. He lamented that in politics, as in religion, Muslims were so overawed by their leaders that they did not dare to think for themselves. The "nation" thus had no political opinion of its own, but blindly followed a few men of authority who formulated all its policies. He was however glad to note a change-the awe of Muslim leaders, and the myth regarding the soundness of their policy had been shattered. In the ensuring political change the "nation" had felt its power, and tried to reflect on its own rather than merely following its leaders, which for him signaled signs of national (*qawmi*) life and spirit in the *millat.* [52]

To Azad Muslim League was not a political party that grew naturally as a result of the fulfillment of Muslim aspirations but an artificial product created by the British for the gratification of their vested interests. He wrote that 'Muslim League has betrayed the people.' [53] Addressing the League in *Al-Hilal,* in 1912, he said, 'you have insulted the Indian Politics during the last six years. [54] According to Azad the greatest mistake League committed was that its politics was rooted in Aligarh- the tree was already there, but the roots had dried up.[55]

Azad believed that due to the British policy of Divide and Rule, the Muslims had broken off their relations with Hindus 'who were the real active group in the country'. The British machinations had succeeded in dissuading the Muslims from joining the Congress. Azad extols the secular outlook of Ganga Prasad Varma, the editor of *Hindustan* in Lucknow for about thirty years, whose mission was to forge Hindu- Muslim unity. Azad described Ganga Prasad Varma as 'among the great men of India' whose every action has been animated by a spirit of service and pure dedication to the country. Azad admonished the Muslim community for committing political suicide by its complete indifference to active politics. He cited the example of Madan Lal Dhingra, a Hindu youth, who inspired by the burning passion of patriotism had sacrificed himself for the liberation of his country.[56] Azad wrote that by his act Dhingra had shown the path to others. [57]

Dealing specifically with the question of Muslim politics vis-à-vis Hindus, Azad asserts that the fear which the Muslims entertain about their being swamped by the Hindu majority because they are small in numbers is gratuitous. He urged that in politics, sheer number should not matter.

Thus his course of action and efforts marked a new phase in the political awakening of Muslims for the period between 1912 and 1918 and towards the end of 1920 their political ideology had broken through its former mold to take new shape.

Religion and Politics

To Azad religion and politics were inseparable because Islam governs all aspects of life. He wrote that Mosque is the real place of religion and politics. [58]Azad's *Al-Hilal* and *Al-Balagh* weeklies could not be characterized as strictly religious in the conventional sense of the term. For Azad 'Islam opens the key to politics'. [59] Politics, according to him, becomes in its turn chilly and spiritless when striped of Islam. Politics meant to him wielding power. [60] He believed that because Muslims forgot the message of Islam and its heritage, they lost their glory in India and elsewhere. Thus, he reduces political order to Islamic order. For political mobilization of Muslims, he regarded Islam as a potential force. He was convinced that nothing could unite Muslims more effectively than Islam. That is why he exhorted the Muslims not to depend for their future on government but on Islam.⁶¹ With historical examples he emphasized that Islam rejected all types of slavery and stood for liberty and democracy. He wrote: 'Islam taught us to love freedom and not to accept slavery.⁶²

About the nature of politics Azad said that in no case the Muslims emulate the Hindus or the British in politics but depend wholly on Islam. ⁶³ He wrote, come to the book, Koran. That is the answer. Azad motivated his coreligionists to follow the straight path of Qur'an which lay down the following basic principles for guidance:

- The Unity of God.
- Muslims are the blessed of all the communities.
- God has given justice (*adal*) to the Muslims.
- Muslims stand for peace.
- The Qur'an opposes autocracy and arbitrary government.
- Muslims should endeavour to establish a parliamentary system of governance.

The point to be emphasized is that Azad wanted to base politics on the message of Koran.

The five six monthly volumes of *al- Hilal* and one of *al-Balagh* opened with the *fatiha* editorials which revealed the real significance of his papers.⁶⁴ In fact they confirmed his commitment to Islam and Koran which is evident from the following prayer which he repeated in every volume:

O, Lord, in this journey which I had begun, take me o a better place. Though I am weak thou by thy favour and persistence in the conflict between the truth and falsehood, grant me victory.

Al-Hilal's objectives and political message[65] as enunciated by Azad in its issue of September 8, 1912, clearly states that political issues cannot be separated from religion. He said:

.... I look at every aspect of human activity from the perspective of religion. The Qur'an is our sole guide. Save that we know nothing.... (Hence) my politics has been derived from it; how can I separate it from the Qur'an? This is my faith; my religion and it includes my politics.

"It is unfortunate that the Qur'an is not understood in its pristine glory. Otherwise, for our political guidance we do not either have to knock at the door of the Government nor look towards the Hindus.... Al-Hilal (therefore) invites the Muslims to follow the Qur'an and the *Sunnah* of the Prophet (peace be upon him) .... (But) the situation is different; we do not act according to what we profess to be our belief...."

Azad also referred to the Islamic tenet of *tawhid* which means submission only to God and reminds the Muslims that they are the best community and have been made the vicegerent of God on earth; every Muslim is expected to feel that way and instead of misery, cowardice and fear should live with dignity, self-respect, courage and steadfastness. Muslims are called upon, he says, to do good to others, to protect the good, prevent the evil and disorder, help those engaged in doing good and oppose the worldly authority that compels people to accept rule that require their "worship". How could, he asks, a worldly authority or government have the right denied even to the prophets.

"God's helping hand", he asserted, "it's placed over the group. The Qur'an's exhortation is clear on that score. The Qur'an also commands that there should be mutual consultation. Thus, God willed that only that government was a legitimate government which, instead of being in the hands of an individual, was in the hands of the community or nation, and that was the basis of His command for mutual consultation. The Muslims should, therefore, consider it is as their religious duty to make every effort to achieve freedom (from the foreign yoke), which is their legitimate and birthright, and should not rest until they have established a parliamentary form of government (*ours*).

"These are the principles to guide us in making our political policy; we need not go begging either to the moderate Hindus or to the extremists for a political policy. If we frame a policy of our own, we shall be a moderate but fearless group which shall not be a source of trouble and fear for any other party. We shall work for the progress and independence of our country as our religion of mischief and disorder. The Qur'an warns the Muslims against 'doing mischief on earth after it hath been set in order.'[66]

"Undoubtedly, the British government has established peace (in the country) which is congenial to our freedom to perform our religious obligations. Now, it would, therefore, amount to doing mischief on earth if we rise in rebellion and are misled to break the laws of the country. The Qur'an asks us to help one another in righteousness and piety and not to help one another in sin and rancor'[67]

"The government should also remember that if we Muslims become true Muslims, it would be advantageous not only to themselves but also to the governments as well as to their neighbors. It should also not forget that if we are true Muslims, we will hold the Qur'an in our hands, and the hand that holds the Qur'an cannot hold a bomb or revolver.[68] But it must also be understood that the Qur'an has taught us both the things i.e., granting freedom (to others) and seeking it (for ourselves). When we were the rulers, we gave liberty and now when we are the ruled, we demand the same. We consider the will of God that nations should be made free to rule themselves. Europe is free by following this principle. To-day, from Britain, we demand precisely what till the other day, she fervently sought herself....

"This is exactly Al-Hilal's policy, and to this we call the Muslims to follow. This is not the invention of any human mind nor is it the *taqlid* of any particular group of people. But this is the path made open for us by the Lord of the Universe who sent His prophets in this world with Books, Wisdom, Justice and Fairness. Provided I have His blessing, I would devote my life that He has graciously bestowed upon me in propagating this call of righteousness. No dispute, no battle-cry against anyone; no desire to be favored or applauded....

"The Muslim League, if it aspires to lead the Muslims politically, should also adopt this very path of action. 'Allah guides those whom He pleases, to the Straight Path.[69] Thus in *al- Hilal* Azad emerged as a strong champion of the cause of the liberty. Azad greatly admired Rashid Raza who was the pupil of Muhammad Abduh and had inherited the reformist zeal of his master. In the first issue of *al- Hilal*, he published the photographs of Jamaluddhin al Afgani, Muhammad Abduh and Rashid Raza captioned with high sounding titles and highlighting their persistent struggles for freedom, equality and justice in the Muslim world.[70] For the first issue of *Al-Hilal*, he wrote an article '*Al Murshidul Hakeem Sayyid Rashid Raza*'(the great reformer and the wise guide Sayyid Rashid Raza) to give an account of his visit to India and his Islamic mission exalting his passion for liberty and reform. Azad highlighted the abject state of the Indian Muslims:

'Indian soil has been from the very beginning, the playground for strangers and travelers...Considering the royalty and nobility which has thronged to these alluring shores, what attention can a dervish-traveler receive? What had Rashid Raza come for this land of guided and jeweled *mandirs?*

Perhaps Rashid Raza is the first traveler who had come not to plunder the spring-horn of plenty, but to offer his lamentations at the autumnal desolation of this land. He wandered across the country, but unlike Beruni, not in search of knowledge and the arts but because the Muslim traditions of love for knowledge lay buried under the dust of history. Unlike Ibn-e- Batuta, he did not witness Islamic grandeur and power, because in place of valour and virtue are now the nests of crows and vultures. [71] Rashid Raza came forth and went back. There are probably very few who found out about his visit. But if we cannot see the light of the sun the fault lies in our vision. Unfortunately, the Indian Muslims are cut off from the Islamic world. Arabic, which was once the language of the *quom* and performed the function of Esperanto for the Islamic world, is no longer a living language. The day is not far when Allah and the Koran will be pronounced in accents dictated by British lexicons.'

The opinions expressed in the above passages and other parts of the Rashid Raza article were developed by Azad into major points of debate and discourses in the later issues of *Al-Hilal*. In the article '*Al Jehad fi Sabil Al Hurriyat*' (Islamic Crusade for the sake of Independence), Azad spoke words of harsh reproof to the errant race:

The future historian who will record the chronology of events, will write that ultimately whatever had to happen, happened. In the 20th century, no country could remain in bondage and none remained. The British government was a constitutional entity, not the autocratic rule of Genghis Khan. Therefore, it did what was expected of it, and India become free. But the world will always remember that this turn of events owed nothing to the Muslims, whatever happened rebounded to the credit of every other community except the Muslims. The Muslims preferred slavery to freedom, groveling the dust to dignity; Muslims have no share in building this memorial. If amendments were made in the country's laws if beneficial legislation was introduced, if people were rid of ruinous taxation, if compulsory education is introduced, military expenses were reduced and lastly, if the county became self-governing it was due only to the Hindus, respectable Hindus, who set an example before the Muslims by starting the political agitation and continuing it. As for the Muslims, they regarded it a sin and remained aloof. And when they try to start something, *Iblis* (Satan) exhorted them to prostrate themselves before the government, and, with the tear filled eyes, begs for alms. Beg not for a guinea or jewels, but for a rusted copper coin, or a rotten crust of bread.[72] He gave a clarion call to his countrymen and his community to wake up, throw off the foreign yoke and work together for the common good. He wrote in Al Hilal:

"I wish I could get the breath of the Judgment Day, which I would take to the mountain tops, and with one single clarion call wake up those who are caught up in the shadows of stupor and asleep in ignominy, and would have shouted out aloud: Wake up! You have slept too long! Wake up because your Creator wants to wake you up and bestow upon your life in place of death, progress in place of decay, honor in place of dishonor." [73]

Thus, Azad wrote articles to inspire the readers to fight for freedom, equality and justice by propagating Islam.

United India: Hindu-Muslim unity

Maulana Azad had a passion for the Independence of India. For this he first joined the revolutionary party. He was the first Muslim to do so. The members of the party were surprised to find not only a Muslim but an eminent theologian joining them. He was a supporter of Hindu-Muslim unity from the very beginning of his life. He gave the idea to the Muslims that there was no conflict in being a good Muslim and also a good Indian Nationalist.

By 1940 Azad was convinced that there was no conflict between the two- a Hindu, Muslim, or Christian, even as he followed his particular faith, could say with equal pride that he was an Indian. In a manner reminiscent of Iqbal he declared that he was proud to be a Muslim and unwilling to forego even the smallest part of his wealth-i.e. the legacy of Islamic teachings, traditions, history, arts and civilization, which in fact it was his duty to protect. The religious and culture of Islam held a special interest for him, and he could brook no interference in these; at the same time its spirit did not come in the way of, rather it guided those other sentiments which were "forced upon" him by the "realities and conditions" of his life. He was proud of being "a part of the indivisible unity that is Indian nationality", and could never surrender his claim to it, since he was an essential and indispensable element which can go into the building of India, and without which it would be incomplete.

Azad succeeded in mobilizing the Muslims into Independence movement, and made efforts to consolidate Hindu-Muslim unity on firm foundations of faith of Muslims as well as on the shared culture of both the communities. In his 1940 Presidential address to the Indian National Congress in Rampur, Azad said:

"This (immigration of Muslims onto Indian soil) led to a meeting of the culture-currents of two different races. Like the Ganga and Jumna, they flowed for a while through separate courses, but nature's immutable law brought them together and joined them in a 'sangam'. This fusion was a notable event in history. Eleven hundred years of common history have enriched India with our common achievement. Our languages, our poetry, our literature, our culture, our art, our dress, our manners and customs, the innumerable happenings of our daily life, everything bears the stamp of our joint endeavor. Our languages were different, but we grew to use a common language; our manners and customs were dissimilar, but they acted and reacted on each other, and thus produced a new synthesis. ...This joint wealth is the heritage of our common nationality, and we do not want to leave it and go back to the times when this joint life had not begun. ...This thousand year of our joint life has molded us into a common nationality. ...Whether we like it or not, we have now become an Indian nation, united and indivisible. No fantasy or artificial scheming to separate and divide can break this unity. We must accept the logic of fact and history, and engage ourselves in the fashioning of our future destiny."[74] In contrast and contrary to the facts, the Muslim League and Hindu nationalists were arguing that culture was based on religion and that Hindu and Muslim cultures were irreconcilable.

Azad argued in favor of *muttahida qaumiyat* (composite nationalism). He cited the example of the first state established by Prophet Mohammed in Medina wherein all the people of Medina entered into a covenant called as 'Covenant of Medina'. Under the covenant, if Medina was attacked by outsiders, all would join forces to defend the city. However, the Jews and Christians were free to practice their religion. Azad further said, "I am proud of being an Indian. I am a part of the indivisible unity that is Indian nationality. I am indispensable to this noble edifice, and without me this splendid structure of India is incomplete. I am an essential element which has gone to build India. I can never surrender this claim."

For Azad, Hindu-Muslim unity was more fundamental than independence if it was to be achieved by partitioning India. In his address to the special session of INC in 1923 Azad said,

"If today an angel descending from the clouds were to declare from the top of the Qutub Minar in Delhi, 'Discard Hind-Muslim unity and within twenty-four hours swaraj is yours,' I would prefer to sacrifice swaraj rather than Hindu-Muslim unity, for delay in the attainment of swaraj will be a loss to India alone, but if our unity disappears it will be a loss to the whole world of humanity."

When the Muslim League leaders were scaring the Muslims that in united India, Hindu majority would dominate and oppress them, Azad wrote in *Al- Hilal* 1 (8) 2-3,

"*The fact that Hindus are a majority is of no significance. It is the condition to which you have brought yourselves that will insure your destruction... There is no need to fear Hindus. You must fear God. You are the army of God. But you have cast off the uniform He gave you. Put it on again and the whole world will tremble. You have to live in India, so embrace your neighbors... You must realize your position among the peoples of the world. Like God himself, look at everyone from a lofty position. If other communities do not treat you well, you should still treat them well. The greater forgive the faults of lesser.*"

Azad had opposed Pakistan to the best of the ability he commanded. "God's earth cannot be divided into Pak (pure) and impure" he wrote. Azad was most pained by the partition and was never reconciled to the fact. Azad and Gandhi*ji* were marginalized within the Congress Working Committee. *"Two states in conflict with one another did not offer solution to the problems of minorities",* Azad opined, *"as minorities would be vulnerable to retributions and reprisals for acts of their co-religionists in the state where they were in majority."* Azad had staked his entire political career on united India and lost. When the All-India Congress Committee voted in favor of partition on 14th June 1947, Azad's final plea was that even if the political defeat had to be accepted, the INC should try to ensure that the culture was not divided. He pleaded that even if a stick is placed in the water and it divides the water temporarily, water remains undivided. [75]

Khilafat: Maulana's Clarion Call for Revival of Islamic Brotherhood

With the advent of World War 1, the Ottoman Empire entered the war, ill prepared, goaded into it by a billion-gold kroner from Germany's Kaiser and by the desire of the Young Turks to recover the European territories lost in the Balkan wars of 1911-12. The Great War was a disaster for the Ottomans; the empire was occupied and the last vestiges of independent Muslim power anywhere on earth disappeared. There followed intrigue and scheming, with Britain and France as the principal players, to carve up the Ottoman empire. The large Muslim population of India could only watch helplessly as this unfolded. But what rallied Muslim opinion was the move to abolish the Khilafat, an institution that had endured 1300 years of Islamic history. The Khilafat issue agitated all strata of the Muslim community.

Maulana Azad threw the full weight of his oratory and his journalistic skills into the battle to save the Khilafat, sometimes using language that was uncharacteristically strident. He presented the Movement as one related to Islam:

"O my dear believers! The issue is not one of the lives of nations and countries; it is an issue of the very survival of Islam". Addressing a convention in support of the Khilafat Movement in 1920, he quoted from Qur'an and Hadith at length to support the movement. He said:

"Gentlemen: The hand that holds the white flag of peace is a noble hand. But only he can survive who holds a sharp sword: it alone is the arbitrator of the lives of nations, the means for establishing justice and upholding balance....and the shield in the hands of the oppressed...." Behold! We sent Messengers with clear Signs and sent down with them the Books and the balance to establish justice among humankind, and We sent down iron in which there is great power and benefit for humankind" (The Qur'an: 57:25). The Muslims should remember that there is only one sword that can now be raised in defense of the Law of God and that is the sanctified sword of the Usmania Khilafat. It is the last footstep of historical Islam and the last ray of hope for our glorious destiny..."

He traced the genesis and the evolution of the Khilafat and explained the objectives behind this institution which included organizing the Muslim community, administering justice and spreading God's message to the world. Azad stressed the temporal message of Khilafat without which he thought it was not possible to propagate the message of Islam. He regarded Khilafat as a symbol, with which to inspire Indian Muslims and rally them into an 'anti-British constituency'.

Azad explained to the Muslim community that the Caliph was the spiritual head to whom they must owe their allegiance. He further pointed out that in view of the Qu'ranic principles there was no reason for Sunnis and Shias to disagree on this point. He said that it is Muslim's moral duty to defend the institution of Caliph as I was a unifying force without which they will lose their identity and cohesion.

He urged the Muslims to defend the Khilafat by means of Jihad. Jihad, according to Azad is not force but a struggle which could be undertaken not by violence but peaceful means like delivering speeches and writing articles in order to mobilize strong public opinion. He stressed that this struggle was necessary for preserving the Khilafat which was being threatened by the hateful European policy of capturing the holy places. Taking the advantage of the situation he drew a distinction between non- Muslims like the British who were determined to destroy their religion and other non-Muslims like Hindus who espoused the Turkish cause. He pleaded that in such circumstances Hindus ought to be treated as friends and Britishers as enemies.

The Khilafat Movement attracted scholars, politicians, mullahs and the common folk. Maulana Azad worked with Maulana Muhammed Ali, Hakim Ajmal Khan and others to rally the Muslim community and exert pressure on the British government to back off from its attempts to eliminate the Khilafat. It was during this period that the Maulana met Gandhi and was attracted by his non-cooperation methods. Gandhi saw in the Khilafat movement a golden opportunity to weld Hindus and Muslims into a grand coalition for the independence of India and was accordingly chosen by the Khilafat committee as its leader. Maulana Azad wrote: "As far as its relationship (the relationship of the Khilafat movement) with a national issue is concerned, it can be said that its movers were certain well-wishers. I take the name of Mahatma Gandhi who was the first and most honorable well-wisher who supported this movement."

The Maulana remained loyal to Gandhi throughout his life, even when he disagreed with him. The Khilafat movement fizzled out when Gandhi pulled the plug on it after the violence at Chauri Chaura. It died when the Turkish parliament abandoned the Khilafat in 1924. Azad defended Gandhi's decision to call off the Khilafat Movement: "Gentlemen! In every national struggle, where there are many memorable moments, there is also a mention of some error. These errors are as if they are a natural part of the process. I am convinced that the decision about Barawali was one such error in our struggle…."

The Maulana's vision was not limited to the borders of his own country or the confines of his own community. It embraced all of humanity. Mohammed Hamid Ali Khan quotes Asif Ali: "Tolerance to him did not mean religious tolerance. He believed in the absolute right of individual to differ and hold whatever opinion he believed to be correct". He believed not just in the unity of Hindus and Muslims but in the brotherhood of man. In this he had his firm anchor in his religious beliefs:

"The greatest tragedy for humankind and a confirmation of its rejection of its divine nature is that it forgot the universal relationship of its creation but instead established its relationships on the basis of plots of land and divisions of lineage. The earth that was made for love and mutual support was made a stage for mutual differences and quarrels. But Islam is the first voice in the world which sent an invitation for universal brotherhood and unity not on the basis of divisions erected by humankind but on the basis of the Unity of God who is to be worshiped and served."

During the last decade of his life, Azad often elaborated upon the idea of world citizenship, especially while addressing international gatherings. He held that the methods of teaching geography and history should be reviewed so as to "bring out the unity of the world and the unity of man." In his speech of welcome at the Second Session of the Indian National Commission for Cooperation with UNESCO, he said:

We must have new maps for children in the elementary stages in which the world will be painted in one color; we must teach the child that he is a citizen of the world first and foremost, and then go on to tell him that just as a town is divided into different wards for purposes of convenience. so the world is divided into segments. but such divisions do not disrupt the unity of the world.[76]

This notion of world citizenship in effect stemmed from his concept of one God and religious pluralism. It reflected his hopes that reforms in education and a synthesis of culture could resolve both political and social conflicts. The above also underlay his conception of the mitigation of the so-called conflict between the West and the East. He argued for the compatibility of Western and Eastern cultures, the differences between them being, in his view, an outcome of placing emphasis on different aspects of common problems.[77] Paying his homage to the memory of Maulana Abul Kalam Azad, Dr. Radhakrishnan wrote: "National spirit was the driving force of his life. He was an apostle of national unity and communal harmony, the lessons which we have to remember even now, since there are forces which are still at work in this country to divide us from one another." Maulana Azad became independent India's first education minister. For his invaluable contribution to the nation, Maulana Abul Kalam Azad was posthumously awarded India's highest civilian honour, Bharat Ratna in 1992.

References

1 Azad, Abul Kalam, India Wins Freedom, New Delhi: Orient Longman Pvt. Ltd., 1988, p.1

2. *Gubar-i-Khatir* (Sallies of Mind), a collection of letters of Azad, all in urdu,1943, p. 97.

3.Ali, B. Sheikh, *Maulana Abul Kalam Azad, vision and action,* Mysore: Azad Publication, 2001, p. 8

4. Azad, Abul Kalam, *India Wins Freedom*, Delhi, 1992, p.4

5.Mahilabadi, Abdur Razzaq, *Azad ki Kahani Khud Unki Zabani, Maktaba Ishatul Qur'an, Delhi,1965,* p.393

6.ibid

7.*ibid.*

8.Mahilabadi, Abdur Razzaq, *Azad ki Kahani Khud Unki Zabani, Maktaba Ishatul Qur'an, Delhi,1965*, p. 359-61

9.*Gubar-i-Khatir* (Sallies of Mind), a collection of letters of Azad, all in *Urdu*,1943, p.102

10.Azad, Abul Kalam, *India Wins Freedom,* Delhi, 1992, p.3

11.Mahilabadi, Abdur Razzaq, *Azad ki Kahani Khud Unki Zabani, Maktaba Ishatul Qur'an, Delhi,1965,* p.383.

12.Mahilabadi, Abdur Razzaq, *Azad ki Kahani Khud Unki Zabani, Maktaba Ishatul Qur'an, Delhi,1965,* p. 361-62

13.Kashmiri, Shorish, *Abul Kalam Azad,* Lahore,1994, p.27

14.ibid., p.28

15. Malihabadi, Abdur Razzaq, *Azad ki Kahani Khud Unki Zabani, Maktaba Ishatul Qur'an, Delhi,1965*, p.406.

16. *ibid.*, p.405.

17. *Speeches of Maulana Azad,* Febuary,1949, p.75.

18. Khan, Abdul Waheed: *India Wins Freedom, the other side,* Karachi, 1961, pp.22-23.

19. Dutta, V. N., *Maulana Azad,* New Delhi : Manohar Publications, 1990, p.38

20. Sabri, Maulana Imdad, *Imaml-ul-Hind, Maulana Azad,* p.38. Quoted in Dutta, V.N, *Maulana Azad,* New Delhi : Manohar Publications, 1990, p.43

21. Quoted in Dutta, V.N, Maulana Azad, New delhi : Manohar Publications, 1990, P.44 & Malihabadi, A. R., *Azad ki Kahani Khud Unki Zabani, Maktaba Ishatul Qur'an, Delhi,196 5,* p. 253

22. *ibid,* pp. 259-76

23. Dutta, V.N, *Maulana Azad,* New Delhi: Manohar Publications,1990, p.45

24. Al- Nadwa, October 1905, pp. 2, 8;

25. Al- Nadwa, January 1906, pp. 2, 11

26. *ibid,* pp. 2 &12

27. *ibid.*

28. Al- Nadwa, Vol.7, No. 4 (April 1910) pp.11-12

29. Robinson, F., *Separatism among Indian Muslims,* Cambridge: Cambridge University press, 1974, p.174.

30. Malik, Ram, *Abul Kalam Azad,* Delhi,1999, pp.88-89

31. Qur'an, Al-Imran, 3, 104 (Allama Yusuf Ali's Translation) as quoted in Ali, B. Sheikh, *Abul Kalam Azad, Vision and Action,* Mysore: Azad publication, 2001

32. *ibid*

33. *ibid., Ayath,* 3; 110

34. *ibid., Surah Tauba (9) Ayath 71*

35. Malik, Ram, *Abul Kalam Azad,* Delhi,1999, p.92

36. *Qur'an, Al-Haj:* 22:78, as quoted in Ali, B. Sheik, *Maulana Abul Kalam Azad, Vision and Action,* Mysore: Azad Publications, 2001

37. Ali, B. Sheik, *Maulana Abul Kalam Azad, Vision and Action,* Mysore: Azad Publications, 2001, p. 40

38. Qur'an, Al Mumtehna; 60; 8,9. Quoted in Ali B, Shiek, *Abul Kalam Azad, Vision and Action*, Mysore: Azad Publications, 2001.

39. Quoted in Malik, Ram, *Abul Kalam Azad,* Delhi,1999, Pp. 97-98.

40. *ibid.,* pp. 99-100.

41. Kashmiri, Shorish, *Abul Kalam Azad,* Lahore, 1994, pp.251-52

42. Ali, B. Sheik, *Maulana Abul Kalam Azad, Vision and Action,* Mysore: Azad Publications, 2001, p. 42.

43. *Al- Hilal,* 14 July, 1914

44. *Al- Hilal,* August 4, 1912, p.4.

45. *Al- Hilal,* October 9, 1912, p.5

46. *Al Hilal,* December 18, 1912, p.7.

47. *ibid.,* pp.50-52

48. *ibid.,* pp.159 and 174

49. Zaidi, A. M., ed., *Congress Presidential Addresses* (1940-85) Vol. V, New Delhi: Indian Institute of Applied Political Research, 1985, pp. 36-37.

50. Azad on Nation and Nationalism" presented at an international seminar on "Maulana Abul Kalam Azad: An Architect of Indo-Persian Culture" organized by the Centre of Persian and Central Asian Studies, School of Languages, Literature and Culture Studies, Jawaharlal Nehru University, NewDelhi,March1-3,2011
http://www.mainstreamweekly.net/article3125.htmdt.8/1/2016

51. *Al-Hilal,* December 18,1912.

52. *ibid.,* pp.151-56; *ibid* P.146

53. *ibid.,* pp 97-98 and 100-101; *ibid*

54. *Al-Hilal,* December 18,1912

55. *ibid.*

56. *ibid.*

57. *Al-Hilal,* August, 1912.

58. *ibid.*

59. *Al- Hilal,* September 1914.

60. *Al- Hilal,* October 23, 1912.

61. *Al- Hilal,* September 8,1912.

62. *ibid.*

63. *ibid.*

64. *Al- Hilal,* December 10,1912.

65. Douglas, Ian Henderson, *Abdul Kalam Azad: An Intellectual and Religious biography,* Delhi : Oxford University Press, 1988, pp.110-112.

66. Al- Hilal, Vol. I, No.9, September 8,1912, pp. 4-8

67. Reference to Anarchists and revolutionaries

68. The Qur'an, II:213

69. *Al- Hilal*, July 13,1912.

70. The *Rashid Raza* article is in three parts, featured, *Al-Hilal*, 13 July, *Al- Hilal.* 20 July and *Al- Hilal*, 27 July,1912

71. *Al-Hilal*, 18 December, 1912.

72. http://historyof islam.com/contents/maulana-abul-kalam-azad/retrieved on 5/1/2016

73. Azad, Abul Kalam. *Presidential Address to the Fifty-Third Session of the Indian National Congress Ramgarh, 1940.*

74. http://www.ummid.com/news/2015/November/03.11.2015

75. Speeches of Maulana Azad, 1947-55, New Delhi: Government of India, Publications Division, 1956, pp. 150-151.

76. *ibid.,*

77. *ibid.,*

CONCLUSION

The in depth study of the revivalist ideas and efforts undertaken by the various Muslim Thinkers, the conclusions drawn reveal different strands of Revivalist thoughts prevalent during the British Rule in India. The Research Questions are:

- The need for Muslim Revivalism?
- Impact of Muslim Revivalism on Muslims?
- Were Muslim Revivalist Thinkers anti- Hindus?
- To what extent the revivalist trends in their political ideas were responsible for the Hindu-Muslim divide which ultimately led to the culmination of Pakistan?

The history of Indian Muslims since the 1857-59 Uprising against British Rule, the first major anti-colonialist action in India, and up to the victorious outcome of the National Liberation Movement in 1947 is characterized by a great variety of religious, philosophical, social and political trends. Politically, they embraced a religious-separatist movement which resulted in the formation of Pakistan, on the one hand, and a movement for unity of Hindus and Muslims in their struggle against British colonialism, on the other.

Revivalism was one of the leading trends in the religious-philosophical thinking of Indian Muslims, providing a framework for expression of ideas both by those who called for a return to medieval ways and who opposed the development of capitalist relations (the ideology of the *Jamat-i-Islam* Party), and by those who, like Abul Kalam Azad, sought to interpret Islamic precepts according to the requirements of the rising national movement.

During the concluding stage in the struggle for political independence, these two trends were personified by two political leaders: Maulana Mohammed Ali Jauhar and Muhammad Ali

Jinnah who led the Muslim League and the communal movement, and Abul Kalam Azad (1888-1958), an outstanding Muslim figure in the National Congress Party, who stood for the unity of Hindus and Muslims.

Indian Muslim renaissance started with Sir Sayyid Ahmad Khan who was a pivotal figure in the awakening of the Muslims. The study shows how the dedication, hard work and clear vision of a single man changed the destiny of a whole nation. It was due to his extraordinary vision that the Muslims of India could regenerate after lapsing into moral despondency, cultural lethargy and educational backwardness. Without him, it might have taken another few centuries for the Indian Muslims to come out of their medievalism to modernism. He sought to reconcile modern scientific thought with religion sensibility and rationalistic interpretations.

He attempted to rehabilitate the Muslims in British eyes after the mutiny; his educational projects were designed initially to benefit the Urdu-speaking elite but after the language question was raised quickly redirected to benefit primarily to Muslims. His political leadership which during the last thirty years of the nineteenth century taught Muslims that their best chance of preserving their strong position in north India lay in allying with the British. Throughout he fought hard to preserve the Muslim elite position in education, in jobs, and in the developing of a representative system of government. He did not allow any pan-Islamic loyalties to hinder this purpose. Though he, like most Indian Muslims, was sensitive to the international brotherhood of Islam, when it seemed that Indian Muslims might make much of their loyalty to the Turkish Caliph after the Russo-Turkish war of 1877-8, he was adamant that loyalty was owed to the British first of all. He advocated that the British filled the role of 'pious sultan'. Considering Muslims in India, he seemed at first to regard them as *qaum* or nation within the Indian *qaum,* but when faced with the realities of Indian nationalist politics from the mid-1880s he made it clear that the Muslim *qaum* was the *qaum*.

Sayyid Ahmad's politics, his concern for the Indian Muslim *qaum* before all other considerations had been interpreted entirely in terms of the material interests of the north Indian Muslim elite. But the study of his politics in the context of his whole life and work, the picture seems somewhat different. His approach to Islam was awe-inspiring. 'Man cannot forget God', he declared, 'God himself pursues us so tenaciously that if we want to leave him, He does not leave us. Before the mutiny, most of his writing was on religious subjects but after the mutiny almost all his intellectual energy, was devoted to resolve the conflict between religion and sciences. His endeavor to reinterpret Islam in the light of western learning played a central role in his life.

'Today', he told an audience in Lahore in 1884, 'we are, as before (That us, when Islam came into close contact with the world of Greek Ideas) in need of a modern *"ilm al-kalam"* by which we should either refute doctrines of modern sciences or undermine their foundations, or show that they are in conformity with the articles of Islamic faith'. If we do not 'reveal to the people the original bright face of Islam, my conscience tells me. we would stand as a sinner before God'.

He defended Islam against the prejudiced ignorance of Western orientalists so that young Muslims could imbibe modern science and remain Muslims. As a Muslim, he worked to make his people strong. "The more worldly progress we make, the more glory Islam gains" was his motto. He persuaded Muslims to come to terms with the two realities of the times- the political fragmentation of the *Ummah* and British power in India.

Sir Sayyid Ahmad Khan's political stance to a large extent stemmed from his conviction that: British rule was here to stay for none else could govern India. It was a folly to challenge its authority since it had proved itself invincible and its permanence would be beneficial for Indians, and particularly Muslims. In 1860-1861, he published Risâlah *Khair Khawahân Musalmanân: An Account of the Loyal Mahommdans of India*, in which the faithful services of Muslim noblemen were recorded and wherein he claimed that the Indian Muslims were the most loyal subjects of the British Raj because of their kindred disposition and because of the principles of their religion. He tried to demonstrate the religious sanctions for this attitude, ruling out *jihad* or rebellion against the government as being un-Islamic. As for the Qur'anic verses commanding Muslims to fight all unbelievers until all mischief was abolished, he did not hesitate to say that they had only contemporary and local, rather than universal application. He wrote a commentary on the Old and the New Testament, *Tabiyyan al-kalam fi'l-tafsir al-tawra wa'l-injil cala millat al-islam* (*The Mahomedan Commentary on the Bible*). He attached a *fatwa* (religious decree) by Jamal ibn al-Abd Allah Umar al-Hanfi, the Mufti of Makkah, at the end of the book. This *fatwa* stated, "as long as some of the peculiar observances of Islam prevailed in India, it is *Dar al-Islam* (Land of Islam)." This was to counter the religious decrees that had been issued by many Indian *Ulema'*, state that the Indian subcontinent had become a *Dar al-Harb,* the land of war. This political overture was favorably received in the ruling circles.

Sir Sayyid Ahmad Khan played a critical role in the field of education for the empowerment of the poor and backward Muslim community. As a social reformer and a great national builder of modern India he prepared the road map for the formation of a Muslim University by starting various schools. He instituted Scientific Society in 1863 to create a scientific temperament among the Muslims and to make the Western knowledge available to Indians in their own language.

Graham, his biographer, writes: "Sayyid Ahmad's motto was 'Educate, educate, educate.' 'All the socio-political diseases of India may be cured by this treatment. Cure the root, and the tree will flourish." He realized that unless the Muslims received adequate modern education, their condition would not improve and they would not occupy an honorable place amongst the nations of the world. Aligarh Muslim University (AMU) known more as a movement than an academic institution is one of the most important chapters of Indian history as far as the sociology of Hindu-Muslim relation is concerned. Sir Sayyid said:

"This is the first time in the history of Mohammedans of India, that a college owes it neither to the charity or love of learning of an individual, nor to the spending patronage of a monarch, but to the combined wishes and the united efforts of a whole community. It has its own origin in course which the history of this county has never witnessed before. It is based on principles of toleration and progress such as find no parallel in the annals of the east."

Aligarh College became a center for Muslim educational and political activities in northern India, and its doors were open to all communities and many distinguished British as well as Hindu Professors served on its faculty. Sir Sayyid allowed mingling of the Hindus and the Muslims, the class and the mass. He insisted on equality of rights between all communities in his college and elsewhere and refused to create two citizenships. Sir Sayyid believed that the basis of a common nationality was not religion but homeland. In his lectures and writings he stated clearly that he regarded the Hindus and Muslims like two eyes of the same person and that discrimination between them was not possible.

The details given above are reflective of his revivalist actions and his idea of a composite culture in India.

There is a fluctuating pattern in Sir Sayyid's views regarding Hindu-Muslim relations. Although he perceived the antagonism between the two major communities even in 1858, as a government servant he himself displayed no trace of prejudice. Due to his impartial and devoted services, he won the trust and affection of the majority community as well. On a personal level too, he served not only his co-religionists but also compatriots, and began to set up various academic and political organizations in which the Hindus also participated actively.

In 1867 when he asserted the geographical basis of nationhood, and considered Muslims as an inalienable part of the native Indian population, Sir Sayyad believed that like Europe India was not a single nation, but comprised numerous similar nations and accepted the notion of composite culture.

But the Urdu-Hindi conflict greatly affected the life and thoughts of Sir Sayyid Ahmad Khan. Before this event he had been a great advocate of Hindu-Muslim unity and was of the opinion that the "two nations are like two eyes of the beautiful bride, India" but *bhasha* movement completely altered his point of view. He put forward the Two-Nation Theory, predicting that the differences between the two groups would increase with the passage of time and the two communities would not join together in anything wholeheartedly.

Although he was pained by the events following the controversy that he despaired of the two communities even working together as a nation, the very next year he set up an organization to send members of both groups abroad for study. In 1870, while he repeated that the issue would greatly damage Hindu-Muslim relations, he admitted that it would be in Muslim interests to keep these healthy; and expressed his desire for the welfare of all Indians irrespective of faith

During a speech in Patna on January 1883 Sir Sayad described Urdu as the language of neither Hindus nor Muslims, but a new creation- the product of their through interaction. Urdu was thus for him a symbol of their composite culture, and any attack on it was a blow to their solidarity.

In 1883 he founded an organization to help Muslims to go abroad for study, but assured the Hindus that he was not motivated by partisanship or lack of sympathy for them, but only the fact that Muslims faced greater hurdles in this respect

Only a year later, in his speeches of early 1884 Sir Sayyid described both India and Europe as single nations despite their religious and racial diversity, reaffirming the territorial (as opposed to religious) basis of nationality. He appealed for concord among all Indians, who were one nation, for the welfare of their common country, and particularly for Hindu-Muslim unity He repeatedly described them as single nation, while emphasizing the social and cultural bonds between them. By defining a "Hindu" as a native of Hindustan rather than the member of a religious group, he tried to prove that far from being aliens, Muslims were also "Hindus." He believed at this stage that their children should be brought up and educated together as brothers, and clarified that by setting up a college for Muslims he did not intend to set them apart from the Hindus. Addressing a big gathering at Gurdaspur on January 27, 1884 he said:

"Hindus and Muslims! Do you belong to a country other than India? Don't you live on this soil and are you not buried under it or cremated on its Ghats? If you live and die on this land, then bear in mind, that Hindus and Muslims is but a religious word; all the Hindus, Muslims and Christians who live in this country are one nation."

In January 1884, Sir Sayyid undermined the territorial basis of nationhood by saying that Islam had abolished it to create a new national bond that was spiritual; and since Islam was the basis of their identity. Muslims must remain true to it. But he added that their compatriots of all faiths were also their brothers-in social and cultural matters, and Islam preached good neighborliness towards all. While he defined his nation as the *ummat of the* Prophet *(Pbuh)*, which he loved and desired to serve, he explained that his efforts for its educational upliftment were meant to contribute towards the progress of India as a whole. Yet despite these pronouncements he did not hesitate to express his conviction that neither community separately, nor both together, could rule India.

A marked change was detected in Sir Sayyid's attitude in an undated article, wherein he expressed the desire to make Muslims a nation, whereas in early 1884 he had used the same phrase for both communities together. He now held that merely education was not sufficient, and a spirit of nationality must be created among Muslims through collective education in their own national institutions. He now believed in the need to teach them Arabic and Persian (which he described as the languages of Muslims), and to impart elementary, if not advanced religious education not as earlier, to popularize education, but in order to strengthen their national consciousness.

In 1884 while justifying the setting up of a college specially for Muslims he defended the need for a separate educational institution for Muslims. He reasoned that not only did the education of Muslims suffer by studying amidst other nations (*quawm)* due to their different needs and modes of life, but they could never thus "become a nation." Their mutual sympathy and "national feeling" which were born by living together would be stifled, and would gradually become extinct by being educated in government colleges where they were very few as compared to other "nations".

In order to keep alive Muslim nationally (*qawmiyyat*) a feeling of "national unity and sympathy" must be generated, which was possible only if students shared all aspects of life together. To illustrate this point he cited the example of the students of the M.A.O. College, who he believed experienced religious enthusiasm and a feeling of nation (*quawmi*) pride, pleasure and sympathy at the thought of studying in their "national college", which he felt was lacking in progress", and it was only by such education that Muslims would become a "Nation".

" For this it was necessary to ensure that they remained Muslims, and the reality of Islam remained firm in their hearts- they should therefore be taught religious tenets and as far as possible made to observe religious obligations. As before, he emphasized that this was necessary alongside elementary religious education since Muslim brotherhood, national unity and in fact nationality itself was based solely on Islam.

Therefore, Sir Sayyid believed that Muslim students should be taught Islamic history, and about the spread of Islam, and Islamic brotherhood, which was stronger than familial bonds. In order to keep alive their nationality (*qawmiyyat*) which he felt was threatened by English education, they must be taught Arabic (The language of their religion and of their forefather) or at least Persian.

The Indian National Congress was formed in 1885, and Sir Sayyad opposed it openly in December 1887. He reverted to the view that the different Indian people had not so far intermingled to form a single nation, and nor were they equally matched. He reiterated his earlier opposition to the implementation of pure representation, and felt that due to their backwardness and fewer numbers, Muslims particularly were unfit to compete with others. He therefore advised them to concentrate only on trade and education, and abstain from the political agitation of the Congress. He also feared that the strong and vindictive arm of the government would fall most heavily on them. His reaction was obviously conditioned by his experience of 1857: he continued to believe that since Indians could not harm the government in the least but would only insecure themselves by a confrontation, it was wiser to secure benefits by winning its trust through loyalty. He felt that the activities of the Congress would spark off a power struggle between the various Indian communities; and that through it the Hindus hoped to politically subjugate, and even annihilate the Muslim community.

Yet soon after his tiff opposition to political co-operation between the two communities, he reaffirmed his earlier desire for religious amity and social unity.

Sir Sayyid opposed the pro-Turkish tendencies of Indian Muslims in 1897, as being in conflict with their duty to remain loyal subjects of their British rulers. He completely undermined the right of the Turkish Sultans to the universal Islamic caliphate which he held had ended thirty years after the demise of the Prophet *(Pbuh)*, and their authority over Indian Muslims. He rejected the possibility of a world-wide Muslim state with a single caliph as its head. Having earlier employed religious arguments to buttress his case for loyalism, he now held that religion must be kept apart from politics. Accordingly, he reasoned that it was unjustified to given wholly political wars a religious coloring, and to defy the government even if its policy was against Muslim states. In 1898 for the last time he opposed the efforts of Hindus against Urdu, which he defended virtually from his death-bed.

To conclude, Sir Sayyid was not concerned with theorizing about Muslim identity in India, his sole aim being the socio-economic, educational, and cultural rehabilitation of his community; and all his efforts were geared towards this end. Accordingly, he supported British rule in India, Hindu-Muslim unity, and the united Indian nationhood which stemmed from the latter, because he felt it was conducive to the attainment of these ends. Yet even in the early period he was astute enough to perceive the inherent antagonism between the different Indian communities. Even before the formation of the Congress he felt that Muslims could not compete with the Hindus in politics, and later opposed it due to the threat that it posed to the permanence of British rule. It was perhaps for him also a symbol of the resurgent Hindu nationalism which he had felt rearing its head during the Urdu-Hindi issue, and perceived as a threat to Muslim progress and security.

Therefore, it is difficult categorizing Sir Sayyid's views. However, both strains are present in his thought, the "nationalist" and also the "separatist" which were the natural outcome of the ever-changing socio-political situations in a colonial and pluralist society of India in which Hindus and Muslims were struggling for their political and cultural gains.

Mohammed Ali Jauhar a product of the Aligarh movement and a principal figure in the historical processes that resulted in the emergence of Pakistan. H.G. Wells wrote of him: "Muhammad Ali possessed the pen of Macaulay, the tongue of Burke and the heart of Napoleon."

Maulana Mohammed Ali represented a synthesis of apparently conflicting trends and currents of Muslim religious and political thought of India. He stressed the need of modernity and science as well as the need to follow the spirit and values of Islam. While criticizing the system of western education which was in vogue in India, he said,

"The present generation is an immature product of modern education with crude, half-formed ideas, not familiar with orders of thing new as well as old," and that the western education, "tended to breed in the student an arrogant omniscience, and to destroy along with age-old beliefs in superstition all respect for Tradition and Authority." Mohammed Ali advocated the genuine spirit of enquiry, for truth as well as respect for tradition. He complained that the modern education had produced men who were "more communal than religious" and who know "so little of their religion and their orthodoxy was more than suspect."

Mohammed Ali favored militancy and the method of mass agitation. The influence of Tilak made Mohammed Ali the leading exponent of extremist Muslim nationalism. Mohammed Ali realized the necessity and significance of mass contract or associating the common people with the political movement. Tilak and Mohammed Ali both, of them used religion to provide a mass base to Indian politics. Mohammed Ali's anti-British stand was the outcome of the British policy towards the Muslim countries. Mohammed Ali played an important role in the awakening and strengthening of the supranational character of Islam and the latent feeling of Pan-Islamism amongst the Muslims in India. Mohammed Ali asserted that Pan-Islamism is nothing more or less than Islam itself, the "Supernational Sangathan of Muslims in five continents." It recognizes neither the sanctity of colour nor the virtue of geography, and by offering a set of common ideals, offers the only rational basis for unity and cooperation among its flowers.

For Mohammed Ali the basis of Pan-Islamism is one God, One Prophet, One Ka'ba and One Book, the Qur'an. Pan-Islamism is not an institution. It has been more an abstract and emotional factor than a pragmatic concept. The defeat of the Islamic countries at the hands of the European countries disheartened the Muslims all over the world and touched the chord of religion in the sub-conscious being of the Muslims. Though essentially a political issue, Mohammed Ali made it religious.

Mohammed Ali does not differentiate between the spiritual and the mundane. Secularism, he said is a western notion, which cannot be applied in the East. The problem according to Mohammed Ali essentially was one of defining the province of religion. In the West politics had set the limits of religion whereas in the East politics were still determined by religion. Mohammed Ali said that "What is politics to the West today, religion is still to the East."

Mohammed Ali finds no conflict between the Khilafat and the independence movement in India. To him freedom of India was only a springboard for "the realization of Eastern Federalism." Therefore he advised Muslims to fight for the country's freedom. For, a "slave India will be of scant help to the Turks and the Khalifat." This gave birth to the idea of Islamic Nationalism. Both Khilafat and Islamic Nationalism were the logical result of the Pan-Islamism of Mohammed Ali.

The Khilafat movement was a blend of the two irreconcilable lines of thought – Islamic universalism and Indian (Muslim) nationalism. The struggle between the two is apparent when Mohammed Ali declared,

"Where God commands I am a Muslim first, and Muslim second, and a Muslim last, and nothing but a Muslim.....but where Indian is concerned .....I am a Indian First, an Indian second, an Indian last, nothing but an Indian."

In 1920 as the head of the Khilafat Delegation, he said:

"I belong to two circles of equal size, but which are not concentric. In one circle was the word "India"; in the other circle was Islam, with the word "Khilafat." We as Indian Muslims came in both circles. We belong to these two circles, each of more than 300 millions, and we can leave neither. We are not nationalists but supernationalists, and I as a Muslim say that "God made man and the Devil made the nation." Nationalism divides; our religion binds. No religious wars, no crusades, have seen such holocausts and have been so cruel as your last war, and that was a war of your nationalism, and not my *Jehad*.

In India the Muslim are "the blood-brothers of the Hindus" but outside Indian there are millions who share their faith. It "is a priceless heritage, the wonder of the age, the most vital and binding human cement."

On Hindu –Muslim unity he said:

"But where our country is concerned, where the question of taxation is concerned, where our crops are concerned, where the weather is concerned, where all associations in those thousands of matters of ordinary life are concerned, which are for the welfare of India, how can I say "I am a Muslim and he is a Hindu"? Make no mistake about the quarrels between Hindu and Muslim; they are founded only on the fear of domination."

And finally the fiasco of the Khilafat Movement obliged him to think in terms of Islamic nationalism. In practical politics it was an emphasis on separateness of the Muslim community as a distinct cultural and political entity.

The failure of the Khilafat movement compelled the Hindu and Muslim communities to face one another and try to work out a modus operandi. To give voice to Muslim sentiments, Maulana Mohammed Ali restarted the *Comrade* weekly in 1924, soon to be followed by its Urdu counterpart, *Hamdard.* But the India of the 1920s was a changed India from that of the 1910s. Communal riots rocked Nagpur, Meerut and other cities. The Hindu Mahasabha gained traction and in 1925, its president Golwalkar proposed the two-nation theory. A disunited and confused Muslim leadership held several meetings to chart out a vision and a course of action for the future. An all-parties conference held in Delhi in 1925, which included representatives of the Indian National Congress and the Muslim League, failed to agree on guidelines for a future constitution for India and instead delegated the task to a committee headed by Motilal Nehru.

The Nehru report was a watershed in the independence struggles of India and Pakistan. Maulana Mohammed Ali failed to convince Gandhi and the Congress party to change these provisions of the Nehru report.

In bitterness he became a critic of Gandhi, broke away with fellow Muslim leaders like Maulana Azad, Hakim Ajmal Khan and Mukhtar Ahmad Ansari, who continued to support Gandhi and the Indian National Congress. Ali attended the Round Table Conference in London 1931, called by the British to discuss a dominion status for India. It was also attended by Jinnah, Dr. Ambedkar, the Agha Khan, Sardar Ujjal Singh, Tej Bahadur Sapru, B.S. Moonje and others. It ended in failure because the Indian National Congress, the largest political party in India, boycotted it.

Muhammed Ali died in London and was buried in Jerusalem as he had wished. Maulana Mohammad Ali is remembered as a fiery leader of many of India's Muslims. He is celebrated as a hero by the Muslims of Pakistan, who claim he inspired the Pakistan movement. But in India, he is remembered for his leadership during Khilafat and the Non-Cooperation Movement (1919-1922) and his leadership in Muslim education. The famous Mohammad Ali Road in south Mumbai, India's largest city, is named after him. The Gulistan-e-Jauhar neighborhood of Karachi, Pakistan's largest city, is named in honor of Maulana Mohammad Ali Johar. Johar Town, Lahore is also named after him.

Muhammad Iqbal the poet philosopher, a jewel in the Muslim community was acutely aware of the problems of Muslim decadence and backwardness. He took upon himself the task to shake the Muslims of India and other countries out of their lethargy, urging them to take the path of progress, so that they can gain an honorable position in the polity of nations. He used the medium of poetry to arouse socio-religious consciousness among Muslims. As a result, Islamic religious and social themes predominate in his poetry. Iqbal's vision of a revived religion was far from conservative. He sharply criticized many of the institutions of historic Islam (of the institution of monarchy, for example), and his vision of a new world derived from the Islamic notions of egalitarianism and social justice. He rejected dogmatism in religion, advocated rethinking of the

Islamic intellectual heritage, and stood for the establishment of a forward-looking community.

Iqbal's ideas were a product of the Indian situation and a response to the impact of the west on India. Its process started even before the mutiny with Zakaullah and others and it gathered force in the last quarter of the 19th Century and in the beginning of the 20th century. Iqbal enriched the process of Muslim renaissance though he was not its initiator. He was "the product rather than a generator of the movement." He was undoubtedly "the poet of Islam's re-awakening in India in the 20th Century." Like his predecessors – Sir Sayyid, he "devoted himself to the war against *Taqlid* and to the resurrection of Islam from lethargy and tradition."

The raison d'etre of Iqbal's poetry is the elucidation and elaboration of the wisdom of the Holy Qur'an and of being 'a vehicle of its secrets', as well as to be the instrument of the renaissance of the Muslim *Ummah* and its consolidation into a united entity, as required by the Holy Qur'an, is clear from a study of his works as well as from his own admission. He says:

Do not consider my seemingly disjointed song as poetry

As I am aware of the inner secrets of the tavern

I have opened the secrets of *qalandari*

Iqbal in the early years of his life stood for composite Indian nationalism. His Urdu poetry before 1906 and specifically poems such as 'The New Temple' and 'The Indian Anthem' bear ample testimony to this fact. His visit to Europe was a turning point and his thoughts altered from composite Indian Nationalism to Muslim Nationalism.

It was during his stay in Europe that he was able to closely observe the political developments in Europe. He explored the basis of their political models. In this exercise he highlighted the inherent flaws which were responsible for creating tensions between countries and according to Iqbal it was territorial nationalism or nationalism based on love for land. Territorial Nationalism was prime factor to provoke selfishness among the countries to protect their national interests and concluded that territorial nationalism was of gross misuse. It was, according to Iqbal a weapon of European Imperialism which destroyed the unity of Muslim world. After his return to Europe Iqbal's abandoned the concept of composite Indian nationalism and adopted Muslim Nationalism.

"As I look back on the year that has passed and as I look at the world in the midst of the New Year's rejoicings...the same misery prevails in every corner of man's earthly home, and hundreds of thousands of men are being butchered mercilessly. Engines of destruction created by science are wiping out the great landmarks of Man's cultural achievements. The governments which are not themselves engaged in this drama of fire and blood are sucking the blood of the weaker people economically."

Iqbal raised a pertinent question:

'Do you not see that the people of Spain, though they have the same common bond of one race, one nationality, one language and one religion, are cutting one another's throats and destroying their culture and civilization by their own hands owing to a difference in their economic creed?'

According to Iqbal this single event demonstrates clearly that 'national unity' is not a 'very durable force.' He asserted that only one unity is dependable, the unity of brotherhood of man, which stands above race, nationality, colour or language.

Hence, he argued that: as long as this so-called democracy, this accursed nationalism and this degraded imperialism are not shattered, so long as men do not demonstrate by their actions that they believe that the whole world is the family of God, so long as distinctions of race, colour and geographical nationalities are not wiped out completely, they will never be able to lead a happy and contended life and the beautiful ideals of liberty, equality and fraternity will never materialize.

He carved out his views on Islamic universalism and said that the European concept of nationalism cannot be applied to India. He asserted that according to European notion India is not a land with one nation. Because two major communities living in India i.e. Hindus and Muslims do not share common language, common culture, common history which is the basis of nationalism. Rather Muslims posses separate identity with their own religious and cultural values. These views were expressed in his poem 'The Anthem of the Islamic Community.'

To Iqbal territorial nationalism and Islam were contradictory and irreconcilable. Iqbal reasoned that mission of Islam was to demolish idolatry, it could not approve of patriotism (born out of nationalism), which was nothing but "a subtle form of idolatry".

He wrote a poem 'Territorial Nationalism' and in one of its couplets said:

Country is the supreme among all the contemporary idols.

Its cloak is the shroud of Islam.

Territorial nationalism creates division in the Muslims community. He said that:

God's creation is divided into nations by territorial nationalism.

The roots of Islamic nationality are destroyed by it.

Iqbal advocated that Muslims have their own basis of nationalism whose origins lie in Islam. Islam did not follow the confined scope of nationalism. Its membership would not be determined by birth or domicile, it did not consider the natural, historical and cultural differences of different races but it is based on common faith. Muslims living in different parts of the world with variant socio-cultural backgrounds, ethnic divisions and cultural values constitute a single Muslim nation i.e. *ummah*. It was Islamic universalism which was a basis of Muslim nationalism.

Iqbal's political philosophy is deeply embedded in his broad and comprehensive Islamic conception of *tawhid,* the unity of God, the unity of life, the unity of the *ummah,* and the unity of humanity. His rejectionist approach toward secularism, materialism, western democracy, and nationalism is based upon his concept of *tawhid.* His philosophy of self-hood *(khudi)* and its related concepts like "man of belief" (*mard-i-momin)* "perfect man" (*mard-i-kamil*), and his conception of the Islamic social order and divine vicegerency are not only related to each other, but also are steeped in his dynamic conception of *tawhid.* Hence, all of his concepts and ideas, which bear the message and mission of *tawhid,* are contrary to the ideology of nationalism, which is rooted in secularism and materialism.

In his writings on Islam's social order, Iqbal states: Islam "finds the foundation of world-unity in the principle of *tawhid* and Islam, as a polity, is only a practical means of making this principle a living factor in the intellectual and emotional life of mankind."

Two important points are deduced from this statement: Islam is a practical means to make the principle of unity a reality in humanity's intellectual and emotional life, and *tawhid* supplies the foundational principle for world unity.

The first point forms the basis of his concept of *tawhid* and strikes the secular origin of nationalism. By portraying Islam as a practical means for making the principle of *tawhid* a living factor, Iqbal implies that Islam unites and integrates all aspects of life (e.g., intellectual, emotional, social, political, and others) into a unified whole. In other words, Islam totally disagrees with the artificial division or compartmentalization of life into "religious life" and "worldly life." This unified and holistic perception of life is religious" domains. At several places, Iqbal elaborates upon Islam's unified approach to life. He writes:

> That according to the law of Islam there is no distinction between the Church and the state. The state with us is not a combination of religious and secular authority, but it is a unit in which no such distinction exists.

Iqbal's upholding of the unity of life and the unity of the spirit and matter can be seen in many of his statements. For example, he states: "All that is secular is therefore sacred in the roots of its being" and "All this immensity of matter constitutes a scope for the self-realization of spirit."

In other words, unlike Hegel, Iqbal did not make a synthesis of "reason" and "spirit" in order to form a state. For him, the state by itself is spiritual because all that is secular is spiritual in Islam. He writes: "The state according to Islam is only an effort to realize the spiritual in a human organization."

The Qur'an (Sura 49: 10) instructs that all the believers are brethren. Iqbal said that if nationalism as a political concept is accepted as an Ideal, Islam will cease to be a living factor. Nationalism "comes into conflict with Islam only when it begins to play the role of the political concept, and claims to be a principle of human solidarity demanding that Islam should recede to the background of a more private opinion and cease to be a living factor in the national life."

Iqbal, however, was not opposed to that type of nationalism which has all the potentialities of uniting the people of a particular country for the achievement of freedom. This, according to him, was not inconsistent with the spirit of Islam. But what could more effectively unite the people is religion and not nationalism. The westerners wanted to use nationalism "to shatter the religious unity of Islam to pieces."

Iqbal was against the growth of western nationalism in India and believed that India is not a nation mainly because the Muslims are in a minority. Therefore, to Iqbal the ultimate goal of Muslims should be the strengthening of Muslim nationalism for the attainment of Islamic universalism. For this purpose Muslims should be concerned with the problem of survival and protection of their separate identity. Muslims are not just the community but a separate cultural entity and attainment of political power was essential to retain uniqueness of Muslims. He envisioned an ideal state which works for the creation of Muslim *ummah*. It should be designed on divine law of Islam, and free of all artificial distinctions between men.

There is an impression that the Muslim League carried Iqbal's concept of Muslim Nationalism to its logical end. But this does not appear to be valid.

Firstly, Iqbal never thought of partitioning the country. He suggested the idea of a separate Muslim State in the North in his Presidential Address to the Muslim League in 1928. This demand was only for "a state within the state", and not for an altogether separate state. No question of partition was involved. Probably he would have been satisfied with the establishment of a true federation in which full internal autonomy is guaranteed to the constituent units. Edward Thompson states that Iqbal was disillusioned with his idea of 'a state within the state' regarding it as disastrous to the British, to the Hindus as well as to the Muslim community. Thus Iqbal's scheme seemed to have no relation to the League demand for partition. Jinnah and the others of the League were closer to Choudhary Rahmat Ali than to Iqbal regarding the concept and scheme of partition. There were others who had also advocated such schemes before Iqbal. But the League leadership exploited Iqbal's name to give strength and sanctity to the demand for Pakistan.

Secondly, Jinnah and many other Muslim leaders in the forties were rallying anti-Hindu forces under the guise of Two

Nation Theory. Here, too, the League was more profoundly inspired by Rehmat Ali than by Iqbal. Iqbal had great respect for the non-Muslim communities.

Iqbal believed that no religion teaches hatred of others religious communities. Iqbal said to Renée G. Shahani "I am sprung from the same stock; India is older than Hinduism and Islam, and will remain when we and our creeds have become one with Yesterday's Seven thousand years…"

"It is wrong to utter a bad word;

To infidel as well as the faithful is God's creations;

Humanity consists in respect for man

So acquaint thyself with the dignity of man."

-Translated by S.A.Vahid

On the issue of the demand of Pakistan, Iqbal felt "that Islam in its pure form had a contribution to make towards the building of new India". From this, it can be concluded that Iqbal was very much opposed to sectarian and narrow nationalism inside and outside India as the basis of polity. But the nature of opposition was more Islamic than political. By attacking nationalism, he never wanted to create obstacles in the way of Independence of the country. On the contrary he had a passion for India's freedom. He sounded a note of warning that nationalism, the product of the west, will be anachronistic and dangerous to the interests of humanity. His aim was to expose the game of the west and explode the myth of nationalism. Iqbal thought that a government based on the concept of One God (*Tawheed*) will be more stable and better than democracy of the western type. The principle of unity of God is a "living factor in the intellectual and emotional life of mankind." The other cardinal principles of Islamic democracy will be 'obedience of law', 'tolerance' 'universalism.'

After the establishment of Pakistan, he came to be considered as "the spiritual founder of Pakistan."

Dr. Zakir Hussain was one of the finest flowers of Indian renaissance. He was a man who was wedded to the highest values of his land namely knowledge, truth, beauty, service, sacrifice, love and humanity. He struggled all his life to bring about a creative integration of a composite culture which is the hall-mark of India, and which finds expression in unity in diversity and identity in multiplicity. As an educationist he was of the view that a genuine and broad-based national renaissance could not be ushered in through the narrow gate of politics; it must have its moorings in, and draw its inspiration from a renascent education and culture. Zakir Hussain said that man is an organic whole, and one cannot compartmentalize him into different units saying that one unit is independent of the other. Social, cultural, educational, economic and political affairs are all inter-related, and one would not understand them better if a comprehensive outlook was not developed. Therefore he emphasized on the need for moral education. He believed that morality and ethics were closely interconnected with religion. Every religion aims at making its votaries conform to the laws of nature through the principles of ethics.

Zakir Hussain introduced Jamia as an Islamic institution to the country. Jamia had come into existence for a purpose to inject nationalist feelings amongst the youth and to restructure the courses according to the "cultural goods" of the country. Zakir Hussain injected the finest elements of the Islamic culture into the courses.

Through Jamia Zakir spread a message that a true muslim is a true patriot as well. It was wrong to think Muslims were against the national movement, or they had not fought or struggled for the country, or that their religion stood in the way of a speedy march towards freedom.

In his speech of 1933 on the occasion of a discussion group on the ideals and the objectives of the Jamia, he said,

"The Jamia is an Islamic institution and its main objective is to provide education for Indian Muslims. Islam and Islamic culture is the basis of education at the Jamia. Islam signifies in this context the faith which frees one from the worship of anyone other than Allah. It binds one to serve the One True God and thus lays the foundation of a universal brotherhood and fraternity. Islamic culture stands here for the role model set by Prophet Muhammad (Peace and blessings be upon him). In recognition of the local culture and conditions, we may pursue some other objectives as well, as for example, a keen desire to attain our independence and to serve the cause of Urdu."

In August 1937 while addressing a gathering of Hamdard-i-Jamia, he said, "The biggest objective of Jamia Millia is to prepare a roadmap for the future lives of Indian Muslims with the religion of Islam at its core ......" If the objective of this university is rooted to the core of a religion, can it not be called a movement for Islamic revivalism? From the very beginning its first Vice-Chancellor Mohammad Ali stressed the teaching of Islamic history and Qur'an and ensured that the teaching day began with a full hour devoted to the rapid exegesis of the Qur'an based on the preaching of prominent Deobandi Ulema.

He was a reformer with a restricted task of rescuing his drowning community. He proved to be to the Muslims what Raja Ram Mohan Roy had been to the Hindus, whom he had induced to prefer modernism to traditionalism. Sir Sayyid asked the Muslims to be loyal to the English, whereas Zakir Hussain asked the Muslims to be loyal to the country. Sir Sayyid condemned vernacular languages in strong terms as "there is but very little difference between a man ignorant of English and a beast", but Zakir Hussain installed Urdu on a high pedestal and made that the medium of instruction in Jamia. Sir Sayyid had kept the Muslims away from the mainstream of Indian nationalism, Zakir Hussain was knee deep in it, and desired that his community too should fall in line with their compatriots.

Zakir Hussain made Jamia the educational front of the struggle for freedom. He emphasized in his essay 'Eternity or Toy' the need for moral education. Morality and ethics were closely interconnected with religion. Religion has two aspects, one is faith and other is righteous deeds. The two together would make a man truly religious. Any religion would not become good or bad until its votaries bring a good name or bad name to it. A good Muslim could also be a good nationalist. He would also exhibit fine qualities such as generosity, action, love and service. Every religion aims at making its votaries conform to the laws of nature through the principles of ethics. He was sorry to see only formalism, and the absence of true religious zeal and spirit at Aligarh.

Through Jamia Zakir spread a message that a true Muslim is a true patriot as well. It was wrong to think Muslims were against the national movement, or they had not fought or struggled for the country, or that their religion stood in the way of a speedy march towards freedom. During the time when the country was ablaze with misgivings and misunderstandings, Zakir Hussain remove this cobweb of confusion by arguing that the true understanding of Islam by the Muslims would promote the national cause. He explained to the Muslims that no one was in greater need to understand the spirit of Islam than the Muslims themselves, who have become the prime factor for making the Islam the most misunderstood religion of the whole world. To repair this damage, Zakir concentrated on Islamic Studies in Jamia, to excite in Muslims true patriotism in order to make them love their land, know their land and serve their land. True patriotism is a true sentiment of good faith which regards all humanity as one family.

Nationalism was an important principle of his philosophy. He thought that loyalty to the land was the first duty an individual owed to himself as the citizen of the country he belonged to. He proudly declared, "It is out of the earth of this country that we were fashioned and it is to this earth that we shall return".

Zakir Hussain successfully instilled the values of nationalism, patriotism and other human values in Muslims so as to enable them to join the freedom struggle and contribute in the progress of the country. He made Jamia an institution where a nationalist could take pride in being a Muslim and a Muslim would be proud of his being a nationalist.

For over a decade (1937-47) Zakir was preoccupied with the Jamia Project and actively involved with the National Basic Education drive. It was a period of political turmoil. The Hindu-Muslim issue became very dangerous and explosive. Muslim League carried out the propaganda that Congress was an enemy of Muslims. Muslims were drawn into large numbers towards Muslim league.Since Dr. Zakir Hussain was devoted to the Basic Education drive, the Muslim League looked upon him as a staunched Congress man who cannot represent the Muslim viewpoint. After the Pakistan resolution in March 1940, the Muslim League attracted the Muslims like a magnetic force. It was taken for granted that every Muslim must join Muslim League. In the given circumstances it was essential to defend Jamia against sectarian politics. Zakir Hussain had a serious concern of the political milieu of the day. Hindu-Muslim issue became complicated and got further compounded with passage of time. He got very much upset over these developments. Zakir Hussain with a educationist heart expressed his concern to the people and appealed to the political leaders to act with maturity and sagacity.

Dr. Zakir Hussain was not a politician yet the politicians treated him with respect. They considered him an honest and sincere person, one who had dedicated himself to the task of nation-building. His eminence as an educationist rose still higher and he was even considered for the Interim Government in June 1946 when he was busy in making preparations for the Silver Jubilee of the Jamia scheduled to be celebrated in November, 1946 instead of October 1945. Yet such was Dr. Zakir Hussain's sense of self-abnegation that he refused to serve the Government unless his name was jointly sponsored by the Indian National Congress and the All-India Muslim League, a proposition which the latter could never have accepted.

On the occasion of Jamia in1946, Zakir managed to bring together outstanding leaders of the Congress and Muslim League both at the same platform. One could see the crisis that India had to face in the following year: Mr. and Mrs. Mohammad Ali Jinnah, and Liyaqat Ali Khan were on one side of Dr. Zakir Husain, the Vice Chancellor, on the dias; Pandit Jawaharlal Nehru, Asaf Ali and Sir C Rajagolapachari were on the other side. The main function was presided over by Nawab Hamidullah Khan of Bhopal.

All bridges of understanding between the Congress and Muslim League had collapsed, bloodshed and violence had taken over in Calcutta, and in retaliation gory riots and inhuman carnage took place in Bombay, Nowakhali, Bihar and Punjab. Humanity and civility were nowhere in sight. It is against this backdrop that one can measure the immense value of D. Zakir Hussain's appeal even today. Even today it can move those youth, if God enables them, who are vulnerable to sectarian and communal propaganda. For such evils are not only present in our country; they have even consolidated themselves. These forces thrive on communal discord and prefer hatred to love, chaos to unity and confrontation to integration.

The atmosphere was vitiated by the communal riots that had become a usual feature. Delhi itself was in the grip of a communal holocaust and suffered from curfew. Some felt that the celebrations would be an utter failure. But Dr. Zakir Hussain worked against all odds. It was a most memorable scene. Dr.

Zakir Hussain narrated the story of the Jamia in brief. Taking advantage of the presence of the distinguished leaders of both the Congress and the League, he made a moving appeal to them for promoting unity and fraternity in the country. It was perhaps the last unsuccessful appeal to them for this cause. It represents a milestone in the career of a great teacher who transcended ephemeral gains and losses. He apprised them of the prevailing communal atmosphere thus:

"You are all stars of the political firmament; there is love and respect for you not only in thousands but in millions of hearts. I wish to take advantage of your presence here to convey to you with the deepest sorrow the sentiments of those engaged in educational work. The fire of mutual hatred which is ablaze in this country makes our work of laying out and tending gardens appear as sheer madness. This fire is scorching the very earth in which nobility and humanity are bred; how can the flowers of virtuous and balanced personalities be made to grow on it? How can we provide adornment for the moral nature of man when the level of conduct is lower than that of beasts? How shall we save culture when barbarism holds sway everywhere, how shall we train men for its services I How shall we safeguard human values in a world of wild beasts? These words might appear harsh to you, but the harshest words would be too mild to describe the conditions that prevail around us. We are obliged by the demands of our own vocation to cultivate reverence for children; how shall I tell you of the anguish we suffer when we hear that in this upsurge of bestiality even innocent children are not spared? An Indian poet had said that every child that is born brings with it the message that God has not altogether despaired of mankind, but has human nature in our country so lost hope in itself that it wants to crush these blossoms even before they have opened? For God's sake, put your heads together and extinguish this fire. This is not the time to investigate and determine who lighted this fire, how it was lighted. The fire is blazing; it has to be put out. It is not a question of the survival of this nation or that nation; it is a question of choosing between civilized human life and the savagery of wild beasts. For God's sake, do not allow the very foundations of civilized life in this country to be destroyed as they are being destroyed now."

His stirring speech moved the hearts of the people. It had an emotional appeal and created such an impact that even the leaders present were seen wiping out the tears from their eyes. Now it was left for them to act as Dr. Zakir Hussain had done his duty by awakening their conscience.

The partition on the country caused heavy pain to Dr. Zakir Hussain and he openly opposed Mohammed Ali Jinnah's two nation theory. Though he was a devout Muslim, he was equally a nationalist Muslim and a great son of the soil. It is said that when Pandit Jawaharlal Nehru's Interim Government faced a crisis as the League members made its working difficult, Dr. Zakir Hussain was highly concerned as the demand for Pakistan grew apace and was ultimately accepted by the new Viceroy, Lord Mountbatten. Freedom dawned upon India on August 15, 1947 but not without a scar on its psyche. Dr. Zakir Hussain was greatly upset on the partition of the country. The ideal of a composite culture to which he was wedded had been shattered. The Jamia was also insecure as it could be attacked any moment by the fanatics. However, Pandit Jawaharlal Nehru took care of this. The visit of Mahatma Gandhi further created the feelings of security in the Jamia community. General Kariappa also visited the Jamia and stationed troops for its protection.

Dr. Zakir Hussain fell ill. The jubilee celebrations had shattered his health. The communal hatred sapped his mind. All his life he had fought against the communal virus and did not lose any opportunity to appeal to the good sense of the people. Dr. Zakir Hussain served humanity in words and deeds. In one of his talks from the All India Radio he said:

You might say man is not just a part of Nature. He is not a stone, or a plant or an animal, remaining just as Nature made him. Man is man; he makes and destroys his world. This is true. That is why I call you 'Friends'. Nature has not made brothers out of you and me by bringing us into existence in the same country. We have for centuries lived together of our own free will, we have shared each other's joys and sorrows, we have been generous towards each other, ignored each other's faults, looked for the good in each other, learning and teaching, making up each other's shortcomings. We have rubbed shoulders with, tested, understood each other; loved, fulfilled the obligations of loyalty, been immersed in each other's hearts and soul; we have lived through the dark night of slavery in the flickering light of these relationships. Now that the sun of freedom has risen, why are our hearts becoming estranged, why do our eyes refuse to recognise each other. Friends follow the rules of friendship, do not look upon friends as enemies, do not uproot centuries-old friendship in the frenzy of the moment. Think of what you can do to those who are afflicted with madness; they, too, are your brothers and they, too, will become your friends. Do not demand guarantees of friendship and loyalty from them as from enemies, strengthen through your friendship the foundations of loyalty. Friendship is a plant that does not take root in the soil of suspicion, distrust and hatred. Be affectionate and trustful, have faith in human nature then see how this plant of friendship thrives, how its flowers fill with their fragrance the atmosphere of vengefulness and rancour, how the bright beauty of their colours dissolves the surrounding turbidity. Brothers! Cultivate friendship, follow its principles, fulfil its demands and ask others to fulfil them.

When in January 1948, Mahatma Gandhi undertook the fast for communal harmony; Dr. Zakir Hussain addressed him thus: "We have no doubt that you are guided by a superior wisdom, and that you have chosen the right moment to urge your people to purify their hearts. God has given you strength and a confidence which does not fail, and a faith that adverse circumstances cannot shake. God is with you and you must succeed. Only we are overwhelmed with shame that free India should have nothing to offer you but bitterness and distress ... May God spare you to lead us onwards towards the higher freedom for which you have been striving and of which, in spite of all our blindness and misdeeds, you still believe us worthy. If anything can transform us, it is your faith that the highest in us must, and will, assert itself.

Mahatma Gandhi's fast was meant to arouse the conscience of the nation and normalcy seemed to be returning. But, ultimately, the apostle of non-violence became a victim of violence and was martyred on January 30, 1948 at Birla House, New Delhi. This shocked Dr. Zakir Hussain beyond measures. But who can fight the will of God?

Very few religious individuals show the daring and courage to criticize their own minds and to fight a battle against their own prejudice. Of the leading tolerant Muslims who have left a deep impact on the idea of pluralism in Islam, Maulana Azad stands out unique. Abul Kalam Azad was a man of constant introspection and critical self-examination. His contribution to Indian nationalism and Hindu-Muslim unity in India, but also to the idea of universal humanism is tremendous. As such Maulana Azad will not only be remembered in the history of India for the role he played in the national liberation movement of the country, but he will also be considered as a Muslim leader who stood for a dialogue among Muslims and Hindus.

Azad started his career of politician and activist as a revivalist Muslim and as an upholder of pure Islam. His early career from 1906 to 1920 was influenced by his religious teachings. During this period Azad firmly believed that the Muslims were the leaders of the world. In his early writings and speeches which appeared in his journal Al-Hilal, Azad talked about the superiority of Muslims over the followers of other religions and called for an "Islamic Way" to independence. In these writings he appeared as a Muslim fundamentalist who is in favor of a linkage between politics and religion. His response to a correspondent of Al-Hilal in the issue of December 29, 1921 characterized his fundamentalist tone in those days.

"You have suggested separation of politics from religion", underlined Azad in his article. "But if we do this what, then, is left with us? We have developed our political thinking from religion....We believe that every thought which draws inspiration from any institution (including politics) other than the Qur'an is *Kufr* (infidelity)."

In the mind of young Azad one can see at the same time an enthusiasm for Muslim nationalism and a passion for the Pan-Islamic theory of Jamaledin Al-Afghani. For Azad every Indian Muslim was first of all a member of the world Muslim brotherhood. By advocating political separation of the Hindus and the Muslims, Azad declared:

"There is no greater shame for Muslims than to beg from others for political education. The Muslims must not join any political party. They were the leaders of the world. If they submit to God, the whole universe will bend to their will but it is strange and astonishing that the same Azad, in the last two decades of his life, began writing on the Hindu-Muslim unity and gave speeches on the idea of a united nationalism. In his presidential address at Ramgarh session of the Indian National Congress in 1940, Azad spoke the issue of unity and affirmed: "Our language, our poetry, literature, society, our tastes, our dresses, our traditions and the innumerable realities of our daily life bears the zeal of a common life and a unified society...Our social intercourse for over one thousand years has blended into a united nationalism."

The evolution of Azad's outlook from Pan-Islamic to secular nationalist, was determined by his friendship and collaboration with Mahatma Gandhi and by the rise of the communal problems in the Indian liberation movement. Through Gandhi, Azad learned that communal harmony played an important role in the future of India. He believed that in spite of religious, ethnic and linguistic differences, India was one nation. Azad believed that the "two-nation theory" offered "no solution of the problem of one another's minorities, but only lead to retribution and reprisals by introducing a system of mutual hostage."

Like Gandhi, Azad considered Hindu-Muslim unity as a necessary principle for the national reconstruction of India. In his famous address to the Agra session of the Khalifat Conference on August 25, 1921, he referred to Hindu-Muslim unity as a moral imperative for the future of India. He proclaimed: "If the Muslims of India would like to perform their best religious and Islamic duties…then they must recognize that it is obligatory for the Muslims to be together with their Hindu brethren… and it is my belief that the Muslims in India cannot perform their best duties, until in conformity within the injunctions of Islam, in all honesty, they establish unity and cooperation with the Hindus. This belief is based on the imperative spirit of Islam."

Azad's contribution to the realm of religion and literature is unmatched. His dream of making the Muslims remain in the main stream of national movement, restoring Khilafat to its earlier position, and preserving the unity and integrity of India was all shattered to pieces with the partition of India. But his deep religious scholarship has enriched the world of Islam to earn for him a high place in the galaxy of Islamic thinkers.

He differed from both Sir Sayyid and Iqbal and believed in the traditionalism of the Middle Ages. He does not think Islamic laws deserve to be changed. On *ijtehad* or rational interpretation he is more conservative than liberal. Iqbal had placed man at the centre of the universe with capacity even to change his destiny, but Azad thought that it was more than sufficient if man were to live up to the ideals and principles already established. Despite his conservatism Azad was more humanistic. He thought the social contract implied in Islam is essentially human, and that Islam recognizes no affinity other than human brotherhood. Azad envisaged an idealized extension of pan-Islamism into an idealized humanism.

It is strange that modernism and liberalism of Aligarh school of thought separated Muslims from Hindus, whereas Azad's conservatism integrated Muslims with Hindus. In Indian politics Iqbal the philosopher with his western enlightenment advocated separatism, whereas Azad the traditionalist fought for composite nationalism and religious universalism. Iqbal touched the hearts of the people through his soul-stirring poetry; while Azad's majestic prose delighted the elite. The common ground between the two was, both were the bitter critics of the west, both had a passionate love for Islamic principles, and both were great thinkers, reformers and activists, one rising high in the Congress and the other in the League.

A comparative estimate of Sir Sayyid and Azad could be done. Both were gifted with great intellect and immense energy. Both wanted to bring about a great social, religious, cultural and political change in the community. Both used their print media as an instrument for their programme. Both wrote commentaries on Qur'an. Both believed ethical values of Islam were timeless, and that the social solidarity of the Muslims depended upon the cultural heritage of the past. Both were powerful writers, speakers, thinkers and reformers. Both were maligned at the hands of their own community, one for his loyalism to the English and the other for its opposition, but both were loved and appreciated for their stand at the end. Both contributed immensely to Urdu language and literature. Both served the cause of the country and the community, Sir Sayyid stood for cooperation with the English to build united India, and Azad for the elimination of the English to build a secular and modern India. Both were great in their own way, as both left deep imprints on sands of time.

Azad had deep roots only in the Islamic learning, and yet he supported the western concepts of nationalism, secularism and democracy. Jinnah was a legal luminary, highly westernised with hardly any touch of Islamic scholarship. An orientlist Azad stood for united and integrated India, but an ultra-modern Jinnah stood for a state based on religion. East was for unity and west was for division. Politics knows no principles.

In short Azad was the only leader who stood solid like a rock for united India. The Congress which boasted for the unity and integrity of the land miserably let down Azad at a critical hour. Even Gandhiji who had declared partition would be only over his dead body fell into the trap of Sardar Patel hardly a few hours after that declaration. Mountbatten had mesmerized all. Political craft had earned India for the British in the past and the same craft would still have its hold through remote control. It could shoot two birds in a single shot. It could please the Congress by making it rule over the vast creamy part of India, and it would win the heart of the League by conceding its demand for Pakistan.

The Mantra of divide and rule the British had learned from the Romans was nowhere so effectively and for so long used as in India. India is yet to pay the price for the mischief Mountbatten did at the time of parting. Kashmir is still a sore in the body-politic of India. How flimsy was the principle on which India was divided became obvious when within 25 years Bangladesh fell apart from Pakistan. The holocaust and the human tragedy that followed the partition had no parallel in history. The only person who anticipated all this and did his utmost to avert it was Maulana Azad.

Azad failed in his efforts for a free United India. Success is not the criterion for glory. Socrates, Jesus, Imam Hussain, and Napoleon, had all apparently failed in their mission, but posterity placed the crown of honour on them.

The findings of the research study clearly indicate the impact of revivalism on Muslim masses. All the five Revivalist Thinkers were great men who had great love for their nation India. They succeeded in awakening the Muslims, to bring them out of the cocoon, to stir them into action, to interpret Islam in new perspective without damaging the soul of the religion, to motivate the Indian Muslims towards education to be in the mainstream of the Indian society. They always advocated Hindu- Muslim unity because the considered themselves to be Indian. They dreamt of a free India with composite culture and a federal political system which provides space to all in a pluralist society like India. Some political situations and decisions as referred in the chapters of the research made Sir Sayyid Ahmad Khan, Maulana Muhammed Ali and Mohammed Iqbal are considered to be the promoters of Two- Nation theory, whereas Dr. Zakir Hussain and Maulana Abul Kalam Azad stood for united India.

Sayyid Tufail Ahmad in a book towards Sayyid Ahmad, says: "The Indian Muslims realized their decay and downfall only about 1870, and this was the time when Sayyid Ahmad started his movement of reform. At that time the Indian Muslims realized for the first time that the responsibility for their progress and welfare, which was being formerly shouldered by the Muslim government, had now to be discharged by themselves and their wellbeing in future would depend on their efforts. In short Sayyid Ahmad's movement made them self-conscious and they began to use their limited resources to regain their lost glory."

Sayyid Ahmad filled a big void created in the life of the Muslim community by the disappearance of Muslim rule. He gave the Indian Muslim a new cohesion, a new political policy, a new educational programme, a new prose, a new approach to their individual and national problems and built up an organization which would carry on his work. Before him there was all disintegration and decay. He rallied together the Indian Muslims, and became the first prophet of their new nationhood. He could very well say about seventy million Muslims of India: "They were like a multitude that had cost its bearings in the wilderness; I gave my clarion call, and to, they became a compact caravn."

K. M. Pannikar in his book 'A Survey of Indian History' writes "Indeed it could well be claimed for Sayyid Ahmad that not only had he arrested the disintegration of Islam but in the course of a generation he restored it to a position of great importance and undoubted influence." Choudhary Khaliquzzaman referred to Sayyid Ahmad Khan as "Father of Muslim Indian" and "Father of Modern Muslim India" who certainly he was.

Choudhary Muzzafar Hussain in *'Khutbath ka Asal Mazu'* wrote, 'Iqbal demonstrated in his thought an evolutionary process. He stood as a revivalist and struggled hard throughout his life since 1905 until his death for the revival of Islam and Islamic civilization.' He wrote, 'Now along with the renaissance of Muslim communities the renaissance of Islam also is needed. I pray to God Almighty that He, for the sake of his beloved, the Prophet, peace be upon him, produces such an interpreter among Muslims who gets at the 'lost wisdom' once more and offers it to *ummah*. Our demise is not near at hand. The Qur'an still holds on.

Maulana Azad under the influence of Jamaluddin Afgani and Rasheed Rida produced a new blend of tradition, religion and liberalism to create a new brand of politics with specific reference to Muslims. Al-Hilal stirred the Muslim mind and gave rise to a country wide agitation. Sayyid Sulemain Nadvi once commented, 'I must in all fairness say one thing, the time Maulana Abul Kalam Azad was bringing out *Al-Hilal*, the Muslims mind was set on fire by his passionate words. He sounded loudly and fiercely the trumpet of Jihad, whose name people were afraid to mention, so that the forgotten lessons were on the tongue of the people again...*Al-Hilal* spoke in a language of a 'High souled Prophet', throughout he had a stamp of a *Mujtahid.*"

Muhammad Ali's contribution to revivalism could be described as infusing a sense of pride towards teachings of Islam not only for the native Muslims but was votary of pan-islamism as reflected in his support to the cause of Khilafat. Muhammad Ali through his journalistic flair contributed in 'Hindustan Review' and later in '*comrade*' and his guidance to sub-editors in bringing out *Hamdard* in Urdu for the masses with the objective of improving the lot of Muslims.

Zakir Hussain a champion of Indian intellectualism and nationalism, placed before us the concept that the goal of mankind is knowledge, and not pleasure. His dream of a free India and his zeal to bring the Muslim community into the mainstream of national life, his patriotic fervour in the struggle for freedom, him to rank as one of the most creative thinkers and statesmen of modern India. A distinguished educationist who enriched vastly the national education and headed admirably two great institutions of higher learning- Aligarh Muslim University and Jamia Millia Islamia, New Delhi, working ceaselessly for the success of the later speaks volumes for his commitment to the cause of education and revivalism of Muslims.

And thus the movement of Islamic Revivalism needs to be continued even in the twenty first century to bring forth the true spirit of Islam. Holy Qur'an promotes peace, harmony and oneness of God. The right interpretation of Islam is now required because it has been the most misinterpreted and misused religion by its promoters in a most inhumane way against humanity. It started from the very beginning of the present century. Islam as presented by Azad in his monumental work *Tarzumanul Qur'an,* intents on discovering on unity of all religions rather than maintaining that Islam was the one true faith. *Shariat* or "the path" of rules of conduct may vary from religion to religion but as Azad rightly said "they do not differ in the roots but in leaves and branches, not in the spirit but in the outward form or body."

GLOSSARY

Alah-o-Akbar	Literary meaning, God is great; a mode of greeting among the followers of *Din-i-Illahi*.
Alim	A learned man, scholar of Islamic Literature, a Muslim theologian.
Amir-i-hind	The leader of India, a title of high order among the Muslim community.
Anna	A coin equal to 1/16 of a rupee.
Azad	Meaning free from all restraint.
Caliph	Literally successor refers to the successor of the Prophet Muhammad, the ruler of Islamic theocracy.
Dars-e-Nizami	Syllabus of Muslim education prepared by Mulla Nizamuddin Sihalvi; a contemporary of Emperor Aurangzab.
Dastar-Bandi	The ceremony of tying a sash around the turban on an auspicious occasion.
DiwanKhana	Main audience chamber in Muslim household.
Darul Islam	The abode, or land, of Islam.
Dkhir	A devotional practice whereby the name of God is repeated in rhythmical manner.
Darul Harb	House of war.
Fatwa	Religious injunction, legal opinions or legal decrees.
Fiqa	The science of Muslim jurisprudence.
Hadith	Traditions attributed to the sayings of Prophet Mohammad.

Harem	The apartments for females.
Haram Sharif	The sacred mosque in Mecca, containing the Kaaba.
Hartal	Cessation of work; strike.
Hidayat	Divine grace.
Hijrat	Departure from one's country and friends; preparation of lovers and friends in particular, the flight of the Prophet Mohammad from Macca to Madina.
Hilal	Crescent Moon
Hijra	Muhammad and his follower's emigration from Mecca to Medina. Literally, "Migration".
ID	Feast festival, the Muslim festival.
Ijtihad	To exert with a view of forming an independent judgment on legal questions, to establish the ruling of a Sharia upon a given point.
Iblis	A jinn banished to Hell for arrogance and disobedience.
Ijma	The consensus of either the *Ummah*(or just the Ulema) one of the four basis of Islamic Law
Islam	Submission to God. The Arabic root word for Islam means submission, obedience, peace and purity.
Imam	Leader of the congregational prayers of Muslims, the spiritual leaders of the Islamic community as successors to the Prophet.
Jazia	A tax charged in an Islamic State from the non-believers.

Jihad	War waged in the name of Islam.
Khilafah	Man's trusteeship and stewardship of Earth; Most basic theory of Caliphate.
Madardsh	School, University
Maulvi	Religious cleric or teacher
Mecca	The Holiest city in Islam
Medina	The city of Prophet
Mujahid	A fighter for Islam
Mulki	National
Mawlana	An Arabic word literally meaning "Our Lord" or "Our Master". It is used mostly as a title preceding the name of a respected religious leader
Taqlid	Following without questioning
Tawheed	One God.
Quam	Nation

www.ingramcontent.com/pod-product-compliance
Lightning Source LLC
LaVergne TN
LVHW091540070526
838199LV00002B/138